HARD TIMES, GOOD TIMES AND THE CELTIC TIGER

James Woods

ORIGINAL WRITING

978-1-908282-55-2

A CIP catalogue for this book is available from the National Library.

Published by ORIGINAL WRITING LTD., Dublin, 2011.

Printed by CAHILL PRINTERS LIMITED, Dublin.

I would like to dedicate this book to my mother,

for being a mother.

About the Author

James Woods is from Gort an Choirce, Contae Dún nGall. Among the list of dos and don'ts on his CV is that he is a contributor to both national and local media.

I would like to acknowledge the part that all the characters and individuals have played in my book; without them there would be no book.

My own personal stories that I have related to in this book are one hundred percent true. Stories recounted to me are based on sincerity; others are based on historical and factual evidence. I have plenty more in reserve for future reference, if need be.

CONTENTS

Part I – The Early Years

Telling my Story

I don't want to start off by sounding like someone whose head's getting a wee bit too big for their shoulders, or being full of one's own importance could be another way of putting it. In saying that, however, I think I got a bite of the salmon of knowledge somewhere along the way, as there is this never-ending stream of happenings swirling around in my head non-stop. Even when I'm asleep, I automatically change over to autopilot and keep thinking of what I could write about next. By the time I wake up, most of it is gobbledygook and needs some tender loving deciphering before making head or tail of it.

I would be sitting with my laptop on the table in front of me, and what should be on a kitchen table pushed to one side. While going through my thoughts, trying to salvage a bit here and there, the second finger of each hand would be ready to start tapping away on the keyboard, before I had forgotten what it was that I had remembered in the first place. Some would say that being able to forget is as important as being able to remember, depends on the context I suppose. If I did forget I'd get annoyed and more than a bit frustrated with myself for letting it slip away. It happens, as is often the case, when there is far too much information going through your head. Confusion reigns when the memory stick is not capable of shelving it properly.

Later, my wife Anne Marie was sitting in front of my laptop, obviously reading. "I've read the first chapter but I can't find the second," she said. "Well," says I, "you won't be reading any more until it's finished and that's that. I'm writing a book. It's a bit like going to confession except it's in print". My daughter Tara's ears pricked up on hearing book, and zoomed in immediately on the mistakes I was making. "Daddy you have no full stop there; that's two sentences instead of one, blah, blah." So I told her to go off and write her own seeing as she knows so much. "Ah c'mon daddy I'm only trying to help, you're getting old y'know".

Yeah. Her thirteen and me nearly fifty.

Anne Marie still had the surprised, jaw-touching-the-floor look on her face. "You writing a book! It's the first I heard of it". "That'd be hard because I never mentioned it before." "You writing a book," she says again and started to laugh. She always thought, "Oh that's him writing more letters to the papers", something I had been at for a long time, giving a whole band of our chubby-cheeked politicians a well-deserved lashing.

I took an interest in politics when I was about eight or nine year's old whilst listening alongside my father to the radio, or the wireless as he called it, about Catholics being burned out of their homes in Belfast and Derry in the late sixties, early seventies. It sounded like the end of the world to me at that time as I thought they were coming to get us as well. That little episode planted a seed at that tender age which has steered me along the virtuous path that is Republicanism, and it has stayed with me throughout the years. It also means I still have as keen an interest in politics today as I had listening to that terrible news on the radio all those years ago.

Anyone in this country at the present time who has an interest in pursuing a political career will find the going very tough following Republican core values of ideology; that is, unless you're willing to settle for less. Then it's only a matter of kissing a few important posteriors along the way and your path will be a lot easier to navigate. It's a fact of life in Irish politics, I'm sorry to say. I have barely skimmed over the subject in this book, and intentionally so, because that would be a book in itself.

There were people out there that did not believe I was capable of putting pen to paper at all, but sure that suited me down to the ground. I would tell some people that when I thought of something to write, I'd get my blank piece of paper and pen, lay it out nicely on the table, turn off the light and off to bed. In the morning after a good night's sleep, out I'd go, and there it was filled out by the elves, and all I had to do was send it off to the papers. Plausible in the extreme, but not credible.

Earliest Memories

If you write to satisfy your soul, then hopefully you will satisfy your readers.

One of my earliest memories is being put into a tea chest to stop me running around pulling at things that I could reach. I think it was the nearest thing to a cot that was in the house at the time. Another one that retains its own wee slot in my ever-diminishing collection of brain cells is that of me holding on for dear life while perched on a shaky carrier on the back of one of those old black men's bicycles with the bar on it.

The ladies' bike didn't have the luxury of the bar, so it would have been awkward enough for my mother, who was doing her best at the controls and peddling for all she was worth. She was taking me to the dentist in Gort an Choirce. Along the way she kept taking the odd speed wobble and I was finding it hard to keep my balance right as the carrier was only a wee narrow thing and there was nothing to rest my feet on. God, I nearly forgot to say why I kept moving about. It was the pain in my arse caused by the end of a spring sticking up. It did not matter how I moved it seemed to move with me. When I think back, I think of the poor wee man, that's me I'm talking about, with my jaw swollen up because of the throbbing toothache. It had nothing whatsoever to do with eating too many sweets, because we never had any. All the same, I wasn't sure which tooth was causing me the pain, the whole pain, and nothing but the pain. I'd say I was about four or five at the time. No taxis then. Well there was one at Harry Curran's garage, Paddy Bui always drove it but that was only for emergencies and this, on the scale of things, was not classed as an emergency.

As we were going in the door to the waiting area of the dentist I got the shivers. I could hear the squealing and crying coming from one of the rooms. It was a boy I knew from up the road whose mother was on the same mission as my own. He was after having a tooth pulled and as this was my first visit I was at a stage now where I could've very easily wet my pants. My mother had told me that the dentist was a very nice man and I had nothing to be afraid of, and that he wore a nice white coat. This was to try to make me feel better about the whole thing, but after seeing the other boy in such a state, all that was in my mind was him standing in his white coat with blood all over the front of it and a pair of pliers in his hand. I was suddenly not as brave as I had thought, but all the same, I was determined not to cry, or be seen crying more like it. It was dentist Bonner. He planted me up on a chair and let the back down at an angle. I think it was gas of some sort that he used to numb the gum surrounding the bad tooth and, after a bit of twisting and turning, had my tooth out in no time at all. He was all praise and telling me I was a soldier. Well I think that remark made me a foot taller, and in my innocence I thought, yes, that's what I'm going to be when I grow up, a soldier.

On the way home again, my mother would stop off at Anne and Sarah McDonald's shop to pick up a few bits and pieces like sugar, tea and square tea biscuits that I thought were the bee's knees, even though they tasted a bit like cardboard. My mother would never buy shop bread because the bread was kept in a tea chest and once you came in the door a big cat would jump out of the chest. There were no wrappers on loaves like there are now so more often than not there could be a hole eaten into the end of the loaf. I think they didn't mind too much where the cat slept as long as it kept the mice away. The worst part of the visit that I remembered was Anne offering me a sweet and me having to refuse it because of my missing tooth. Them chances were few and far between. This was the same shop-house where Padraig Pearse, on a visit to Donegal in 1907, while doing a reading in Gaelic in McDonald's was leaning on a chair. Whatever way he twisted, the leg broke on the chair, so after being fixed, that chair was always known as Pearse's chair. It has found a good home since and is still in the Parish.

As I said my mother very rarely bought shop bread for the simple reason that the money wasn't there. She would get the four stone bags of flour. Sometimes there would be signs of long-tailed visitors with holes having been sewn up, or when my mother would be in the process of baking a scone, she would start cursing because she had found mice droppings in the flour. So the offending particles and any other evidence was removed and the baking continued and no one died because of it.

Porridge was always the last bite to eat, before bed. I hated it unless I could get what was on the bottom of the pot; I suppose it tasted better because it was burned. It would sort of remind you of a Charles Dickens story about the bowl of porridge made with oats, water and a touch of salt; how times have changed. I wouldn't eat mine now unless it was made with milk and a generous tablespoon of honey in it. I do remember getting rice on the odd occasion. I don't know where it came from but it was a treat, that was for sure.

Lighting the Paraffin Lamps

We used to have one or two of the paraffin lamps. The paraffin that was used in them was a bit thinner than diesel oil but not as thin as petrol. Imagine trying to light a lamp with petrol in it, you would blow the place up. I would have to hold one while Michael would be milking the cows on the dark evenings in the cow byre; the light from them wasn't much better than a good candle. Then we got a Tilley lamp at home to give us a much brighter light, the same as most of the other houses at the time. There would be howls of laughter by any young person today if you told them about the whole rigmarole attached to getting a bit of light going. Well I suppose the amount of work that had to be put into it rather than just flicking a switch would be considered the dark ages in today's world. First it had to be filled with paraffin oil. Then it needed to be pumped up to build up the pressure. Then you'd dip the tongs in metholated spirits, which would then be lit using a piece of rolled-up paper that you had lit from the fire. You had to place the tongs on the stem below the mantle that resembled a one-legged pair of bloomers that would glow brightly after a while and create the light similar to a twenty-five or thirty watt bulb. It would then need pumping up every fifteen minutes or so to keep it fairly bright.

The Travelling Man

There was an old travelling man that used to visit us. He would give my mother books, mainly western or detective stories that he would swap again the next time he came around, in payment for food and a place to sleep for the night, not that she wanted anything from him anyway. It could be weeks or months before he'd show up again. I remember that during his visit, he would drink all the metholated spirits in the house if he could get his hands on it. I thought he was a rare buck indeed, so it had to be kept well hidden.

I remember when we did eventually get the electricity connected for the first time, I think there were about three or four houses in the townland that had refused to get connected because they thought that there was no need for electricity and that it would cost a fortune once you were connected up. I suppose it's just like everything new that comes along, people are wary for a while until it's tried and tested.

Nearly Drowning

In the field behind our house there was a large, deep hole in the ground. I think it was left after quarrying out, or digging stones for building the high wall that surrounded, as we called it, the back field. When it rained it would fill up with water and was very dangerous, so obviously it had been drummed into my little head that I was never to go near it unless there was someone older with me.

My father had made me a boat out of a piece of tin that had been lying around. One day, my grandfather was sitting out on a small boulder that he used as a seat in the back field, close to the large hole that was now filled with water after the heavy rainfall that we had had over the few days previous. So now, this was my chance to try out my new boat. I got my grandfather to tie a length of string to the boat, as I knew he always gathered up any bits and pieces he would see and put them in his pockets. I then put a few small stones in it to balance it out, gathered up a few spiders and any other insects I could catch to give it a bit of the Noah's Ark look, and started to walk around the edge of the hole pulling the boat after me on the water.

I had been sailing the boat for some time when I must have slipped. The next thing I knew I was under the water. At that time I remember, for some strange reason, I was terrified of ladybirds, and all I could imagine was hundreds of them attacking me in the water. But thank God help wasn't too far away. My older brother Michael had happened to come into the back field looking for me when he saw me falling in. He ran as fast as he could and grabbed me by one of my wellington boots that was sticking up out of the water and dragged me out. What made the whole situation worse for me was that my grandfather was still sitting on his stone laughing his head off at me. I suppose after the relief of seeing me rescued what else could he have done but laugh? The shock must have kicked in at that stage as I started to bawl my head off. I was only four at the time. If Michael had not seen me falling in, I probably would not be writing this now. My grandfather would never have been able to reach me in time because he walked with the support of a walking stick. Years beforehand, he got a kick from a horse when he was trying to shoe one of them that left him with a nasty limp. This fright gave me a reason to be afraid of the water. When Michael took me with him to get water from the well, which was quite a distance from the house, I'd be afraid of my life to go too close.

I remember clear enough the day my grandfather died. The coffin was in the porch, as it was the only suitable place for it while he was being waked. I would get my sister Mary Bridget, who was younger than me, and coax her into looking at him lying in the coffin. When I would get her close enough, I would give the coffin a shake so that his head would move. I'd then shout at her "Quick! He's coming to get you!" and she would run away squealing her poor head off. Sure I thought this was great craic until I would start getting afraid myself and make off in the same direction as her.

Sunday Best

Sunday was a big day as my mother had a job getting us dressed up in our Sunday best clothes, scrubbed behind the ears, making sure the fingernails were as clean as was expected and off to mass. Most of the men would be dressed up in suits, ties and waistcoats. I would have a habit of staring at them because I found it hard to associate the men in their rough working clothes with the clean cut polished look about them now. My granny took me to mass one day. I know it wasn't a Sunday, it could possibly have been a holy day, and I was about five years' old. Always up as near to the front seat as possible. On this occasion I felt mother nature calling. As my granny was very busy praying, I was afraid to say anything to her about the predicament I was in, so the inevitable happened – I shit myself!! It wasn't funny for me at the time because I was wearing handed-down short trousers that had nothing to do with style, but necessity. As soon as I stood up it slowly but surely worked its way snakelike right down to my ankles. Well granny did even more praying then; well I think it was prayers. I got raced out fairly speedily. By the time I got to the bottom of the steps, it had worked its way well into my socks. Over the road where there was a stream running alongside the school next to the chapel she stripped me off and gave me a cold water scrubbing. After walking the whole way home, walking like a saddle-sore John Wayne, was I glad to see the inside of the house, even though I had a scalded arse for about two weeks.

Tractors and Lorries

My father would have been one of the first people in the surrounding parishes to have a tractor. I think it was around 1949 because he was telling me that he would get two pounds an acre for ploughing, which was good money at the time, and he would manage about three acres a day, sometimes a bit more if you worked a long day. Most people still had horses, so once they got the ploughing done with the tractor, which was a lot quicker, they would do the rest of the work then with the horses. He bought an Austin lorry in 1953. He used that for hauling turf home from the bog. If it was a single load he charged sixteen shillings, and if he was hauling for the one person all day he would charge less. Another job was taking home loads of sea sand from the beach (you wouldn't dare do that now) or seaweed for spreading on the fields. People would quarry gravel in some of the gravel pits dotted around the townland for spreading on streets and lane ways. No diggers then, it was all done by hand with the trusty pick and shovel.

Building the Church in Gort an Choirce

Once tractors became more common my father sold up and eventually went off to work in Scotland. Before he did that the quarrying was going on for the building of the new church in Gort an Choirce, and one person from every house in the parish had to do a week's breaking and carrying stones, unpaid of course. He did a few weeks at different stages of the quarrying. The priest, Fr Carr, would be out and about acting as foreman on the construction of the church, keeping an eye on things so that there was no slacking or messing about on the site. All work and no play. It was a slow process to begin with as there would be a line of men, one holding and twisting the jumper as the other man with the sledge hammer that had a broad head on it was belting away, making holes that went down four or five feet into the rock for the gelignite used to blast the rock. There were no machines for drilling at that time, although they did get one later on. When it was all set up and ready to set off the charge, bales of straw were packed around the holes. Sometimes the blast would be too powerful and burst through the straw and some of the stones would break slates on nearby houses. This was voluntary, but wages were roughly four to five pounds a week when work started on the church itself.

My Father in Australia

When he came home from working in Scotland he then headed off to Australia. I think it took about a month or six weeks on the boat. He ended up working on one of the first hydroelectric dams in the country. It was situated in the snowy mountains where he was working right in underneath a huge mountain where they were constructing gigantic control rooms for the dams. When that was near completion, he was sent with a number of other gangs planting black sally bushes higher up in the mountains to prevent soil erosion. He spent from 1956 until 1958 working in a huge opencast coalmine operation in Victoria, one of the smallest states in Australia. He told me that the coal wasn't black like what you see here, it was brown in colour and resembled logs of wood. He also told me of men called swagmen, who travelled throughout the country. The name came from them carrying their belongings with them in a rolled-up bag carried on their back. They depended mostly on truck drivers for lifts and would work a few days on a farm splitting logs for firewood or fencing in return for food, bed and a few dollars to help them on their way. Sometimes they could end up stuck in the middle of nowhere, hundreds of miles from a town or farmhouse so a rifle was an essential part of the swag bag. There were rabbits everywhere, so this was the reason for the rifle, getting your diner and cooking it before it got too dark. An Italian co-worker had owned and run a tobacco farm before starting work at the coalmine, because there was more money and less hardship to be made at this type of work, strangely enough. He showed pictures of the place to my father.

Now the farm was out in the bush. There was something that didn't quite fit into the picture at all, which was tied to a big tree near to the farmhouse. What was it but a big barge!! "What the hell is that doing there?" he said. The Italian started to laugh and said, "I knew you would say that" and went on to explain that they would get huge floods and that was his way of solving the problem, his own version of Noah's ark.

Joe McGonigle

Some days I would go for a dander across the field to the next-door neighbour. He was an old man who lived on his own. To me he seemed really ancient or as old as the hills might be a better description. I was around five so he was very interesting to me because he lived in an old thatched house that looked a bit scary. I used to watch him thatching and when he would come down for another bundle of rushes or maybe even a cup of tea, he would lean over an old stone wall and do his best trying to explain to me how to thatch and why it should be done like that, and while he was giving me all this information that wasn't registering too well with me at the time, he would have the pipe hanging from his mouth. As well as that he would have this lump of crowbar tobacco in one hand and a small knife in the other paring away at the tobacco. Then when he had enough cut he would spend ages rolling it between the palms of his hands, which were much the same color as the lump of tobacco, before carefully filling up his pipe. It was done in a way that made it look like a part of some sort of ritual.

There was only one room in the house with a tiny little window. Well there were two rooms at one time but the roof over the other room had caved in and it was never fixed. I suppose he didn't see the point with him getting on in years, because with the bed in the kitchen near to the heat of the fire he had no need for it anyway. When you would get as far as the door he would shout, come on in, come in. I would take a step in but it would take a long time for your eyes to adjust to the darkness inside. His name was Joe McGonigle and he would be sitting up beside the fire smoking his pipe where it would be roasting hot and you could make out the outline of his black cat laying stretched out in front of the fire. There was an old dresser where he had his cups, plates and other bits and pieces, including lozenges that he kept in a small paper bag, a very hot sweet that people used to chew on. It helped to keep the cold away. He would tell me to sit on a stool beside the fire. It was heavy for me to move because he made it out of a big piece of bog oak and he put three legs on it. If the fire was too hot he would throw some water on it that he kept in a jug beside it. He kept a small pile of ashes beside the fire and he explained to me that before he went to bed he would cover the fire with the ashes and it would keep smouldering away until the morning. After smoking the pipe and telling me some more stories he would get up, go over to the dresser, and reach up and I would hear the rustling of the paper bag. Then he would give me one or two of the lozenges the same way as he always did and if he wasn't in I would get up on a stool and help myself to one as I knew exactly where he had them hidden in behind a cup at the corner of the top shelf. Sometimes the draught in the chimney would be so bad, the whole house would be full of smoke. You could hardly breathe, but it was strange, the smoke never did go down as far as the floor, there always seemed to be about three foot of fresh air from the floor up. It was always the direction of the wind that determined whether you would have red eyes or whether you could breathe freely or not. Big black stone flags covered the floor that sloped towards the door. The reason for this slope was twofold. He would often have a calf tied in the corner closest to the door, and all the water ran straight out. I think it was like this in most of the thatched houses long ago. I never remembered him taking ill, coughing or anything like that. To me he was tough as leather and a pure tanned color to match, mainly dyed with the smoke.

If old Joe did not happen to be around the house and I couldn't find the sweets I would just continue on to the next neighbour's house, where an old woman and her son lived. She had a wooden leg and this used to amaze me because I thought that she was born with it. She could manoeuvre around no problem when she would make her way to the table and cut me a big slice of bread, lather it with butter, spoonfuls of jam, then finish it off with a thick layer of sugar. She would talk away for ages. I think she liked to see children coming in; it helped pass the time. I thought this was mighty stuff altogether and would not let on about it when I went home, because my mother would not let me next or near the sweet stuff, as she kept telling me that too much sugar would rot my teeth.

Bringing Tea to the Turf Cutters

My mother said to me one day "C'mon we have a job to do. We have to go up to the bog to make tea for the men working at the turf." I did not really want to hear that because I knew it meant a long walk. It wasn't something to be looking forward to in the middle of a roasting hot summer, when your legs were about the same length as your wellies. As far as I remember every summer seemed to be the same when I was young, your skin would peel off, helped along by picking at it, just to see how big a piece you could get off in the one go. No such thing as protection from the sun then, just the warning that if you stayed out too long you would get burned, and if it happened, it happened. I would dawdle along behind, doing my best to keep up, but would keep getting distracted by bumble bees looking for their fix of pollen through the purple or pinkish flowers on the heather. If it wasn't that it would be birds or maybe even a bug of some sort trying to make its way to the verge on the other side of the road. Then I would hear the shout "Hurry up there's a badger in the heather and it will eat the ass off you if you don't blooming hurry up," so I'd take off running and catch up, until such time had passed that I forgot the warning about getting the ass eaten off me.

When we'd get to where my father, Michael, and a neighbour were working, my job was to gather up some small pieces of turf and a bit of fir roots, trees that were part of forests that covered most of Ireland during the stone age. The fire would be going nicely in no time at all. There was a stream nearby that came out from a spring in the rocks. Pure, clean, fresh water where my mother would get the water using a tin can. That would be placed on top of the fire until it started to boil. Then she would throw in the tea and leave it for a few minutes before giving the men a shout. You'd get very hungry working in the bog. Maybe it was a mixture of tough physical work and of course the fresh air. On this one and only occasion I thought I was bigger than I was, or I wanted to impress the men by carrying the can over to them. So my mother, against her better judgment, let me carry the boiling hot can. I hadn't taken that many steps before I tripped over a sod, spilling the scalding black tea over my left arm. There was some squealing and shouting then, I can tell you. My mother grabbed me and off to the stream like an Olympic sprinter and held my arm under the ice cold water for ages. I remember looking at my arm with the skin all shrivelled up on it. The tea had to be made a second time before we headed for home. I was sitting on a big sod of turf blubbering and feeling very sorry for myself when a paper that was lying in front of me, after falling out of the lunch bag, suddenly lifted off the ground and started to zig-zag over and back as it floated slowly upwards into the sky. It was one of those small whirlwinds you would see on a very hot day, but for me I thought it was some sort of sign. With that and a loud warning from my mother ringing in my ears - don't ever go next or near hot tea again - we got a lift part of the way with another neighbour on his new tractor that he was after buying. No doctor or no hospitals, just get on with it.

Starting School

I vaguely remember my first day at school, I would have been five years' old. It was about two to three good miles away and we had to walk, unless there was heavy rain, hail or snow, when we would be kept at home or squeezed into the cab of the tractor, a Super Dexter. When walking, my brother Michael had to take me by the hand and sort of drag me along as I found it a bit hard to keep up sometimes. I don't think he was too happy about that because a little brother can be a hindrance at the best of times, never mind when he was in a hurry and he could not run off to play with his schoolmates; these were the neighbouring boys and girls who you happened to meet up with along the way. Just like any school anywhere in the country there'd always be a bit of bullying going on or someone picking on you, or you picking on someone else for one reason or another. But I was lucky enough to have an older brother at that stage to watch out for me, which gave me a false sense of security. Something I would find out about not too far into the future.

There was this other boy who was older than I was at the time and for some reason I had taken a dislike to him. Maybe I had seen him picking his nose or something, and for some time now I had been calling him names and none of them very nice either. As it happened, one day Michael was not at school. I suppose I could see the dark clouds coming my way; it was payback time. This boy came over to me and challenged me to call him names now, and, with me being as stubborn as I was, I couldn't hold back so I called him some other name thinking that it didn't sound as bad. Well that was a mistake. I can still feel the searing hot pain of the slap I got straight across the gob, and I suppose I did learn two good lessons out of that encounter but it's a pity I had to learn the hard way. My lesson was no more unneces- sary name calling, and, secondly, never depend on anyone else to fight your battles. After that I just sort of learned to speak up for myself. I suppose it was just another learning curve for me, and, like a lot of boys, you had to try and fight your corner. If you didn't the chance was that you'd get picked on, so you had a choice to make. The strange thing then was I sort of took a liking for the odd bit of shoving and pushing. I think it was the challenge. There was never any big harm done in our scraps at school because it amounted to no more than a few slaps, a bit of shouting and hot air swearing. It was all fine as long as it went my way, which I have to admit was not always the case.

School wasn't so bad as long as you didn't step too far out of line. One thing that I think is the hardest thing for any boy to do is to sit still in class. There were times when I thought that purgatory would be a walk in the park compared to having to sit still for longer than ten minutes. When I went into my first teacher, a job which at the time was classed as very much a privileged posi- tion in society, and with good reason too I suppose, I remember her as being a kind teacher with a very good temperament for dealing with children. There was one incident I remember quite clearly in her class. Someone had given me a marble. I think it may have been a swap for a pencil or something along that line. I remember sitting at my desk only half listening to what the teacher was saying. I had put the marble into my mouth and was swirling it around with my tongue. Whatever happened it went half-way down my throat and in a panic I tried to swallow it but that only made it worse because it wouldn't go up or down, which meant I couldn't breathe. So in a panic I grabbed the shoulders of the girl who was sitting in front of me, and when she saw the look on my face, she started shouting for the teacher, who then ran across from the blackboard and hit me a whack on the back with the palm of her hand. Needless to say, the marble shot right across the floor. I got an awful fright plus the telling off which I never forgot.

Tuesday was always a good day because it was dole day. So there would always be a few old men who'd be a bit under the weather due to a few drinks too many. They were old to us anyway, but in reality they were probably somewhere between their thirties and fifties. They would buy a few handfuls of sweets in Nial Rua's shop across the road from our school and they would throw the sweets down over the fence to us in the playground as they passed by. Our playground was below road level, so the crafty older boys would sneak out to where a man was standing on the outside, because as he took the sweets from his pockets a fair few would end up on the ground. But that was a risky business because more than likely you would get told on by the school 'tell tit' or by some other one who didn't manage to get any, and was feeling sore for it, and if someone did tell on you then it was the sally rod and no sweets. Sometimes it was a lose-lose situation, a bit like stocks and shares. The rewards were there, if you were willing to take the risk. On a Sunday coming out from mass, I would see the same men that would throw the sweets to us standing outside the chapel gates with a good few other men. This was them after rushing out before the mass was over and then stand talking for half an hour outside.

I don't know if it was after my first year or second that I was shifted into my next teacher, who was fairly new to the school at the time. She was very sharp indeed. She caught me copying off Richard Conlon, who sat in front of me. He was someone who never got a sum or an answer wrong, so if you copied his work you didn't get any wrong either. Or Barney Coyle, he would be beside me or sometimes directly behind. That worked okay until she put you sitting beside someone who was up to the same sort of tricks as yourself, and if that happened then it was up to the Gods whether you got your work right or wrong.

There was a story to tell about her as well. One day things just weren't going right for her. This meant that she would be in a bad mood. Fortunately that didn't happen too often, but on this occasion she was dishing out a bit of the ruler treatment; anyone would be punished if they were not paying proper attention in class. She was very strict but good, but in her haste to get to the offending rascal she tripped and sort of stumbled without falling, but her head we thought had come off; it went across the floor and ended up under a seat. Well it was the first time in my life to see a hairpiece or a wig. Her hair was always very prim and proper and now we knew why. Finally we had found her weak spot but never took advantage of it because of the fear factor.

Next in line was a teacher whose bark was always far worse than his bite, but he had a great way of relating all the historical stories about Queen Maeve of Connacht, the Normans, Cromwell, the Plantation of Ulster, and the Flight of the Earls from Mulroy Bay. These were the history lessons that I enjoyed most and still remember fondly if I may say so. I remember the inkwells in the desks. At that time we had to write with ink pens and I remember writing with a feather that he brought in to show us what was used to write with before the ink pen came into use. There'd be ink on your hands, then you'd scratch or rub your face, then you'd try to clean it off with the sleeve of your jumper. You'd get some eating when you went home in that sort of mess. The first time could be classed an accident but the second or third time would be stretching your luck a bit too far.

On another occasion myself and one of my mates at school, Eddie, in an act of bravado, decided to run out of class after the teacher had gone to the leithras (toilet). Out the door and around the corner we went and across the yard. There was a wall about a meter in height with a stream running along behind it. Well with our adrenalin flowing we cleared the lot in a single jump. Red Rum wouldn't have held a candle to us that day. We made our way through the bushes and out onto the main road a bit further up and came out in front of where An Bear Mór is now, but at that time it was Hughie McClafferty's Oiche Loistin (bed and breakfast), and us thinking we were the bravest lads on the planet. But lo and behold, there is always a price to be paid at the end of the day. We had hardly got our breath back and us huffing and puffing, when who did we run into only Eddie's mother. She immediately asked us what we were up to. We blurted out that we had got a half day and that we were first out and we were trying to be home before everyone else. She seemed happy enough with our explanation so off home we went.

The following morning I made out I was sick and got to stay at home, but poor Eddie wasn't so lucky. He had to go to school and face the music for both of us, although all he got was a good telling off and was warned not to even think about doing it again. I managed to keep up my story of feeling unwell and got to stay at home another day, so by the time I did walk into school I think the teacher had more important things to be dealing with, or so it seemed, because he never, ever mentioned it to me.

I recall another occasion on my way home from school; it was during the summer. When you turned off the main road, and up An Lane Mhór, as it was always known, there was a stream running down just in off the road and part of it was dammed up. This was because it was used as a source for household water by a few of the surrounding neighbours. It was handy for us because we'd spend ages there with a couple of sticks and a piece of string and a hairgrip, stolen off granny, for a hook. But this day anyway, Elish, one of my sisters, was leaning in a bit too far, when the next thing I saw was her disappearing, head first, under the water. In sheer panic I tried to grab her but I fell in as well. I managed to get back on my feet fairly quickly, but I couldn't get Elish out as her hair was tangled in briars under the water. I was struggling away trying to free her, when there was a big splash. This older boy Johnny Doogan had landed in beside me, pulled out a pocket knife, and in a flash cut the briars and pulled her out. I don't know how she was still breathing after drinking half the water in the stream, but lucky for her, Johnny had been on his way home on his bicycle after leaving sheep up on the hill. When he saw the two of us fall in, that was a stroke of luck for us. Or was there someone higher up keeping an eye out as well?

My next move at school was into what would be the last class I would attend at that school. The teacher was the headmaster and so was a different kettle of fish altogether. Everyone would be scared stiff when it came to their time for going into his class. I think he relished the fact that he could administer his version of corporal punishment in whatever manner he wished. There would be a lot of boys who would not forget their time with him in a hurry, including me. I saw boys who were a fair bit older then me pee their pants with fear whilst standing at the blackboard trying to do sums that they were clearly not fit to do and then get the big stick down on the palm of the hands. Each strike left a visible welt that you wouldn't forget in a hurry. One of the legs came out of his chair as well, which was used in the same way as the sticks on the palm of the hands, although not as often. Another extra bit of torture that wasn't too pleasant either was that you were sent out to break your own rod off the tree. You would then try and break any small jaggy bits off it on the way back in again. You'd spit and rub the palms of your hands together in the hope that it would somehow dull the pain that was as inevitable as the big smile he had on his face as soon as he saw you entering the classroom.

We were doing sums or measurements one day. One of the boys was having some difficulty with what he was tasked to do, so the teacher told him to go and measure a pane of glass on the window. He did that and returned to his seat. He was asked what was its size. "Nine by twelve," he replied. "Wrong," the teacher said and told him to hold out his hand where he got a good few raps of the stick. This was repeated three times before he took the ruler and measured it himself. Wasn't the young boy right all along, but of course there was no such thing as apologies issued and he continued on as if nothing had happened.

It would be very easy to use excuses and say dyslexia wasn't recognized back then as a factor in children having difficulty learning. You were classed as plain stupid or just too lazy to learn so the stick was always on standby for teachers who followed this line of thought. The good side of being in a new class was that you were now mixing with the older boys, as a few of the teachers had too many classes to deal with. Some of them were always up to something or hatching some sort of far-fetched plan for after school. There was a little shop across from the church in Gort an Choirce, it's now known as An Panc. Tommy Rooney owned the shop then and he had very bad eyesight and one boy would keep him talking while the others would grab whatever they could and by the time poor Tommy copped what was going on, they'd be off out the door and him after them. The next day he would be at the school going mad but he would not be able to point out who exactly had been in his shop because of his bad eyesight so everyone was barred from going near the shop until such time as things calmed down in a week or so.

Another one of the many pastimes that only happened on certain days of the week was, on the way home from school, the delivery lorries or vans would coincide with us going past what was Harry Curran's garage and McDonald's shop in Bedlam. We would wait until the drinks lorry, which was open backed, pulled off from the garage. They were very slow in them days with plenty of smoke coming out the back, so the fast boys would always jump up on the back and throw off a few large bottles of lemonade or coke. Then we'd hide behind the hedge and wait for the bread van to come along. It was all a matter of timing. When that van arrived the delivery man would open the back doors. He normally did two runs into the shop with loaves of bread. Then he would do the one run with whatever cakes or biscuits, so he was usually an extra few minutes making up his bill. He always kept his pen or pencil behind his ear. How I remember this is more than once him dropping a loaf or a cake and as he was picking it up the pencil fell off and he would start cursing because he couldn't pick it up with his arms full and he would have to come back out for it. But these few minutes was enough time for us to carry out 'the great cake robbery'. It was nearly always just sweet bread with raisins and fruit but they were good enough for us and did the trick. It was a matter of piling in behind the hedge again to share out the spoils. The cakes would be broken into shares for whoever was there, and then the bottles would be passed around. So you had to try and be first or second in line for getting your drink because by the time it came around again it would be full of bits of cake. In saying that, it still didn't stop anyone from taking their slug from the big bottle. You just had to pretend to yourself that it was all your own crumbs and spit.

Remembering

Some of the things you remember, maybe you shouldn't. Life for everyone is full of ups but occasionally a few downs would come my way. One of those downs came in the form of a man who had some grievance with my grandfather. So this man decided that it was fair play for him to take some of his spite out on me and because of the difference in size, him being a big man and me no bigger than a grasshopper, almost every day he would pass me on his bike on our way home from school and throw a dirty big spittle. You could hear him draw in his breath in readiness for his strike. It reminded me of those cowboys in the westerns with the spittoon placed at a nice vantage point from where they sat at the bar chewing tobacco. All they had to do was turn their head round a bit without looking and spit. He was just like that. It always landed around my feet. This was after Michael had left school so it was just me and one or two of my sisters. I always meant to get my revenge on him when I got older, but by that time, he was more to be pitied than laughed at, and I never did find out what had caused the friction between himself and my grandfather in the first place. He could have had it for a number of reasons. It's possible the sour puss was over gates that were put on a right-of-way to keep animals in and prevent them from straying. It could have been about bog, fences, or who bought what at the fair day; even what side was taken before or after the civil war would have caused a lot of strife. Back in them days people were very territorial about right-of-ways and fought for little or no reason, but anything to do with land and you could have a fight on your hands before you knew it. Like most unsavoury things of that era, the way I see it, it's all in the past now and best left there.

Plans to Emigrate

The first hint I got that all was not as it seemed was one day my father came to pick us up from school on the tractor. Now this only happened if the rain was pouring from the heavens but it was always exciting as my father was one of the first people to get a tractor in the townland. On our way home I could not quite figure out why every so often he would stop and shake hands with different people along the way. I remember when we arrived at the house I jumped down from the tractor and ran in to see my mother. I asked her why my father was acting so strangely, and what were all the handshakes in aid of? I was young, about eleven, at the time but I still got a shock when she told me what it was all about. We were emigrating to Australia she told me. Michael and my father were to go out first and organize for the rest of the family to follow at a later date. It unnerved me to the extent that over the coming weeks I was considering running away from home. When you are young like that it was impossible to stop your imagination from running riot. I was imagining all sorts in my head.

I have no recollection of the day that my father and Michael left for that faraway land, I blanked it out somehow. But one thing I can remember is being very upset, and I would spend some days away up over the hills with the dog, searching for rabbit's burrows or chasing the odd hare thinking I could catch it. Other days I would spend hours climbing through bushes along parts of the local Glenea River, where we had land running alongside part of it. I knew where all the crossing points were, all the deep or dangerous holes. I also knew that a neighbour of ours whose mother used to give me the bread, jam and sugar sandwiches, would spend a lot of his spare time fishing along this patch of river so if I caught sight of him I would sit and watch him fishing. It was great watching, especially when he hooked a big salmon or a sea trout. He could spend half an hour playing the salmon trying to tire it out, and then he would let me hold the fishing rod while he reached into the water to grab the fish before it had time to regain its strength.

I remember every year my father would have cabbage, carrots, turnips and other vegetables planted on part of this land near the river, and when it was cold and frosty I would often break off the outer leaves of a cabbage like crisps, until I could get into the hard centre and put my head down and chew off big chunks, or pull a carrot and clean it on the grass and eat it on the way up the road. I remember the sweet taste of the carrot in my mouth now. If you haven't tasted a home-grown carrot fertilized with cow or horse dung then you haven't tasted a carrot at all. These sort of innocent activities kept my curiously mixed-up mind occupied for the time being, while all other thoughts were shoved into a part of the brain that you would not visit too often.

The Cousins are Coming

The next shock to my world was when my mother told me that my uncle and his family were coming home from Glasgow where they were living and that our house was now theirs. That scared me shitless to put it bluntly. Loads of their stuff began to arrive within the next couple of days, including a bike, so I begged and begged my mother to let me have a go on it. Eventually she gave in so off I would go on the bike acting all sensible until I got out of sight. Then it was a different story. Down the road I'd go, peddling as hard as I could with my knees nearly hitting my chin. Down the road past Hughie's I'd go; he had a bike of his own. At the time to me it seemed like he had everything, all the toys, everything that I didn't have, so this was my chance to pretend that I owned a bike. Myself and Hughie had some sort of a falling out as children do, so there was no talking for a while, just huffing and puffing like two penguins. Of course when the talking got off to a stuttering start and we were best buddies again, I could not tell him that it wasn't my bike so I had to let him have a go on it. All very exciting while it lasted, which wasn't long because when the cousins landed, I told him that my mother gave the bike to them.

Fishing with Hughie

Hughie's father was a foreman out with the County Council, which in those days was considered, and still is today, a very good position to be able to get yourself into. Every Sunday in the summer months he would go fishing on the lakes. He hardly ever had to fish on the same lake twice as there were so many of them within driving distance. He drove a small blue mini and the excitement of the whole thing was great, because the two of us would be able to tag along as well and sometimes get in the way in our rush to take trout off the hooks and letting them drop into the water, and off they'd go.

Before leaving the house, the board, or the otter as they used to call it, would have to be checked out. In case you don't know what I'm talking about, it's an apparatus that was used for fishing instead of a fishing rod. There were two types of otters, the single board or the double board, the double being, in my opinion, the more effective one. It involves a piece of board with some lead fixed to the bottom to make it stay upright in the water. The line is then fixed a little below the water level, near to half ways in length. When it's left in the water and pressure put on the line by pulling it, walking at the same time, the board will steer itself out from the bank and the more line you release the further out it goes, with the fly hooks hanging down from this line. That's how you catch your fish.

It was me and Hughie's job to take the trout off the hooks. Sometimes he could have up to five trout on at the same time. What used to happen more often than not was just as you were about to catch the fish it would fall off, splash into the water and shoot off like a flash, because it wasn't hooked on properly in the first place. But again it all depended on the type of weather. If it was too hot it was no good, because the trout stayed down in the cooler waters. If it was too windy it was no good, and it depended what direction the wind was blowing from. A lot of things depended on the wind in those days. So things weren't as simple as throwing a hook in the water and catching a big trout. When we'd get back to Hughie's house, his father would roast the trout over the open fire. They were delicious, especially when they were done enough so that the bones sorted of melted; then there was no fear of being choked on a fish bone.

The Cousins Arrive

There was a lot of excitement and rushing around on the day my unknown relatives did arrive, sort of unexpectedly, in a way. It was the first time for me, or us should I say, to meet our cousins so there was a period of getting to know one another over the next number of weeks or months. Unfortunately we had to move house due to an unforeseen conflict of interests, stress, and circumstantial hearsay leading to arguments. Two families in the one house just does not work, no matter how hard you try, so it just made the move inevitable. It was only across the fields really so no big changes. This would have been about 1973 to '74. Me, Joe and Michael Woods, my new cousin who was older than me, began to get up to all sorts of tricks. As home entertainment goes it would be hard to get better.

Bartley was an old boy who lived on his own just down the laneway from our house. He always smoked them old clay pipes. He gave us a few that had the shanks broken off, but that did not stop us from trying them out. We collected old leaves off the trees and dried them out nicely before the trial run, which turned out not too bad. But the next batch of homemade tobacco nearly killed us. We went through the same process of drying and all that but decided at the last minute to add a few extra ingredients. Sure there would be no harm in it. When we did manage to light up, there was a foul taste but we continued to smoke away like old pros. When the dizziness started we knew something was amiss. What I went through over the next few hours and a sleepless night was terrible. I felt I was turning every color of the rainbow before sticking on green. When I woke up the next morning the only thing I could compare it to would be like someone in the horrors of drink or on drugs. One minute the window was beside me the next it was miles away at the end of a tunnel. Next I was walking across the ceiling. That was the end of any idea I had of becoming a pipe smoker.

There were a few fields close by that we would use as a shortcut where some of our neighbours would have rams tethered up around about lambing time. So we would catch the rope from where it was pegged into the ground and keep pulling until we caught the ram. Some of them would be wild and try to butt you, so one boy would distract it while the other would sneak up from behind and jump on its back and off you went. For us it was as good as rodeo horses, just hold on for dear life to see who could stay on the longest.

Trying to Do Away with the Dog

I remember this big stray dog following us around one Sunday evening where we'd hang around passing the time outside Nial Rua's shop in Gort an Choirce. We tried loads of times to chase it away but it just would not take no for an answer. A bright idea came to me when it rolled onto its back wanting to play and me doing my best trying to get rid of it. I lifted the air hose and stuck the end of the nozzle up to the dogs arse and gave it a blast!! Well if you seen the takeoff it made it was like a Ferrari leaving the starting line at the Monaco Grand Prix. That was okay, but for the fact that it made a fart like a motorbike backfiring and the smell was the foulest stench that I ever had the misfortune to breath into my lungs then or since. The over-friendly canine was in serious need of some colonic irrigation, which it got by way of an air hose. The dog followed us the whole way home and parked itself outside our door. A few days later some of the, neighbours who owned sheep came to our house raring up, that our dog was harassing the sheep. My mother, who had more than enough on her plate at the time, could have done without this added hassle so the three of us decided the only thing we could do because it was our fault was to drown the dog. So down to the river we go. Tied a rope around the dog's neck and tied a big stone on the other end and threw both in at the same time. We felt bad about doing it so we began walking off.

We were only half way to the house when the dog comes bounding up to us wagging its tail with the stone still attached. Back to square one. So we got a bigger stone and tied it as best as we could. All the while the dog is licking away at my hands while I'm tying it, as if I was its best friend ever. The poor dog. Over to the edge again and in it goes. To be honest I felt relieved then as we began walking up along the hedge. We had nearly reached the same point as we had the first time when it raced past us with its tail wagging like mad, as if it was saying, let's do this again its great fun. But there was no again in it. The dog was tied up, learned a few survival tips and became part of the family after that. The mutt was lucky twice, I wonder whose side would the luck have been on if there was a third time?

My Uncle Joe

My Uncle Joe was a very quiet type of a man, never one to give too much away. He was very handy. He could fix almost anything, as long as it was mechanical, lorries, tractors, cars, or watches. He was the first person, as far as I know, that had a car running on gas back in those days; it was around about 1971 I think. He had a mini, which he adapted with all homemade gadgets to run on them yellow bottles of gas you see outside of most hardware shops. It did work very well but unfortunately it proved too costly to run, so he reverted back to the petrol some time afterwards.

On the Move Again

We were on the move again after about a year. I think we ended up in a house in Ray, Ned McHugh's, a two-story house that was damp, draughty and a bit squeezed for space. I don't remember what time of the year it was when we made the move, but what I do remember clearly is trying to pack newspapers in around the window frames and anywhere else that we could to stop the cold air coming in. There was that much of a gap at the bottom of the door that a cat could walk in and out without having to touch its belly on the floor, so a couple of coats with a piece of timber on top were used to stop the wind from howling like a banshee in around there. But at the end of the day I suppose, beggars can't be choosers. That's how the saying goes anyway, as I've been told often enough. It didn't help me when I'd be in under the bedcovers with my knees up to my chin trying to escape the cold and get to sleep at the same time. The Harkins, Mary, Dan and one of their sons Danny, were our next-door neighbours. Danny had an old grey TVO tractor and was always taking it apart and fixing at it. I made it my business to help him, but the truth of the matter was that I could have been more of a hindrance than a help. He would spend ages explaining all the dos and the don'ts about the makeup of the tractor. He even told me how many pumps of the hand pumps it took to fill the big wheel with air; it was a few hundred as far as I remember, not that I ever really wanted to find out because it sounded like an awful lot of hard work.

Doing the Housework

At that stage our family consisted of my mother, granny, three boys and eight girls, so we would have been used to a lot of squealing and shouting. Another function that had to be carried out, and it seemed to be a never-ending process where you were playing catch-up the whole time, was all the washing. My mother and granny had to do it using a washing board, all the clothes, including nappies which weren't like the disposable version that are used today; it was just a towel, sometimes doubled to soak up the pee. My mother would have the sewing machine out making plastic pants to pull on over the nappy to prevent leaks and a much bigger washing job if it were to happen. Over all the years people came to her from all over the place to have clothes altered, zips replaced, trousers shortened, dresses made, and so on.

It was fairly important that there was always a good fire kept on the go. The well for clean drinking water was just down the laneway so all the water had to be carried up to the house, It was no big deal as long as you didn't mess around. The first thing you had to do was boil a big pot of water then pour it into a big basin or bath, stand the washing board nearly upright, bend over it with your ass pointing up in the air and get to work. You dipped the garment into the water, rubbed soap on it, then scrubbed it up and down on the board, which had lots of ridges running crossways on it. Some of them had a glass plate with the ridges on it. These types were better as the ridges did not wear off like the wooden ones. We, the older ones of the gang, had to take our turn on it as well when the pressure came on. Then the clothes had to be rinsed out in clean water and your poor knuckles would be nearly rubbed off you. I think sometimes I can still feel the tingling sensation in my hands from the ripples going up and down on the board, and my ears still suffer from the effect of all that shouting and squealing. A lot of my mother's time would be taken up with knitting jumpers or knitting socks. In the middle of all the organized chaos she would be darning the toes or the heels of the socks that were letting the daylight in.

My Mother Growing Up

My mother was originally from Ballybofey, where she was brought up on the family farm by her grandmother and a farm labourer who looked after her through thick and thin. Her mother had committed the unthinkable at that time, and had run off with another man and never again laid eyes on her daughter. My mother was only three years' old at the time. Many times I have tried to place myself in her mother's shoes to see if I could come up with a rational explanation other than a selfish one that would cause a person to do this. But in hindsight, it is easy to judge and apportion blame for what did or did not happen in these unexplainable circumstances. It would be much easier to forgive if you knew why. Her father also did the very same thing a short time later, only returning once to carry out one of the lowest deeds that a father could do. After her mother had left, her grandmother gave her a ewe and a few lambs. The purpose of that I would imagine would be to take her mind off the turmoil that was taking place around her. She may have been at a tender age but she could see and hear what was going on and carried that heavy burden with her every day since.

A couple of days after her father had been around, she had gone out over the hills to check on her sheep. They were not to be seen high or low in their normal grazing spots, which was unusual. Eventually she spotted a neighbouring farmer rounding up his sheep not too far away from where she was, so her and the dog ran towards him and as she got closer she could see that her sheep were mixed in through his flock. She asked him if he could help her separate them. He looked a bit puzzled at her request. Then he said, "Did your father not tell you? He came and asked me if I wanted to buy them so I did". The farmer was very apologetic but it broke her heart and it was something that she never got over.

I saw her father once in my life without realising who it was. I was home from England on holiday when a car came to the house asking for my mother. As I was on my way out I did not pay too much attention as to who it was because there was always someone coming or going at our house. But I remember on coming back and finding out who had been to visit, I could see that my mother was upset by his visit. But I had also to understand that at the end of the day he was still her father and in a strange way perhaps she gained some peace of mind from his visit. In my mind there was too much water under the bridge at this late stage to make amends that would be considered rational. In my mind his visit was not made to seek forgiveness but clearing his own conscience for not being there as a father to her when she was growing up or walking up the aisle to give her away when she got married, a very important thing in most young women's lives. When a parent abandons a child as in this case, the reasons for doing so must be very strong to override the inbuilt instincts that all parents subconsciously inherit; in other words, a connection that should happily exist.

All in all she did spend many happy years on the farm. She told us about the rationing that went on throughout the Second World War when she would accompany the old woman, her granny, with the horse and cart and bring back tea chests full of tea, sugar and stuff like that. If you got caught with your black market goods the penalty was that you lost the lot. It was never a moneymaking concern, it was about having the bare essentials that we take for granted today. There was a bit of bartering and haggling that would take place then between neighbours and such like, in place of exchanging money. When her grandmother died she left the farm to my mother who was still only a young girl, on a written condition that Michael Murray, who was the farm labourer, would spend the rest of his days on the farm. He had always classed it as his home anyway. A just reward for a kind and generous man. When it came to the stage where he was having trouble doing things for himself my mother brought him to live with us, where he spent the rest of his days. There was one thing that he was great at when he had his wits about him. When there were children around he would start telling ghost stories and scare the living daylights out of them. The downside of that was they would be too frightened to go to bed on their own then or pee the bed at night as I had done plenty of times after listening to him telling ghost stories to me when I was young.

Long Lost Relatives

If I can briefly skip ahead a few years, after Michael Murray, or Mick as we knew him, had passed away my mother had a sixth sense that all was not what it seemed, and subsequently, as I understand it (I may be a bit sketchy on the dates and stuff like that, but it started around 1992), she started making some enquiries and found out that she had a brother Jim (who passed away before I got to meet him) who was married and living in Antrim. He had also been trying to get in touch with her after catching bits of rumours and hearsay. They did meet up and started trying to piece together all the blank bits, finding out that their mother and the man she had eloped with had made their way to Australia. But that's where the trail went dead. My mother's relatives on both sides must have been sworn to secrecy, because as far as they were concerned they had vanished off the face of the earth and they did not know of their whereabouts. But there were more shocks to come. My mother received a letter from Australia through the Salvation Army. She was shocked at the contents of the letter; a web of deceit was at long last beginning to unravel. Apparently a family whose mother had died found an Irish birth cert in her belongings and the surname did not correspond with theirs, and neither did the birth cert stating that she was born in Ireland. Baffled at first, curiosity then took over, but it was my mother receiving the letter that really set the ball rolling. To cut a long story short, it turned out that she had a brother and sister born and brought up in Australia that were as much in the dark about the shocks that were beginning to unfold.

Throughout their whole lives, nothing had ever been mentioned to them that would raise any suspicions about what they had to come to terms with now. After a lot of exchanging of photos, birth certificates and all that sort of stuff over the coming weeks and months in an attempt to prove beyond all reasonable doubt that no one was making a dreadful mistake or barking up the wrong tree, a length of time passed, enough for everything to sink in. I was at home from London especially to be there, when my mother's newly found sister Kathleen and her husband Peter made the journey of discovery home. It proved to be much more fruitful than they at first thought it would be. There was a lot of soul searching done, and in the process dusting down the cobwebs that covered the truth for reasons unknown to us. They enjoyed their time immensely. We did our utmost to make them feel at home, even though trying to get to know relatives you never knew you had in a short space of time is exhausting; more so for them because of the long journey, as you can imagine.

My newly discovered Uncle Jack and his wife Nola also made the long journey from Australia, where they met up with my mother and my Uncle Jim for what was a very emotional family reunion. After a few weeks of visiting relatives and sightseeing, they flew over to London as they had it fixed into their schedule because they knew that there were a good few of the family over there as well. So when we met up with them it was just great. My uncle was the spitting image of my mother, with the same temperament as well. His wife was playing second fiddle or being sidelined the whole time. Of course it was not meant to be so, but our uncle was the focus of attention as if maybe he had all the answers. They did a bit of sighting around London unescorted, as I may not have had the same sights or tastes in mind as them. When they left he promised to be back. He kept his promise and returned for a more relaxed holiday and fitted in like a glove that had been lost for a while. He got more enjoyment the second time around because he did a lot more sightseeing throughout a good few counties. Joe, my brother, then went out to visit and spent a month with them seeing the sights, including the trusty old kangaroo, and travelling around different parts of the country.

Of course today with the advancement of modern technology a person on the other side of the world can be brought right into your living room via Skype on a PC or laptop. There are no hiding places left.

The reason for telling this part of the story is for people who knew and were friends of my mother and would never think that there was so much turmoil in her life, because she was one of the happiest people you could meet. Everyone in the parish knew her laugh and those who didn't talked about it.

As long as there is a reasonably happy ending to a story, as there was in this case, it means that a ray of sunshine has shone on a skeleton that was confined to a cupboard unnecessarily, in my opinion, for far too long. There are many cases similar to this one, where families were split up due to poverty and desperate times. After the famine some who got the chance of going to Australia or America lost touch, never meeting up again to mend broken fences.

Melting the Butter Mountain

There was a small shop down at the end of the road near to where the grotto is and that was run by Mickey and Mary Doherty. Over the road another wee bit was Seamus Neil's shop; both of them are long gone now. But I remember having to carry the shopping bags up the hill, getting distracted, then leaving the shopping lying there and going off for an hour or so. By the time the shopping eventually got to the house the butter would be dripping out the bottom of the bag after melting with the heat of the sun. There was a butter mountain in the EEC because of over supply so everyone got so many coupons for free butter. But a lot of ours left trails along the side of the road I have to say. Sometimes I would pinch a few pennies from the purse when it was full of change because I thought my mother would never notice. I think she did because she stopped giving me the purse and would pay herself later for whatever was got at the shop. A lot of people nowadays would not know what it was like living in a house with no spare money whatsoever. I hope I don't have to live through those sorts of times again during my lifetime.

Me and Joe, James and Willie

Myself and Joe started to hang about at the end of the road just watching who might be passing by. Two boys would pass up or down now and again but wouldn't speak to us, which annoyed me I have to say. But then, sure I didn't speak to them either. My mother bought me and Joe a bicycle to share between us so I was coming up the hill walking with the bike one day when I saw the two boys coming down the hill towards me. There was a bit of staring going on when we came abreast of one another so I says, "What are you looking at?" The younger boy starts asking me about the bike. Meanwhile the older boy gets around behind me without me paying too much heed. Next thing I see stars after getting a good hard smack of a fist right on the ear and he makes off running and me at this stage tangled up in the bike. After getting over the shock of the clatter on the ear I made a dash after him, forgetting that I was still half astride the bike. Hence the falling over. So after getting my wits about me I was off in hot pursuit but he had a good start at this stage. To tell the truth, he would have been too fast for me anyway, so all I could do was watch him disappearing, as he made good his getaway. Well with me huffing and puffing I had to turn back as my bike was still lying in the middle of the road. The younger boy made out it had nothing to do with him. He told me the boy that gave me the clatter was his brother James and that his name was Willie. I used to hang around the same spot every day for a week or two hoping to get revenge but it wasn't to be. We became friends some time after that so that schoolboy incident was soon forgotten about.

There was one other incident when James showed off his speed. Both of us set off one day to do a bit of fishing on a lake. We had two smallish fishing rods. I think we had tried the worms first but were having no luck. Then we tried a few fly hooks with a bubble at the end. As luck would have it the trout kept going for one of my hooks. It was a red and black fly. I don't remember the name for it right now. I think I caught about six and he had no luck at all. So on the way home I was proud as punch holding my plastic bag up just in case we met any cars on the road so that they could see that I caught something. Thinking back they wouldn't have been much bigger than sardines. As we got nearer to our houses he tried to make a deal by giving me a few pennies that he had, which was tempting because the pennies were very hard to come by. But I wanted the trout. Then after another while he wanted to see what size they were so we took them out of the bag and laid them out on the road for a closer inspection. Poor me. Before I knew what was happening he made off running with a few fish. I took off after him but it was a waste of time, he was far too fast. He still wanted to do the deal so he left the few pennies laying on the road for me. I had no choice then but to go along with it. That's how we walked the rest of the way home, with him keeping a nice distance in front so that I had no chance of catching him. At the end of the day we both went home with something to show for our trek to the lake.

Carrowcanon National School

I think seven of us had to enrol at Carrowcanon National School at that time, it was 1974. Again we had to walk about two and a half miles or so, although as far as I remember we did manage to get on the school bus after a few months. I was nervous on my first day going in because I was used to speaking and doing all my classes through Gaelic at school up to now and I found it hard to settle in and find my place. But if you can't beat them join them, and that's just what I did to the best of my ability. The teacher, who everyone knew in the school as Darby, was the headmaster and I ended up in his classroom. It was very unnerving as I was placed up at the front of the class. God only knows why, as I was completely out of my depth when it came to lessons. If you were not paying attention or day dreaming as I would quite often be, next thing you'd get the rap on the back of the head. He had a knack of keeping the middle knuckle extended. I don't know who christened it the Darby knuckle shot and I could never duck it because he could always sneak up on you, seemingly from nowhere. Maybe it was because I would spend most of the time twiddling my thumbs anyway, but in all fairness he had his good days as well. He wasn't all that bad, as he would put me and Perri, as he was known, together. I don't know how he picked up the nickname but I always assumed it was because he had a fondness for Perri crisps. It was handy as he had the two of us sitting at the same desk. If there were any errands going up the town to the bank or fixing punctures on his bike we got the job. We looked forward to Monday morning because he would hand us all the weekend's newspapers and we'd spend the rest of the day going through them.

I still have a great affinity for reading and writing, although at the time it might not have done a lot of good for our future work prospects, but there you go. There was another teacher you had to watch out for. I can't remember his nickname but he was very sharp and he liked to get results, although I wasn't in with him that much, only if my teacher was off sick or some reason like that. But the times that I was unfortunate to be in, I won't forget his methods of getting the message through to you. When you got a slap from him you got the back of the hand on one cheek and the palm on the way back, a sort of a rabbit punch and if he really got annoyed with you because you could not answer questions he would twist your arm up your back and hit you a thump where the arm joins the shoulder and it left you with a dead arm for ages afterwards. He probably picked these tips up from watching Bruce Lee films, they were very popular at the time. So it wasn't only the pupils who were practicing their kung fu moves. It was really up to the teachers as to what punishment you got. Even the drumsticks were used for more than beating a roll on a drum. That's the way it was and was accepted because there was not a lot you could do about it.

I began mating around with another boy down the road from us called Brian Ferry. He was mad into fishing so we began to spend a lot of time along the Ray River. I never caught much. I didn't have the same patience that he had, or the know-how for that matter, so he caught the salmon and I got to carry the odd one home. He had an older brother, Patrick, but we always called him Benjy. So one day the two of us spent the whole day trying to cycle our bicycles backwards. I lost count of the times we fell off but neither of us would give in just in case the other boy got the hang of it. That would not be good for a boy's credibility so we hung in there until we got it mastered more or less simultaneously. It was great showing off what we could do to the rest of the boys, but the novelty of it soon wore off.

When we all got together at night, mainly Joe, Brian, James, Willie, Owen Curran, wee Barny and me, you just never knew what was going to happen in the hours ahead. Most nights we'd meet at Seamus's shop. We were always on the lookout for empty mineral bottles that were returnable. Every dump that we knew of would get a visit at some stage in the never-ending search for bottles. You'd get a few pence each so that would keep you going on sweets. There was always one or two fly boys who would just rattle the bottles brazenly that were stacked inside the door of the porch as they went in, and just say that they had left so many in a crate, then buy some goodies with the money. It was always a great place for the craic, especially when the slagging would start, one trying to tell a taller story than the next. There was one character who everyone knew as wee Hughie. He was around four foot nothing in height, an old saying I would hear my mother use, which in this case wasn't too far off the truth. All he ever talked about was women. You had to pick the right words to get him revved up. All you had to say to wee Hughie to get him hopping off the ground was sure you have nothing anyway (endowed) and he'd get into a temper and threaten to produce his manhood. "Get it out there now and I'll measure up with you," he'd start shouting, but that's as far as it would ever go.

The real attraction for us if the truth be told was that a good few of the local girls, who all wore jeans and brogues (that was the style then), would meet up and hang around there as well. So there was always the odd bit of innocent starry-eyed flirting going on, holding hands if you were lucky. We were about eleven or twelve at the time. I watched a few DIY ear piercing jobs carried out by a few of the girls. All that was needed was a needle and some disinfectant, half a potato and some ice cubes, and a couple of short pieces of thread. Freeze the ear lobe with an ice cube on each side then put the half potato at the back (which acted as a cushion and stopped the needle from sticking into the neck) and push the needle through, pulling the thread after and tying it in a loose circle so that it could be kept moving back and forth until the hole healed up, then the earring was popped in. If there happened to be older boys around, as there were on many occasions, the girls would soon lose interest in us. We might move on then to Ballyboes where we had a good spot for dropping big sods down onto passing cars with only a slim chance of getting caught. Then maybe knock on a few doors and run like hell. It wasn't so bad if you knew there was a few of the boys slower than you, because if we did get chased they would be the first to get caught.

I remember me, Brian, and Joe trying to catch a corncrake. We tried it loads of times, sneaking in through the corn fields. Each time it sang or croaked, we would move towards it. If it stopped we stopped. When you got close enough to be able to pinpoint exactly where it was you would turn on the torch and there it would be right in front of you. But it did not matter how close we got, we never managed to catch one. They were very plentiful way back then. You would hear them in every field of corn in the whole place.

Old Grainne

James and Willie's old granny often got a visit. She liked us coming in as long as we were behaving. Old Grainne had very bad eyesight so she never really saw half of what went on. There was no running water in the house at the time so she always used to keep a big galvanized bucket of clean water for drinking or making the tea sitting on the second or third step up on the stairs. One night we decided to have a game of football using a tennis ball in the kitchen. Grainne used to sit on this big old armchair beside the open fire. When the ball would start to get belted all over the place it could knock ornaments, statues or the odd cup down that would end up in smithereens. In some cases the bucket of water got the upside down treatment, which it did on too many occasions. Well this time it was rather different. When the ball was bouncing around it must have gone into the fire and out again without any of us noticing until we saw the smoke rising up from the chair Grainne was sitting in. A hot coal must have got flung underneath the bloody chair. There we were trying to get her out of it and her thinking we had gone mad pulling her out of her chair. We turned it upside down and one of the boys grabbed the bucket of water off the stairs and poured it over the chair. We turned it up again and put her with a cushion under her back into it without her knowing a thing. She thought the ball had got stuck under it and that was why we had to get her out of it.

Grainne used to get a visitor calling one or two nights in the week. He lived about twenty minutes' walk away. He was well known throughout the townland. He would bring in turf or water for any of the old people that he used to visit. On this particular occasion in Grainne's, when we came in we started messing about because he had a couple of packets of Nice biscuits and he would not let us have any. We kept annoying him so eventually he chased us out and locked the door. He made tea for himself and Grainne and started tempting us with the biscuits as we were looking in the window and our tongues hanging out. So we came up with a plan. Somehow with help from the other boys I managed to get up onto the barge of the roof so I made my way up onto the chimney and sat on the chimney pot to stop the smoke getting out. After about fifteen minutes the house was full of smoke and George came outside coughing and spluttering. At this stage he did not know why the chimney wasn't drawing properly. He didn't know that I was perched up on top getting my backside roasted. By then I couldn't take any more, I had to get off because with the heat my back end was nearly like a barbequed piece of rump steak. He soon figured out then what had been the cause of the smoke. Well the next day when someone who had been visiting old Grainne came and told my mother what we were up to the night before, I think I was about twelve at the time, but I can tell you I had a hot ass, a burned ass, and a very sore ass for the second night running. It was a while before I was allowed out again.

Making Butter and Other Foods

I liked watching the whole process of making butter. I would watch my granny skimming the cream off the milk every morning and putting it into the churn that sat beside the range. It needed that little bit of heat to make it ferment. I think it took about two weeks to collect enough cream to make it worth churning. The churn would be brought into the middle of the floor and whoever was there was given their turn at plunging the dash up and down. Your arms would start to ache after a while if not used to it, or maybe you being too young and not strong enough would be a good enough excuse as well. It had to be done at a nice steady pace. If you became too impatient and started going too fast your butter would be a very pale colour; the combination of the cream fermenting properly and using the dash the way it's supposed to be used would leave you with beautiful, yellow, tasty butter. You could never see the change, it happened so quickly. One second it was cream you were looking at, and in the blink of an eye butter appeared. It was then lifted out in lumps and had to be beaten until all the water was taken from it. Then it was salted to taste and that was it. Job over, apart from the buttermilk, which was lovely and creamy. I liked it when it was left for a day or two so that it would have a slight sting in the taste. Of course we were encouraged to drink it because of its benefits for the digestive system.

There were a few other dishes or cures that I was force fed on and off. One was bogbean or bogbine, which was long roots that would be found in bog holes. It was boiled and you drank the soup of it. It was the most foul-tasting stuff you could let near your lips, but it was believed to be good for cleansing the blood, among other things. Then there was Carrigeen moss picked off the rocks down along the shore. You would boil it, separating it by cooking it in a netted cloth. That didn't taste too bad at all. There was another seaweed dish called sloac that you would find in through the stuff on the rocks, which wasn't bad but a little rubbery. You could just about pretend that you were enjoying it. You had to acquire a liking to the taste for some of those foods otherwise you would have to get your iron intake from some other source. We used to eat a lot of fish as well. There were a few men from Inishboffin Island going around selling fresh fish, which were caught early that morning. The herring were always very tasty, when roasted enough to make the bones brittle enough so that you wouldn't choke on them. I had a few bad experiences with fish bones getting caught in my throat. The only cure for it was to eat dry bread in the hope that it would dislodge it. It always did the trick, but you might have to eat half of a homemade scone that was the size of a tractor wheel and a gallon of milk before it moved.

The Old Man on the Farm

I used to help an old man that had a farm and owned a few tractors that he used to let me drive, putting out cow dung on the fields and doing the ploughing. He was a very rough and ready sort of a man. He would come back from the butchers with, for instance, sheep ribs. He would throw them on the floor, get a block of wood he had for breaking turf on and chop the ribs in half with the same axe he had for the turf. The bread would be lying on the table until hair grew on it and it still got eaten. There was a time when I ran over one of his dogs beside the house and killed it, so he lifted it and threw it on the track where I would be driving up and down with hay, but it wasn't working out as an easy way of burying the dog. So after a week he pulled it out with his hands. It was sort of starting to rot and his fingers were going in through it, so he threw it into a deep drain. He just cleaned his hands on his coat. Shortly after that we went into the house for some tea. He got out a pound of sausages and packed them into a pot to boil them. Believe it or not I was that hungry that I ate those sausages knowing where his hands were an hour before and that he never washed them. For that matter he'd never get sick. Just imagine that now; I think people's immune systems have become weakened due to the fact that we are no longer exposed to a bit of dirt. Now you'd be guarantied to end up with swine flu or mad cow disease, or something definitely along these lines.

Bicycles and Adventures

Vincent Carton was one of the local undertakers but he also had a minibus and used to drive children to school. As well as all that he sold bicycles from a small shop that you passed on the way to the doctor's surgery where it was at that time, on the Muckish road up towards the Falcarragh Hall. You'd always be in having a look at what you could not afford. Anyway I pestered my mother about it until she gave in and bought a bike between me and my brother Joe for fifteen or twenty pounds, a lot of money at the time. I felt bad about getting her to spend the money on it later on when I realised how scarce money was, because any clothes that she did not make for us, she bought at jumble sales. As far as I remember the make of the bike was a Tourer. They were popular enough at the time, similar to a BMX. When I think about it, that bike got some abuse.

I'd be allowed to take it to mass on a Sunday, where there wasn't much point in us going as most of us sat on the stairs at the back of the church anyway. The whole point was that we'd be out early and I could do a good bit of showing off. I remember on the way home from mass coming down Carrocannon Hill, which was fairly steep, with five of us on the bike, myself, Joe, Brian Ferry, James and Willie McGee. Mathematically speaking, five into one doesn't go too well, but it did for us. The brakes would not hold you back so it was straight out onto the main road and hope nothing was coming. Even though it was dangerous it was well worth it. You'd get some thrill, especially if it was a close call as you got out onto the main road. That was the whole point of doing it in the first place I suppose.

Robbing Apples

There used to be an orchard in the Ballyconnel Estate, and the excitement we used to get out of doing the odd raid on it was great. In our eyes it was no different than raiding a bank. There was one time we got caught in the orchard by Connie Hanlon. He used to work there as caretaker. A few of us were up the trees shaking them to knock the apples down when someone shouted to run. There was some scramble to get over the wall that surrounded the orchard. First you had to climb a tree that was close to the wall and then jump onto the wall. Then climb down another one to get down the other side. Connie had a big scar down one side of his face. We did not know that he had got this in a car accident, we just assumed that he got it in a fight. We were frightened of our lives of him, because we were sure if he caught any of us he would take you back to the Ballyconnel House and most likely chop us up or bury us alive. All these mad thoughts would be running through your head when the chase was on.

Well the chase was on and we were running like hell to get away from this imaginary killer. We were in through thick bushes and crossing a stream before emerging onto the road. Just as we were about to go out through the hedge, a Garda patrol car was driving very slowly past. Of course we thought they were after us, so back into the stream with us and we started to crawl through the water. That brought more fear for us. What if there were rats or weasels that might jump at our throats and suck the blood out of us? Talk about getting ourselves into a state. Eventually we crossed the road and went up through the fields and across the upper road. We were that scared we decided to chance crossing through the middle of a cornfield. We were about half way across when the owner, who had been out walking along at one end of the field, started shouting. In the panic we were in we wouldn't have seen him if he was standing right in front of us, and worse than that he had a shotgun with him. At this stage he started to run towards us shouting for all he was worth because we were in the middle of his corn, destroying it. If he knew how scared we were he wouldn't have said a word, and us thinking we had avoided being chopped up. But what was the point, now we were going to be shot anyway!

There was this thick blackthorn hedge surrounding the field but that did not stop us going through it. By the time we eventually made our way back to home ground, with nearly every one of us cut and scratched all over, we were absolutely knackered. All just for a few blooming apples. I remember telling Connie a few years afterwards about how afraid we were of him at the time. As I was telling him the story of how he chased us, he was killing himself laughing. He said he would have given us all the apples we wanted if we had asked him, but then that would have taken the fun out of it and I would have no story to tell you now.

Horror at the Cinema

There used to be a cinema in Falcarragh at around that same time as well. It was next to where McCarthy's old yard is. As a matter of fact it is still called The Yard. It was always a treat to be taken there. I remember one night in particular my mother brought me and it was a horror film where an old woman had died and was brought to the mortuary where she is lying with eyes closed looking fairly normal until the man in charge of the place spots a nice ring on her finger and thinks to himself there is no point in letting that go with her. So he goes to take it off. He's there twisting and turning, nearly breaking the finger. Anyway he gets it off but it slips and falls to the ground so he throws the arm across the body and gets down on his knees to look under the bed for it. The next thing the arm falls down and gives him an almighty clatter on the back of the head. With that he jumps up with the fright, and what made it worse then was her eyes were now wide open. I got that much of a scaring watching that blooming film that I was afraid of the dark for years after it. Not that it stopped me going out, I have to say, because there was that other attraction about the hope of seeing some semi-naked females on the big screen if you were lucky, and a bit of messing on the way home that you could have a good laugh at. Going to mass on Sunday morning people would be wondering how did such and such a man's cows get into that field, or more like, how did they get out of the field with the gate still closed?

The Ray River Inn

There was a nightclub called the Ray River Inn on the spot where Frank Sweeney's garage is situated now. I remember going in there for the first time with Wee Barny. Believe it or not I was only about twelve and he was about fifteen so it was scary enough, with a few flashing lights and a lot of men with fighting reputations that we would hear about. My heart was in my mouth in case I happened to trod on any of their toes. As far as I was concerned I would be as well to be thrown straight into a mincing machine. The licensing laws were very lax at the time so age wouldn't be that much of a barrier. It was because Barny knew some of the bouncers, so that helped as long as you had the fifty pence to get in. As far as my mother was concerned I was just out late messing about with the rest of the boys on the way home from the pictures, because that's what you did. I did see a few fights on the nights that I managed to get in, which was exiting and looked a lot worse to us at that age than what they really were.

My Father's Return from Australia

My father and older brother Michael returned from Australia, where things had not been working out as planned. That was another rude awakening for me because in a short space of time it went from all play to no play, as ploughing, making drills, planting potatoes, and being able to cover them up properly with the shovel took over. Turf had to be cut. Welcome to a man's world. All work, work, work. Right or wrong that's how it was going to be for quite some time, so I was as well to get used to the idea whether I liked it or not. That's what I thought at that time anyway.

Our next move then was to Fanabhui, where we had bought a small farm from Mickey Ferry who lived there on his own, with his guard rooster. Yes, a big white rooster with spurs about three inches long. Not even the parish priest could get to his door without getting the okay from Mickey and his bodyguard, as he was to find out. I think it was Fr Bonner who nearly ended up in the well at the end of the street trying to shake the rooster of his back. Mickey came to his rescue with a swing off his walking stick that sent the poor rooster flying head over heels.

His reason for deciding to sell his home place was he was having trouble moving around. He had two walking sticks, so he was intending on moving to the town where things would be more accessible for him. Mickey had been a member of the old IRA and later the Irish army when it was formed. He was a very active participant in the war against the British. He was one of many who took a courageous stance in bringing the fight to them at every opportunity that presented itself, especially when dealing with the Black and Tans, who were notorious for their cruelty and murderous activities throughout the country. It's a pity that most of these people died without having their stories recorded for historical purposes. The reasoning for this is that the past cannot be improved but the future can. I found his revolver and IRA medals hidden in the wall of the old cow shed when carrying out repairs. In a cruel twist of fate Mickey must have been out trying to move his TV aerial to get a better picture, where it was situated up on a high banking. It was frosty weather and he must have slipped and fallen and could not get up. Unfortunately he was found dead the following morning by a neighbour.

When we moved into the house it was a bit of a squeeze and it was very cold and draughty with the old stone flag floors that would send a shock through the system when you put your bare feet on them as you had to do when going to bed. We began repairing the house bit by bit as there was an awful lot of work involved. After a while we got the mains connected up, which put an end to humping buckets from the well. For me it was more about watching and trying to learn a wee bit as you went along and just doing what you were told. It was very time consuming. All the old walls had to have the old lime plaster picked off using a hammer and chisel; that was one monotonous job.

Part II – The Troubles and Other Tales

I'm thinking this must have been around 1980 to '81, as I remember it being a very turbulent time in our country. Events at this time, for anyone to experience, could not but shape a person's thinking politically for the rest of their lives. Young Irish men were dying on hunger strike in the H-blocks prison for the exact same cause that Mickey and his comrades had fought for many years previously. Our mainstream politicians, whether it was Fianna Fáil, or Fine Gael, were useless and made little or no effort whatsoever to stand up to Margaret Thatcher's dictatorial stance, partly because of an infiltration of pro-British thinking that seeped in over the years. There were marches and protests in almost every town in the country in support of these men, but as always you have the gutless politicians combined with what I would call the curtain twitchers who would watch from a distance and would not venture outside of the safety net of their own comfortable wee world in case it caused them hardship of any kind.

One of my many sisters was working in Dublin during that time and like the majority of young people had no interest in politics whatsoever. But she knew what was happening was wrong and started to attend protest marches, travelling to Belfast on buses that were organized for this purpose. Because of this she came to the attention of the Special Branch and the low level intimidation started. She got the feeling that she was being followed when she began to notice the same two men parked outside where she lived as she left for work in the morning. The same thing then as she left her place of work to return home, they would be sitting on the opposite side of the street. It was obvious these men and those who they received their orders from in Dublin castle cared little for their fellow citizens in the six counties when they had to resort to this level of intimidation to stop people showing that they cared a lot about what was happening to the young men on the H-blocks. I have complete admiration without reservations of any kind for all those who took up arms against a hugely superior force that was the occupying British forces in this country, whether it was the men of 1798 or their descendants in any of the following decades.

I remember my mother taking me to the Drumboe martyrs commemoration in Ballybofey when I was around seven or eight years old. It intrigued me to hear the speeches and see so many people out marching in remembrance of these men, Com. Gen. Charlie Daly, Timothy O'Sullivan, Daniel Enright from Co Kerry and Brig. General Sean Larkin from Co. Derry who were executed by their former comrades at Drumboe castle in 1923.

(Not) Wearing the Poppy

While on the subject of politics and history, there was a program on a local radio station one day discussing whether Irish people should or should not wear poppies to commemorate Irishmen who died while wearing a British uniform. Of course that got my blood pressure up straight away, so I phoned in. First thing I said was that I believed Ireland should be kept as a completely poppy-free zone. There was silence for a few seconds and then it really got going. One lady who couldn't believe her ears completely lost the run of herself when she said live on radio that I should be taken out and shot. I felt like telling her, go away and boil your head. If I was shot every time someone like her wanted to shoot me, I'd have as many holes as you'd find in a pincushion! I must say it was a very unladylike thing to say, but I was laughing that much that I had to hold the phone out at arm's length in case they could hear me. Fair play to her as she did apologise once the temperature lowered a bit. The valid points, in my view, that I wanted to put across were that these emblems commemorate all British soldiers killed in all conflicts, which included the battle-hardened troops that came back from the Somme and Flanders and those let loose from British prisons on condition that they volunteer for service in Ireland. This they readily did, and were subsequently sent over to keep the Irish under the thumb, to put it mildly. Whatever the cost, they wreaked havoc throughout the country, burning, looting and killing. Once you don a British uniform and march behind a Union Jack common sense tells you that you are a British soldier. You will be awarded a British war pension and a few British war medals with the king or queen's head of that time on them once you become surplus to requirement. War was never forced upon on us by any country apart from England and furthermore we did not have to defend ourselves against any other country apart from England. So that old saying, love thy neighbour, is asking quite a lot from us, considering our turbulent history.

British generals sent thousands of Irishmen who were, it's sad to say, victims of their colonial masters to their deaths by marching them into machine-gun fire in a futile war that achieved absolutely nothing, apart from settling old scores and squabbles between different strains of Europe's royal families. My grandfather was one of those who was seduced or coerced by the manipulation of carefully worded rhetoric into joining the British army, and served in the Dardanelles in Belgium. He was one of the lucky ones to have been able to return to their home soil again. He never spoke about it except for the odd murmuring of distaste or regret that I could pick up from him when I would ask him questions about war and shooting with guns. I was that bit to young to realise that you were meant to kill people. The generals who directed some of these ill-thought-out assaults ended up being rewarded with that many medals pinned to their chests that if they fell over they would find it hard to get up again without help.

The Germans marched thousands of Jews to their deaths in the gas chambers during the Second World War. The difference between these two scenarios is the Germans leaders were held accountable and paid the ultimate price, if and when caught, on the scaffold or by firing squad, often without facing a trial of any kind. I think the Irishmen that died in both wars should be remembered first and foremost as victims in the same way as we remember the thousands who died during the Famine as a direct consequence of actions undertaken by the British establishment, who kept shipping thousands of tons of grain out of the country while people were dying in desperate circumstances throughout the country. It is important that we get rid of the slave mentality that keeps too many Irish people in a subservient state.

On January 30th 1972 I was ten years old as I listened to the expressions of disbelief from my father as the news was read out on the wireless (radio). I was a bit young to understand fully the significance of these events at that time, but I thought it was the end of the world. Thirteen innocent civil rights marchers died on what we now know as Bloody Sunday. Another died later because of severe injuries sustained after British paratroopers fired into the marchers, some randomly, and others taking careful aim. The youngest was seventeen, the oldest fifty-nine. Seven of those murdered were under the age of eighteen; in other words they were only children. Some of those same soldiers took part in another massacre of innocent civilians in Ballymurphy, West Belfast, six months later when eleven civilians were gunned down, including the parish priest, the youngest nineteen and the oldest, a fifty-year-old woman.

On Tuesday the 15th of June 2010 me, Anne Marie, Fionn and Tara stood among thousands of people in solidarity with the relatives of the victims outside the Guildhall Square in the centre of Derry. There was an eeriness to the tense atmosphere leading up to the long-awaited announcement of the results of the Saville Inquiry being read out by British Prime Minister David Cameron. A large screen was erected outside the Guildhall so that all could see and hear this historic confession for themselves and not get the information second hand. An immense weight was lifted from the shoulders of everyone, especially the relatives, as the innocent verdict was read out, clearing the victims of all wrongdoing, rubbishing the previously fabricated Widgery Inquiry. Some stood silent in disbelief, not taking in what they had heard; some cried, some cheered and danced, but the fact that it took nearly forty years to extract the truth in a slow, painful manner from the British government is in my view a hollow but essential victory, because a lot of those who suffered as a consequence of relatives names being sullied and dragged through the gutter by agencies of the state have since passed away.

To watch a British prime minister chastise publicly the role his brave paratroopers played in this shooting spree was satisfying, even though there are those further up the ladder who have escaped blame by making scapegoats of others. There are a lot more of these guilty verdicts that will hopefully come to the surface in the time ahead – a parish priest and ten of his parishioners shot dead in Ballymurphy by the same regiment of trigger-happy paras only six months previous to the shooting in Derry. In the Malvinas in the Falklands war, hundreds of young Argentines, average age sixteen to seventeen, were sent to a watery grave on the direct orders of British premier Margaret Thatcher while sailing away from the conflict zone and in international waters.

Ten of the bravest of the brave died on hunger strike in the H-Blocks prison in 1981, as a direct result of the above-named premier's actions in trying to criminalise those opposed to the presence of British troops on Irish soil. Have the British ever been held accountable for their murderous activities? The answer to that is a blatant No. If they at least had to pay in monetary terms, they'd be bankrupt for the next thousand years. What is there to celebrate about these crimes against humanity by wearing a poppy? With clarity in my mind, I for one will never wear one because of the reasons stated above, which should be more than enough for any fair-minded person to think likewise. Never let revisionism dilute your history. Tell it how it really was.

Barny McNulty, or Barny Andy Ruaigh as he was better known in the locality, told me of him as a young boy watching Mickey and other local volunteers armed with rifles firing volleys of shots at the British auxiliary forces, the Black n' Tans, as they made their way in their lorries up past where the lead or iron ore mines used to be in upper Keeldrum, situated along what is now known as the N56 towards An Clochan Liath. No doubt there were plenty of other attacks that they would have been involved in. Both Barny and his brother Phil were a mine of informa-tion. They had unbelievable memories. Barny loved telling sto-ries about the goings on at the fair days in Gort an Choirce and An Fhal Carrach, where fights would take place between some of the local fighting men and could last for hours. Of course alcohol would most likely play a major part in some if not all of those battles. Barny could tell you the exact day, date and what type of day was in it. Phil, he could tell you the length and breath of every field in the townland, where everyone's plot of bog was, where it started and where it finished. They also took great pride in how they built their corn-stacks and how the straw ropes for holding the thatch down were made. They were the sort who were always on hand to offer help to anyone in any way they could.

The House in Fanabhui

We started to renovate part of the house in Fanabhui at first to make it liveable, as it was in a bad state of repair, along with that an old shed that had to be fixed up for a few cows and another one for the hens and ducks. Bit by bit the place took shape and became fully functional.

There was one stage where there were about sixty ducks and God only knows how many hens, so that meant plenty of eggs.

There was one time when Joe would go to gather the eggs from the hen house he started to swallow the eggs raw because they were supposed to be better for you that way. There was that many going missing my father thought the dog was eating them, as he would leave the shells lying around the floor. The dinner menu was varied with all the fine feathered friends about the place. I was appointed the chief executioner. The rules were simple enough: hold your (victim) chicken or duck between your legs so that the wings couldn't flap around; then hold the neck and beak together facing downwards and draw a very sharp knife across the neck. There is only one spot on the neck where you can do this. Done correctly it is very quick and humane.

Me and Joe did go down another avenue thinking it might be better or quicker with a hatchet, but trying to get a chicken or a rooster to lay down with its neck stretched across a piece of timber was no mean feat, and then if you had a tendency to close your eyes as you brought the hatchet down, that carried along with it its own set of problems. Sometimes you would not know if you cut the chicken off the head or the head off the chicken as it was in two halves. There was a few times after getting the head chopped off in this fashion a rooster would jump up and go off running flat out, until the message got through that you can't go anywhere without your head. I can see these sorts of plain-speaking descriptions of how things were done back then sending the shivers up some people's spines.

There was and still is a valley full of all types of shrubbery with a scattering of ash trees, blackthorn and hazel, which would be full of hazelnuts in the summer. It was very handy because as we were herding the cows close by, if you were a bit cold and a cow was lying down, well you would give it a whack or two to make it get up then lie down in the warm spot. Any other spare time would be spent picking hazelnuts. They were a bit sore on the teeth breaking them open but you just ignored that to get at the nut. The place was full of hares, rabbits, a good scattering of pheasant, and of course plenty of foxes. I always had the dog with me and it was always chasing something. I was climbing in through the trees one day when I heard the dog barking like mad. I grabbed hold of some branches above me to pull myself up onto a banking. Unknown to me there was a track running along on top of the banking, and as I pulled myself up to where my head was at the level of the track, didn't the fox appear at the same split second. It made a snap for my face. It was that close I could see its tonsils as it barely missed taking a piece of my fine features with it. I don't know which of us got the biggest fright, but the poor fox never stopped to find out, with the dog close on its heels. It was an encounter that was just that wee bit too close for comfort.

The rest of my brothers and sisters had to go to Cashel Na Gor School, where the head teacher had a reputation for taking no nonsense. A funny thing happened one day when they were being let out to go home. The father of one of the other boys was waiting outside the school gates. As soon as he saw my brother Martin coming round the corner he called him over and put his fist up under his nose and said to him, "If you go next or near my boys again, I'll hit you that hard with this big fist that you'll go straight up into orbit and never be seen again". Martin said afterwards that when he looked at the size of his fist, he believed every word of it. No need to ask whether he ever ventured near his boys again.

Labouring with VT

I think it was around this time that I got a job labouring with a local plasterer, who we shall call VT (very tight), because all he was willing to pay was three pounds a day at that particular time. He had a saying that he was fond of repeating!! "Ah'll give you three pounds a day and your dung home in a bag". I was thirteen at the time and that keen and excited about getting a job in the first place that I would have done it for nothing just to learn some sort of a trade. He always liked to start work at eight. It was impossible to depend on lifts because one day you would get a lift, the next you wouldn't so a lot of the time I would have to be up early enough to get my lunch ready and then cycle as far as his house, about four miles away. It did not matter how early I managed to get up my granny was up before me and had the fire going, and neither did it matter how late you sat up she would be the last going to bed. She had a very hard life, especially when she was young. She was hired out to farmers out in the Lagan gathering potatoes, milking and all the rest of the farm work that was to be undertaken when she was only eleven years old. She very rarely had shoes to wear. During the wintertime was when she needed or got shoes or boots to wear. Then when she got married to my grandfather, I think it was the key of the church that was used to marry them instead of a ring like nowadays, and no honeymoon; poverty was rife. She was left on her own to work the farm when he was coaxed or enticed off to the trenches of the First World War. She did all the ploughing with the horse herself, spread the cow dung on the fields using the horse and cart. As well as that she would have to go to Maheroroarty beach with the horse and cart to collect seaweed. It would have been around a six or seven mile round trip. She could only do one run per day as it had to coincide with the tide being out. She wasn't the only woman that lived a hard life of manual labour, as most of the men were in Scotland working on farms trying to make ends meet. There were a few people who would deliver a cartload of dried seaweed to most areas in the parish for one pound a load. This was during the war years.

I remember as a small boy and her taking me walking for what I thought was forever to get to the beach. Right enough, it would have been about four miles, to pick barnacles off the rocks. But that was too tiresome for me, so what interested me more was getting my legs stuck in soft wet sand that you would bog up to your knees in without too much of a struggle. Sometimes I'd get a bit carried away and find it was almost impossible to free myself without help. Then the squealing would start because this image of the tide coming in and covering me up would frighten the life out of me. She would have to make her way to me then, without getting stuck herself and put the fear of God into me telling me how lucky I was, telling me that lots of children were lost like this.

A New Job

It was often pitch black in the winter time when I would be heading off on my bike to work. There were very few street lights. The only place you would see them was in the town or at some road junctions. There was a dynamo on the bike but you would use it as little as possible because when you did have it on, the bloody thing with the pressure rubbing on the tyre, it would slow you down too much. It was one of them old black bikes that had no gears or anything like that to make it any easier. When you got there, it was hard work. You did not get a minute to stand around. He had loads of work as there were very few plasterers around at the time, and cement mixers were few and far between. Nearly all the mixing was done using the trusty shovel, and bonding or finish were mixed with a plunger, a homemade job that was made up of a drive wheel of a bicycle, without the pedals of course, with a half inch round iron bar cut at whatever length suited your height welded into the centre.

On my first day at work it was a rotten wet morning but we were working inside. VT told me to mix a bucket of bonding, but sure I didn't even know what the hell bonding was never mind anything else. Anyway he gave me a bit of a lesson. He would have got a few stiff lumpy buckets and a good few watery ones, but I got the hang of it. After that first eventful day, things began to improve rapidly. VT was a wild man for telling stories about his exploits. Some true and some where it was obvious the truth was stretched to the point where it had gone completely off the radar, but he could tell it with so much fervour that he would actually believe it himself. Like the one about me when I started on the first day. He told everyone who showed enough interest that when he sent me to mix the bonding, I was taking such a long time that he decided to go and see what the problem was. He said, very convincingly, that there I was mixing a big batch of bonding with the shovel, out on the street. It did not matter how many times that I denied this had ever happened, people would say, "Aye we believe you" and you'd see the doubting smile on their faces that told you what they were really thinking.

He got a fair bit of work on Aranmore Island. At one stage Joe came in to work with us as well, but VT took a dislike to him because when Joe would mix pebble dash you needed a lot of lime in the mixture and it used to burn Joe's fingers raw. You'd think he had leprosy. When we'd go back to the house we had rented for the tea, Joe was always looking for some opportunity to wind VT up, so he'd stick his fingers half way into the sliced loaf for badness. VT would start swearing like mad and calling him all the names under the sun, and I'd be killing myself laughing, you just could not make up a comedy film like it.

When we came out to Aranmore first and got settled in we got all that we were likely to need for work in the morning. So after we finished our first day working we made ourselves some grub, then got cleaned up and all the rest. We went down to this pub where there was a pool table and spent a few hours playing and then back to the house because you would never see anyone else there. We mentioned this to the house owner one day, and he started laughing and said you're far too early, go about one or two in the morning, that's the time everyone goes out. Well we did and the pub was packed.

VT bought a pint for himself and a coke for me as I did not go near the alcohol. There was a few empty seats so we sat down and VT started yapping away to some people he knew. So I was sort of left on my own. No problem there you would think, but it could only happen to me. The next thing this big lump of a man sat down right opposite me and started giving me the evil eye. I did not know anyone there and did not want to get into any fights. After a while he leans over to me and says, "You're nothing but a gobshite". He had a drink on him as well, which did not help the situation one bit. Eventually I got tired of the insults and I whispered to him that I would meet him outside in five minutes. "Right," he says, gets up and heads towards the door. So for a minute or two I sat there thinking about the fixture I was after getting myself into.

I says to VT, "Come on, it's time to go home". No one heard what went on with me and the other buck, so he was wondering why I wanted to leave as he thought the craic was only just beginning. So I said we have to be on the go early because it was going to rain tomorrow evening. So up he gets and out the door we go. It was pitch black outside and I could see no sign of your man. So I shouts, "Where are you?" Next thing, "I'm over here," came the reply. All I could see in the direction of the voice was a small red light of a cigarette. I took a few careful steps towards the red light. As soon as I thought I was close enough I took aim and hit him a real clatter. All you heard was the grunt as I connected with my fist, then a big clump as he landed on the ground and silence. "Let's go," I says to VT as we made our way out on the road. There wasn't a word spoken until we reached the house. He was still in a bit of a shock. I explained to him then what had happened. I found out later that my opponent on the night was fine and no harm was done, he got a bit carried away when he got a few drinks, but he got a good wake up call I can assure you that and learned a lesson in the process.

The Currach

VT brought me and Phil McHugh to a friend of his at Horn Head to look at a currach that he had made using flour bags that my mother had sewn together for him. When we got to where he lived straight across the bay from Dunfanaghy, he already had the currach in the water. The tide was on its way out at the time, so the owner and VT went out for a trial run that went very well. They were very pleased with how easy it was to handle. Then it was me and Phil's turn. Neither of us had ever set foot in a currach before, but so what, we were going to give it a go. We got in anyway without going upside down, all very professional as a matter of fact, so that was good. After a few minutes we thought we were expert seafarers as we headed out into the middle of the bay. We were thinking we were far enough so as I was doing the rowing I was just about to start turning around when Phil shifted on his seat a bit making the currach rock. As Phil tried to steady it up again, didn't he tear a couple of small holes in the canvas with the heel of his size ten boots and the water started to come in. We seemed to be closer to the Dunfanaghy side so I started to row as hard as I could in that direction. We were nearly swimming when we reached dry land, then after jumping out and without realising, we tore the whole bottom on the stones as we tried to pull it up out of the water.

Both of us felt rotten about tearing the ass out of it but what was the point? It was all about damage limitation now for us. When the two boys drove around from the Horn Head side there were no smiles when they saw the holes along the whole bottom. There was some swearing done after all the hard work that the owner had put into it. This was the first and last time for me to get into a currach. I don't know about Phil, he could make his own mind up.

VT liked a bit of the outdoors as well, shooting, fishing, etc. He persuaded me to purchase my first legal firearm, a single barrel shotgun, made in Brazil. The first time I fired a shot it fell apart, so I did a bit of remodelling to try and fix the problem. It did the trick, so I fancied myself as a gunsmith for a short while after that.

We'd often go shooting wild geese and ducks down by the back strand near Falcarragh. Thousands of geese would start coming in from the sea just as it was starting to get dark, so you had to be in place before they started to come in, because they were so alert it was impossible to sneak up on them. You would also have to wait until they were here eating grass for about two weeks or so in the season before going hunting them, because there'd be a terrible salty sea taste off the meat, a bit like eating raw barnacles. But after that, the meat on the geese would be brownish in color but taste lovely.

Poaching

When we weren't at that we'd be poaching salmon on a few of the local rivers, which was exciting, because you had to keep your eyes peeled the whole time to stop yourself from falling into the river or getting caught by the bailiffs. There was one night in particular when we caught sixty fish with one drag of the river at the Waterfoot. You'd think the water was boiling in front of the net and it needed a lot of effort to pull it. You have to remember that all the fish were trying to go the complete opposite direction to you. I think there was about twenty good salmon or so, and the rest a mixture of sea trout and smallish salmon. VT nearly always wore a pair of waders as he did not like getting wet, but you heard the clatter of the tops whacking off each other when he started running for cover at the mention of bailiffs coming.

I remember thumbing a lift coming in from Lifford when this car stopped so I jumped in and started chatting away. When the driver found out where I came from he told me that he worked as a bailiff and started telling me about how him and another man working with him were sitting watching these poachers spreading out their net in a field alongside a certain river. They were hiding in some buses and were that bit too far away to identify or arrest them. He described the spot where this took place and it was then that it dawned on me that I was one of the boys he was talking about. On that day a few of us were heading through some fields to the river when we spotted the two bailiffs lurking around some bushes beside a good salmon hole so we decided there wasn't a hope in hell that we were going to get near that hole, so we decided to wind them up instead. We took the net out of the bag and hid it, then filled the bag with ferns and walked out into the open where we knew the two boys would see us. We then started emptying the pretend net as if we were trying to spread it before getting it ready to set in the river, while at the same time keeping a good eye on the two heads peering at us from the safety of the bushes. We were in stitches the whole time, eventually getting fed up and leaving because we knew they weren't going to run after us. But anyway there I was laughing as your man is telling me his story and him not having a clue that he was after giving one of the poachers he had watched that lovely evening a lift. It was comical, the two of us laughing and him not even guessing that I might be laughing at him, which was exactly what I was doing.

There was some daft and dangerous things done when it came to a bit of poaching. Often on a Saturday night on the way home from the disco at the Pier Hotel at Port na Blath, myself, Eddie, Owen, John, Hughie, and sometimes Pierre would decide to go fishing at around four in the morning. I was the only sober one among them and would have to take the trousers off to cross a small river that ran into the main one. The water just about come up under my tackle, if you know what I mean? But it gave me the shivers because you had to feel with your feet. Sometimes it could be a flat fish or an eel wriggling around your toes. It was hard to concentrate because you had to have an eye on the water and an eye on the boys stumbling and falling along the river bank and telling them to keep quit. If there was a bailiff within a mile of them, they'd be heard no problem.

I cannot ever remember having caught much on these night-time follies apart from a cold or the flu. It was always much better when you knew the bailiffs were around as you were guaranteed a good chase. One night we were sitting in the car at the Back Strand car park having a laugh before getting the net out. I was sitting in the front passenger seat with the window down. It was fairly dark when I heard this tick tick-tick noise. I was just about to ask the other boys what it was, when the next thing we were blinded by lights. Wasn't the tick-tick noise I heard from the bailiff's jeep as they were sneaking up on us with the lights out. When they got within a few feet of us they switched on the full power spotlights. We had an idea then what it was like for a rabbit when it was caught in the glare of a spotlight, but anyway we didn't panic so they started to drive in circles around us about ten times or so. They eventually turned off the lights and sat there. After about ten minutes sitting thinking what we should do next, Michael, who was driving the car, started up and started to go in circles around them and drove off as hard as he could go and headed off in the direction of Gort an Choirce, where we parked beside the Glenea River. After a while along comes our shadows in the jeep and parked alongside us. Again we took off back the way we came to the Back Strand and hid the car in sand dunes in a completely different place where it would not be seen so easily, took the net out and ran to the river as hard as we could and set it in the river. We then hid a bit away from where we had the net set and watched as the bailiffs came and went a few times looking for us, not realising that if they looked that little bit further they would have had someone to chase. They got out of the jeep at one stage and walked along the river where we had the net set without seeing it. We got fed up at this stage and took it out of the river without catching a thing.

On another occasion we tried setting the net out in the bay where the fresh water runs out in a stream. This was just as the tide starts to come in. Then we went away to the town for a bag of chips to pass the time. When we came back, there was some action going on in front of the net, so rather than pull it in at that stage, we got greedy and thought, "We'll leave it another while". So off we went, all pleased with ourselves. To make a long story short, the water was strangely quiet calm around where we had the net set. Anyway we got the end rope and pulled it in. What a mess. It was torn to shreds and not a fish in sight. The only thing we could think of was that a seal had come along and could not believe its luck and devoured all around it, including our net. That little trial run left us minus a net for a long time, but it brought home to us for a while anyway that you shouldn't be too greedy; it doesn't pay good dividends in the long run.

This was the same spot we would end up at around four or five on a lovely summer's morning with the sun just rising and not even a ripple in the water, after getting a lift as far as Falcarragh if we were lucky and walking the rest of the way. Once we got as far as the jetty it was too tempting to pass by without taking the canoes out for a spin. There was never a lock on the door so all we had to do was take them out nice and carefully. It wasn't too difficult, although we had to use bits of old branches as makeshift oars to paddle the canoes. None of us were able to swim, something that never crossed our minds though we could end up half way out in the bay. If you capsized you were a goner without doubt.

Back to the wildlife, where if the times were right, hares and pheasants tasted very good as well and were always in with a chance of being on the menu at some time or another. The menu changed with the seasons so it would never get too boring. Myself and Joe used to catch a lot of rabbits using snares. They were to be got in almost all hardware shops. We got ours in McGinley's in Falcarragh. Hubert worked at the hardware counter and if he didn't know what you were talking about or where it was at, he would just say, "They don't make these anymore" and dismiss you in the one breath. You had to know where and how to set a snare. As rabbits follow a path they leave a patch where they hop each time, so the snare had to be set in between the hops, the right height off the ground about three to four inch's and the right circumference so that the rabbit did not go straight through it. It was easy when you knew how and just as easy to make rabbit stew when you knew how.

The Homing Pigeons

A lovely tame looking bird landed on our roof one time. It was one of them homing pigeons, so we started to feed it bits of bread, or scraps. It must have liked the taste of its food because it decided to stay. This was after it was coaxed down off the roof. It would then eat off your hand, so we made a little house for it that was fixed onto the shed wall. After a while it laid a half dozen eggs and lo and behold we soon had pigeons flying all around the place, including the house, getting to the stage where if the door was lying open anything could happen. I saw us sitting in having the tea after coming in from the threshing mill with a few of the local men who were helping out at threshing the corn, when about eight pigeons came zooming in around the kitchen and out again leaving some shocked and startled faces behind them, never mind the wind and the dust. We'd be killed laughing because we knew what was going to happen so it was just a matter of waiting.

Ructions at The Pier Hotel

The Pier Hotel that I mentioned earlier on was a very rough spot. I was hardly ever there a night that there wasn't ructions of some sort. My very first night in the place I got into a scrap through no fault of my own. The funny thing was, he must have thought he was a foot taller than he actually was, or else he thought that I was a foot smaller than I was. I was sitting down at the time, when he decided for no apparent reason to empty the contents of his pint glass over me. Lucky enough there wasn't too much in it. He went head over heels that fast he must have thought he was struck by lightning. That set a sort of precedent from then on.

The local guards were sitting outside the hotel in the patrol car one night when there was a bit of a ruckus getting going. It was one of them box-shaped Renault fours. Whatever happened, a whole crowd got around the car and tried to tumble it over. While this was going on another boy ran and got a wheel brace from another car, so while the two boys were being rocked over and back and I'd say in danger of getting seasick, he started to unscrew the nuts from one or two of the back wheels. When he got them off he threw them away so they wouldn't be found, so as soon as the guards tried to drive away the wheel fell off. They had to get out then and the whole crowd laughing at them they had to unscrew a nut off each of the other wheels to be able to put the wheel back on and get away in case the same thing happened again. I was relayed all this information by the person that took the nuts off the wheel, so it was from the horse's mouth you could say. For whatever reason (money, flu or too tired), I wasn't there that night.

There was another lively night when a rugby team from somewhere in the six counties decided to push their weight around because there were some big boys among them and thinking that no one would dare go near them started acting as if they owned the place. But at some stage the fists started to fly in all corners and that changed the whole concept of the night for them. I was coming in from the toilets when I met Joe coming out with about ten of these big boys in hot pursuit. As soon as they went past me I followed them out the door and round the back, which was in darkness. I could not see where they went but decided to head on into the darkness because if they caught Joe he was in for some hiding. He knew the place so he had an advantage that way. I made my way further around the back where there was a bright light shining down, but it was blinding me as well. Next thing, I could see the outline of two men moving around in the shadows in front of me. "Is that you Joe?" I says, but the response I got was an almighty crack of a fist that sent me flying back in the direction I came from, tripping over a fence in the process. It took me a while to regain my senses.

When I did I pulled out a fencing post and headed back looking for the boys that clattered me. By the time I got around to the front again it was like the Wild West, and straight into the middle of the lot I go again. The rugby boys learned the hard way that night after coming out on the losing side and I had a painful job of twisting my nose back into its rightful place again. There were a lot of nights that replicated that one, nearly every weekend as a matter of fact.

A few of us were on our way home from the Pier late, or maybe I should say early; we had got a few lifts that got us as far as Falcarragh. We had noticed a gang of lads from Letterkenny talking to some of the local girls earlier in the night outside the Pier and we knew that they were driving a van, so we had a look around some of the usual places where courting couples would park. We were giving up hope when one of the boys spotted the van, sitting in a darkened spot where there were no streetlights so it was too good an opportunity for us to let go. We decided that they had to be taught a lesson. There were plenty of loose chips around so we started firing handfuls at the van, but didn't the guards appear on the scene. Whether they suspected something was going on or not I don't know. We made off in all directions anyway. After a while me and one of the other boys made our way to the main street, not a soul around. Next thing didn't a guard that was stationed in the local barracks appear out of nowhere and off we were again and him in hot pursuit. He was that close behind me I could nearly feel the heat of his fingers on my neck, as he grabbed at the collar of my jacket and me with my back arched like a half moon as if that was going to do any good. I was tight on the heels of your man in front when he took a sharp turn into a garden and I just about managed to follow. Well the next thing was the clatter and the howls as the guard went head over heels along the footpath. I can tell you we made good our escape as we headed home, not knowing where the rest of the boys were hiding.

Next day me, Joe and my father were in the bog cutting turf when we see the patrol car coming up towards us and stopping. Joe goes over to meet them so that they would not come up to us as my father would find out what was going on. No doubt there would be a price to pay then. Anyway he denied that any of us were in the town that night. The guard gave him a good eating and left it at that. Joe told my father that they were looking for directions to one of our neighbours' houses for some reason or another. He said maybe they got caught with no tax or something. They seemed to know everywhere that we were likely to be cutting banks of turf, and they would appear – looking for directions! I think my father began to realise that there was more to these visits than meets the eye. Funny enough he never said anything to make us think otherwise.

Drunken Antics

We intended going home on the bus one night when one of our mates had more than his fair share of drink taken at the Pier. So we had to carry him to the bus, distract the driver for a while and get him into a seat at the same time without the driver noticing he was drunk, because he did not want to end up having to clean up some mess on the seats if he'd get sick. Once he was on the seat for a while you could pretend he was sleeping anyway. Well he was sleeping that much that we could not wake him up when the bus was coming near his house, so we had to get off a bit early and drag him up and down the road for an hour or so in an attempt to waken him. It was bloody freezing around that time as well, but it was no good, we couldn't wake him up. So we sneaked up to his house and opened the door as quietly as we could. We were doing our best not to wake anyone else in the house. We just about managed to get him into the sitting room and left him stretched out on a couch without stumbling over anything and out as quietly as we came in. When we met up with him some time the following day he had another story for us about what happened after we left him. It seems that he awoke an hour or two later and felt hungry, so he decided to put on a fry for himself. He managed to light the gas, or so he thought, and put the pan on, got the bacon and eggs out of the fridge, and put the lot on before going to the bathroom to have a pee. That was when he fell into the bath and was not able to get out of it again. Some time later someone had got up and found him sound asleep in the bath and found the smell of gas. They went into the kitchen to find the cooker in a mess, the gas was turned on but not lit, with eggs splattered all over the hob. He had kept missing the frying pan. He was lucky he did not burn the house down or blow it up in the process. There was another incident some time later when a bus driver taking workers to the factories early in the morning spotted a pair of legs sticking up from behind an old stone wall. Wasn't it the same buck and him stiff as a poker with the cold, but alive, so the bus driver managed to wake him up and dropped him off at his house, which was on his way anyway.

If we happened to be hanging around the town when the pubs were closing, that was the time most of the regulars would head straight for Rosie Mhór's chip shop. It was a good time to act around a bit. Joe was good at pretending that he was legless and steamed to the eyeballs. He would lay half-on half-off the pavement. We would watch from behind a car or van, then you would see a few oul boys that would have a good drink on them on trying to drag Joe in, in case a car ran over him, and leave him next to the wall. No sooner was that done than Joe would start crawling back out and roll under a parked car making sure that his head was right under the wheel, and your boys could not leave him there in case the driver came, jumped in and drove off over his head without seeing him. Then all of a sudden Joe would jump up completely sober and accuse your boys of trying to put him under a car, to kill him, before making off, ranting and raving about how lucky he was that they didn't kill him. Leaving your boys cursing under their breath, not really knowing what to say or do.

You could expect anything to happen in Rosie's. It had its romantic moments, when lovey dovey couples shared a plate of chips. In between all this a fight could break out in a few places at once, then Margaret would be out settling the disputes with the floor brush while Seamus would stay in the background watching and smiling away unless things got out of hand; then he would make his presence felt. One night when the place was fairly busy, I had a few bangers. I can't remember who had given them to me. They were loud enough to leave you deaf for a while when they were let off inside. I had a bit of a brainstorm as I stood at the counter waiting to be served.

There was a table directly behind me with a whole gang sitting around it, so I thought if I throw it under the table on the sly, they're going to get the blame. The time was right when Margaret had her back to me. I lit it. Well I got some shock, the fuse was about half an inch long, which gave you plenty of time to throw it wherever you wanted too, but this time it turned out to be a faulty one and as soon as I put the match to it and me holding it between finger and thumb, I could see the little red flame shoot into it, and then the bang and the cloud of smoke followed. If you could just picture it, me standing at the counter with the remains of the banger still between a completely numb finger and thumb, with a cloud of smoke surrounding me from the waist up, and everyone in stitches laughing at me. It was like something straight out of an episode of Mr Bean. Even Margaret, the owner, who was serving behind the counter, had a smile on her face, and on this occasion she did not bar me because I got caught out so badly.

New Year's Eve at The Pier

One of the best bout of fisticuffs I had at The Pier happened on a New Year's Eve night, when a fellow who I had gone to school with, but hadn't seen for a good few years because he had gone to England, was home for the Christmas holidays. He was out in The Pier as well that night. To cut a long story short, he challenged me out for a square go, over some misunderstanding that happened earlier on in the night. He was big into the fitness side of things, including the boxing ring. That never scared me off before and it wasn't going to now, so the battle commenced with me getting the upper hand thinking to myself this isn't going to last long. I got a bit cocky and complacent, resulting in me getting hit with a haymaker that I didn't get time to recover from. It slowed down the thinking process. This was all taking place on a sloped car park and him being ring-craftier than I was, he managed to keep to the high ground and the outside light that was above the main entrance at his back so I was continually having to deal with the light shining in my eyes. But in saying that and making no excuses, it was a great scrap as far as I was concerned. The adrenalin was flowing, even though I was coming out the worst at the end of the later exchanges. It was eventually stopped when lumps started appearing on top of lumps, as well as being minus one of my teeth. A good job too because I could not afford to lose any more, as I found out to my cost, when I visited the dentist and she told me how much the repair work was going to set me back. It must have been great entertainment for the crowd because there was far more outside watching the action than there were inside singing in the new year. I didn't get any New Year's kisses that night I can assure you. The moral of this story is never take your eye off the ball and don't go fighting on New Year's Eve.

Our poor mother, she was in the habit of nearly drowning you with holy water before you went out. She was always warning us about fighting and staying out of trouble. Then there was that bit of advice she said was important about not putting your hand above a girl's knee. She never really explained what the consequences would be if your hand did happen to go that wee bit farther. That was the grey area that you had to draw your own conclusions on. Once she would hear us coming in at night she would wait for a while until we were in bed then she would go out to the bathroom just to see if I had left a shirt lying in the bath. If I did, she would check it for traces of blood. If there was none, she'd go back to sleep and if there was she'd be praying the rest of the night that there wasn't any harm done. You have to become a parent before you realise just how much worry you had put your own under.

McFadden's hotel in Gort An Choirce (Óstán Loch Altan now) was another place where a boxing ring should have been set up for the nights we were there. We were constantly doing things to wind people up and if they didn't see the funny side of it then that could go any direction. It would more often than not turn into a scrap of some sort. I remember a few of us going into a Fine Gael dance with posters of Paddy Kelly, who was an independent Fianna Fáil candidate at that time, sticking on our backs. I suppose part of the reason was that Blaney put his money where his mouth was and put republicanism to the fore in his split with the parent party Fianna Fáil at that juncture of our history. And with not the slightest hint of republicanism within Fine Gael, well where better a place to go to annoy their supporters but to their very own dance?

More Drunken Antics

I wouldn't do it now, but I would like to for the craic. There was a bit of a battle going on with some Gaoth Dobhair boys one night, and of course I was in the middle, or slightly off centre, of it when I got the feeling that I had an extra passenger on board. When I got a minute I discovered it was one of the local Guards stuck on my back like a leech. He's retired now. I couldn't get him off so I just ignored him and whacked away for all I was worth. When I did manage to shake him off, he said, "What the fuck is wrong with you? There's plenty of women in there and that's what you should be using your energy on, instead of wasting it out here fighting". Many's the time I thought of it afterwards, wasn't he bloody right in what he was saying, but I put it down to being a slow learner. It took me a long time to cop on that being a blaggard wouldn't be the best title to have hanging around your neck. I ended up doing door work there as well.

People came from all parts of the county to The Pier. It was the, sort of, 'in' place to be at the time. Eventually I was offered a job as a doorman to keep me quiet. It was a while before I took them up on the offer but I did eventually after having a good think about it. There was always someone challenging someone else out to fight and some of the words used in the lead up to what would be no more than a wrestling match would make you laugh. One not very big fellow shouting to the bigger boy, "Come out here now and say it to my face ya wee runt". Another funny one was a boy shouting to another boy "Go away ya wee narrow-shouldered whore ya". This new status of being a doorman was grand, as it kept me busy trying my best to prevent trouble and not to get into any myself. But before I took on the responsibility of that job, and as the man says, still thinking about it, we used to go to the Tramore Inn in Downings or the Milford Inn.

How that came about was that there was always competition between the bus drivers on who got a head start leaving Falcarragh first. That way first out was guaranteed to get a full bus. Rosie Mhór's chip shop was the main gathering point. The smell of the vinegar and chips combined would make you hungry as hell. One of the bus drivers started taking us wherever we wanted to go for free. We'd have a whip-around and give him what we could. It would just about cover his diesel. There was a fair gang hanging around together at that stage. It did not seem to matter where we went, there was trouble of some sort, mainly caused by the hangers-on in the group. When the opportunity did arise most of them couldn't whack their way out of a wet paper bag. There was always someone telling you that this person or that person was a so and so, that he said something about you, and needed a good slap, or because he looked at them or didn't look at them, but of course they wouldn't do it themselves. That was where I was supposed to come into the picture, or some of the other few boys who seemed to be doing all the battling. Pure stupid when I think of it now.

There were lots of nights we stayed long after the national anthem was played, when everyone stood to attention. If it was played in some places now they wouldn't know what it was and would continue with their dancing. A few of us were walking up from the pier to the main road when these two boys from Creeslough got into an argument about who was the toughest. "Prove it then," one of them said, so what did the other fellow do but jump out in front of a car, which hit him and sent him head over heels. The car kept going, and your boy got up with not a scratch. Next the other fellow jumped out in the same fashion but went flying up in the air and landed in the middle of the road, and was half knocked out. The car had braked and the driver had got out and threatened to kick the shit out of your man for jumping out like that; the poor driver was more shook up than the clown that was now up and staggering around.

Because of the mad goings on at The Pier and not wanting to miss anything, we would deliberately miss the bus home, so then you were left depending on lifts, and if the worst came to the worst, it was a case of just keep walking till you were ready to drop. Sometimes you could be lucky enough to get a lift as far as Falcarragh. More often than not some would go well out of their way to drop us that far. It meant one thing on them nights, that there was still a bit of energy left to carry out a few changes along the way. If there were people who we thought were not on the best of speaking terms, we'd swap over their garden furniture and stuff like that. We even gathered a field of corn that was in stuks and built a stack in the middle of the road. Great entertainment altogether as long as it wasn't your corn that was ending up in the middle of the road.

Another night we moved most of the materials that were being used to build a house out onto the road. The intention was that they would not be able to get to mass the following morning. No doubt it worked perfectly. We took a horse cart out of a shed in Keeldrum another night and dragged it the whole way to the post office in Gortahork, where we left it parked up nicely. I'm telling you it was not one bit easy, because every time we saw the lights of a car in the distance, it was panic stations then to find an entrance or some sort of opening into a field to hide it until the car passed. If it did pass, that is, because as happened plenty of times after nearly killing ourselves trying to get the bloody thing in off the road, the car or whatever would turn off and head away in some other direction, not coming near us at all and what a job we had a few times trying to get back out on the road again. One time we were going to just leave it there, because one wheel had gone into a drain, so trying to lift and push at the same time is hard work, and it wasn't as if we were getting paid for it.

The Corn Cutters Rest

I got to work the odd night on the door at the Corn Cutters Rest in Creeslough through Eddie Harkin, who was the trainer at the Dunfanaghy Boxing Club. It used to be a fairly tough spot at one time for men to be tearing lumps out of one another. I knew a lot of the customers there so it was a bit awkward at times trying to keep the peace when you were on friendly terms with both sides squaring up to each other, but sometimes that did not seem to matter too much when it was hard to tell the difference between your so-called friends and enemies. A bit of trouble started brewing at the opposite end of the floor to me and as I made my way across to try and calm things down a bit I tripped over a stool and ended up on my hands and knees. Before I could even think of getting up, a little runt no bigger than a decent sized bottle of washing up liquid, who looked like a circumcised rabbit, kicked me right above the eye. By the time I got to my feet he had disappeared into the crowd, leaving me with blood streaming down my face. That was the sort of thing that would happen. It didn't matter whether you were in the Corncutters or one of Peter Stringfellow's lap dancing clubs.

A Bad Accident

Myself and Eddie were walking home from the town one Sunday night, after being in the Shamrock Bar where there used to be live bands playing at the time. We were just doddering along in no great hurry because we had an idea that we'd get a lift anyway. The next thing I remembered was waking up in hospital with a nurse leaning over me, fixing the pillow. As it happens, one of her boobs was nearly poking me in the eye. Being eighteen, the first thought that came into my head was to get a hold of it, and without realising I found my hand reaching up automatically as if on autopilot and squeezed her generous boob. None too gently either I could imagine. Because of the state I was in, unknown to me of course, it did not warrant giving me a good whack, as I suspect she would have done in normal circumstances. Lucky for me that escape clause was there, so I don't think she was overly bothered about it; her prime concern was that I was alive. Seeing as I was so poorly she said she would let me off with it, but lo and behold the opportunity never presented itself again, what a pity.

That was on a Tuesday. Little did I realise at the time, I was given the last rites by a priest, because it was thought I would not make it. It was a close call. To this day, I don't know whether I would have gone the heavenly route or the sinners' highway. I had been knocked down by a driver who was under the influence of alcohol, in a hit and run accident. It was a few days before the driver eventually owned up. No doubt they would have been caught anyway. I did know the person involved fairly well because I had gotten lifts in the same vehicle on many occasions previous to this.

Life's too short to be holding grudges over something like that. After all, even the greatest make mistakes, because accidents will happen whether you like it or not. Eddie got an awful fright, as he said himself. One minute we were talking and laughing and the next I was flying through the air. I got home after a week or so, but I was confined to the bed for at least three months before I ventured outside. It was well over a year before I could even think about work, so in between I read book after book, whether it was fact or fiction it didn't matter too much. It got to the stage where I had a torch under the bedclothes so I could pull the clothes over my head and read away all hours. It was all I could do to pass the time. I had to be looked after hand and foot by the rest of the family. I imagined that I would be able to return to work within weeks. I was afraid of losing my job but I was only codding myself. VT had to get another three men to fill my place I was that good! However when I did manage to get back on my feet and my mother would send me to the shop, by the time I got there I would have forgotten completely what I was supposed to get. I would get so annoyed as I did not understand why this was happening, and would fly off the handle in a split second. It turned out to be something that I had to put up with for a few years before my memory gradually returned to a level that I was reasonably happy with.

I was dying to get out after being cooped up in the house for so long because I was missing the whole weekend fun thing. There was always a mad rush to get using the bathroom on the Saturday night to get the hair washed. You had to get in before any of the girls or else you would be as well to forget about it. Then it was drying the hair in front of the range or the open fire. Many's the time I singed my hair because I stuck my head a bit too close to the flames; then I had two choices: wash the hair again, or go out with the smell of burnt hair hanging in the air. It was the second option most of the time.

Michael's Merc

Michael had gone back over to London and he left a reasonably good Mercedes car behind, so I started taking it out for the odd spin. It was diesel so it was easy enough on the juice. Myself, Joe, Hughie, Michael Doogan and Charlie Whorisky would head off for Letterkenny or Ballybofey for the craic thinking that a stranger in town would have a better chance with the girls than the locals. Thinking back there was something that we weren't doing quiet right because the success rate wasn't that great. Of course there was no insurance or anything on the bloody car anyway, but sure you could nearly convince yourself that it only applied to older boys. One night in the early hours we were heading for home on the way from Ballybofey in the direction of Letterkenny when we passed a patrol car that was half hidden in a parking spot along the side of the road. We had not gone too far past when I saw the car pulling out with the blue lights flashing, so I puts the boot to the board and away like hell, and the boys shouting "Faster!". Then I had a bright idea. I turned off onto a back road that leads down into Letterkenny, but I was not that familiar with it, having been on it only once before in the backseat of some car. Anyway I was going as fast as the car would go, when the next thing in front of us was a humpback bridge, but it was to late to brake before we were airborne for what seemed like ages. We landed with a mighty wallop as the car split over the back wheel arches so the whole boot of the car was trailing on the road. I never lifted the throttle. It was like the space shuttle going to the moon with the big trail of sparks flying out the back. I had to stop a bit further on when we realised that we not being followed. The worst thing was they were probably not even after us in the first place. We had some job on our hands then. We pulled out a few fencing posts to try and jack up the rear. With a mish-mash of wire and the posts and driving in first gear, the sun was shining by the time we made it home and the car ended up in a place along the garden hedge where only nettles grew. When Michael came home he wasn't too happy but of course no one told him how the car ended up in such a state in the first place until about a year or so afterwards.

Hughie and the Mark 2

Hughie had a red Mark 2 Escort. It was his father's, but he was let use it on a Sunday. If his father knew half of what the car was used for, he would never have got next or near it. Anyway, it was a 1.3 engine that was in it, and it was goosed after Hughie got driving it, blowing out oil and smoke everywhere. So we got the thinking caps on and came up with an idea. Michael had a 1.6 engine laying beside the shed that he had taken out of some car to put in a more powerful one. We thought, it has to be better than what we have, so we set about the job one very cold night in Michael Doogan's shed. Out with Hughie's engine no problem, but it did not matter how we tried we could not get the other one to fit. So the next bright idea was to dismantle it and maybe use some of the parts on Hughie's engine. The thing was that not one of us knew what we were doing. It was all guesswork and pure luck. We took the whole thing apart, cylinder head, pistons, sump, bearings. Then we set about doing the same with the original one. We had figured out by this stage that because the piston rings in the 1.3 engine were so worn we should try and fit the pistons from the 1.6 engine into it. We did and guess what? Three of them fitted but the third was too damaged to use, so we spent the whole night working on this rather strange project. By morning time we had nearly managed to get the engine back into the car, but we ran out of steam, along with the fact that we needed someone with a little know-how to put the finishing touches to it.

So that's where Michael came in. He spent a fair part of the next night undoing and putting together properly some of the work that we had wrecked our brains on the previous night. But it was all for the better. It refused to start with the key. We thought, "All that work for nothing," but out came the tractor and towed it up and down the road a few times before it started. It was still smoky, because of the third piston that we could not change, but not half as bad as it was before the big operation. The other unexpected plus was that it had now way more power than it had before. You could not make up a story like that with a lucky ending even if you tried.

We were always trying to do what we thought no one else had done before, like climbing Errigal Mountain and it all snow with little more than t-shirts on us; but we did it and survived. The next one was down at Maheraroarty beach, where we went for a walk along the sand because we had little else to do on a Sunday. We weren't too interested in football or anything like that as there was too much snow and frost about, but it was the same along the beach, so you could imagine how cold it would be. We started following the waves as they went out and running back when the next one came in but someone got pushed and got their feet wet then the next man got his feet wet, so then we began daring one another to go out a bit further. It ended up that we were completely soaked going out till the waves were nearly coming over the top of us. Micheal Doogan went out further than the rest of us. The water was up to his neck. This was us with our clothes on and not being able to swim. Of course it was a stupid thing to do and I suffered for a few weeks after it, having to spend a full week in bed with a severe cold.

Liberating Beer

We, the same few boys, were sitting outside a certain licensed premises one night in an old banger of a car that was barely legal to have on the road in the first place. We were just messing about passing the time. After a while we noticed that the barman would come out every so often and go into the adjoining store and back in with a crate of beer. So each time he was inside we thought why don't we help ourselves to some of the crates as well? It was working so well after a few runs that we had the car half full of bottles, completely unnoticed, before the barman got locking the door. We put nearly all the bottles into the back and some in the front passenger side. We drove off then killing ourselves laughing and wondering what we were going to do with them as no one in the car was drinking at that stage. The laughing stopped all of a sudden because right in front of us in the middle of the road was a guard waving us down and me in the front with my legs sticking up. Talk about bad luck. We had driven straight into a bloody checkpoint without realising it. We thought, "This is it we're in trouble now". The boys in the back were sitting up high on top of all the bottles, so there was no hiding place. The guard came to the window and shone his torch into our faces. He was one of the local guards with a big moustache and waved us on. There was pure silence for about a mile before the laughing started, a bit nervous first but the further we got the more we laughed. It had a happy ending as there were a few old boys around the place that had a few merry nights drinking bottles of beer after it.

The Ballroom of Romance

The Ballroom of Romance started up in the local hall and the local priest was involved in it as well. It used to be mobbed out to the door. The only bouncer was the priest. Although there was no alcohol being served, a lot would be well-oiled by the time they came in. That would lead to the inevitable punch-up now and again with the priest showing them the door. The other thing was the country music and the dancing was all jiving or waltzes with a bit of céili thrown in for good measure. None of us were any good at it so Joe would go out in the middle of the floor and start head-banging and jumping all around the place, which guaranteed him some strange looks, leaving people thinking that he was drinking or in league with old Black Nick himself. The priest warned him a few times. In the end he put him out, so that was Joe's honour – getting barred from the hall for dancing, which he was proud of. I think it was a first.

Sheep and Goats

A good few of the older men from around the locality used to meet up in some houses to play cards during the winter time, telling old yarns, some true and some not so true. One night we were on our usual rambles, wondering what sort of tricks we could play on someone to pass the time, when we thought of the boys meeting up in this particular house. There were a fair shot of sheep in the field next to the house, so the best course of action to take was to get the sheep rounded up into a corner so that they would be easier caught. We then formed a bit of a conveyer belt system to the door and as quiet as you like we had the hallway so full that we had trouble closing the door. Then it was a matter of getting the best vantage point to watch the action unfold, and what a hullabaloo. The shouting and cursing as men and sheep came out the door together. The swearing would be directed at us more than the poor sheep. Great entertainment altogether. It was funny how opportunities for a bit of craic seemed to appear out of nowhere. It was as if you had your own invisible Minister for Fun trotting alongside and presenting you with these golden gifts of devilment for you to enjoy at someone else's expense.

There was a goat tethered in a garden beside this house, so we decided one night to take the goat for a bit of a walk. We were lucky that the rope was fairly long because as it turned out it was a bad-tempered article, something we copped on after being butted a few times. It was that troublesome that we took it no further than the nearest house, tied it to the door, then gave the door a few bangs, ran and hid behind a hedge; as luck would have it, there was plenty of small gaps to watch through. It was a few minutes before the door opened. It was obvious that he must have been watching TV as we could hear it loud and clear and him in the process of putting on his shoes before coming out. He shouted "Who is it, who's there?". Coming from being in the light out into semi-darkness it would take a minute or two before your eyes would adjust, but when his eyes did and all he saw was this big goat standing up on its hind legs ready to make a race at him, he let out a big roar and made a turbo-charged turn to get inside the door. It was like one of them Tom and Jerry cartoons where Tom is standing flat out running for a couple of seconds before he moves, then takes off like a rocket. The funny thing in this case was that the roar your man let out must have scared the living daylights out of the goat, because your man was just barely in the door, when the goat, who had made off in the opposite direction, came to the end of the rope, which meant the door slammed that hard that it nearly took the whole lot with it, including the door frame. We knew then it was time to be going, so we made off as fast as your man going in the door, or maybe even faster.

Carpentry

I went on to do a course in carpentry under the stewardship of Ruairi McMonagle at a Rehab Centre in Gaoth Dobhair. I was fortunate that I had such a place to go to. Although it was not that long in existence before I became part of the furniture. He had me turning out everything from turf barrows to children's custom-made slides. While there doing work, it was at a pace that suited you, because you were there in the first place to re-cuperate or, if need be, learn new skills to be in a position to get back in the workforce, if there was work to go back to. There were days when I could do nothing because of a sore back, or pains in my head that would leave me not fit for doing anything, but thankfully these occurrences gradually faded away over a period of time.

Ruairi often came in after lunch break to find me hanging up-side down doing exercises or flat out skipping. I'm sure some rare thoughts crossed his mind at times, like what sort of a header have I got in here. I must have spent roughly two years there but had to leave prematurely because of a disagreement with the manager who was a hot-headed old goat as far as I was concerned. Much the same as I could be myself but it was his way or no way, so it was only a matter of time before there was a rare-up; how it didn't happen before that I do not know. Anyway the result was that due to me flying off the handle in a split second I gave him a fair oul slap, which I did apologise unreservedly for. I think he saw money signs when he was upside down, because he insisted on getting an ambulance, which took him off to hospital. It was away over the top for a man who did more than a fair bit of talking about all the fighting he had done and in his eyes was still capable of doing.

But my time there was well worth it for what I learned. There were other people attending who found themselves in a similar situation to what I was in myself or much worse, survivors of serious car accidents, but I was lucky twice, fortunate to be alive, and very lucky that I was not left in a position where I could not work, or earn a living.

Salthill for the Weekend

I was nearly back to my feet again, having recovered enough to be able to go out at night again. A few of us decided to go to Salthill in Galway for the weekend. I had a Toyota van, so it was a matter of just packing in. There was me, Blondie John, Conner Kelly, Pauge McLean and John Harkin headed off. Martin Jim was supposed to go but could not make it. We headed off with our bits and pieces with us, the planning for all the fun we were going to have was being thought out as we headed towards Donegal Town, where we got stuck behind a coach full of tourists. I did not have enough power to overtake unless there was a good stretch of road ahead for doing so. The bus driver wasn't making it any easier as he was keeping out to the white line the whole time, so Blondie John says, "I'll show him what we think of him" when we did manage to pass. He pulls down his trousers and plants his bare buttocks up to the window. We were all killing ourselves laughing at how quickly John was able to get the trousers down and get into position. As far as we were concerned then that was the last we would see of them as we sped off leaving the bus behind.

Well that was how it should have gone, until we saw the signs telling us to slow down. Wasn't the council doing some roadwork ahead. The laughing stopped when we realised that the coach was now right behind us nearly touching the bumper and the driver giving us dirty looks. What was going through my mind at that stage of the proceedings was the driver will get the registration number and phone the guards and that will put an end to our weekend in Salthill. As good luck would have it, the driver obviously had more important things on his mind than telling the Guards about some eejit flashing his ass at him, so on we went. When we got as far as Sligo we came upon our first set of traffic lights, but of course I hadn't a clue, so on I go ignoring the glaringly red lights. I knew something was up when every car we met started flashing the lights and waving like mad. We were going the wrong direction along a one-way street. It was the first time to see a one-way street never mind drive on one. There was no such thing as road rage in them times, most people would try and help you and so we were soon directed back onto the right road again.

The first thing to do was to look for somewhere to stay, so our first port of call was a big hotel, which was a very fancy looking place. In we went anyway. We noticed that the place was full of well-dressed people. It did not take long to cop on that a wedding reception was taking place. We forgot all about booking in and made our way towards the music. Straight away we were out on the floor flat dancing. No woman was safe. At one stage I was out doing a slow waltz with a chair. Someone, I think it was John Harkin, ended up running around the floor with an old women getting a piggyback. I was getting off with one of the bridesmaids. The only problem was that she had a boyfriend and she did not know how to sneak off without him noticing, because he was watching her like a hawk. We sort of took the place over for a good while until we were eventually asked to leave. We thanked them for letting us gate crash their wedding and were sorry if we upset anyone.

The next hotel we tried, it was decided that we were to pretend that we were foreigners and I volunteered to do the talking. I made my way to the reception desk taking a good deep breath on the way, and started off in my best attempt at a stuttering French accent. The receptionist was doing her utmost at trying to explain house rules to us. I felt that I was doing a very good job, because I was getting her to repeat herself over and over again. It was going great until I got a strange feeling of being alone, I looked around only to see the rest of my fellow foreigners half way out the door laughing their heads off. My courage left me at that moment, so I did a runner for the door as well, leaving the bewildered receptionist, who was doing her best in trying to help us, with an open mouth.

We tried out some of the nightclubs and had good craic, but I cannot remember if any of us scored or not. I know I didn't and it wasn't from the want of trying. I think if I remember correctly some of our rooms were left in a bit of a state. I think we laughed the whole way home.

The only incident to happen on the way home was a dog ran out onto the road, giving me no time to stop. I whacked it anyway, whether I wanted to or not. It was a golden Labrador. But the funny thing was it went sliding along the road in a sitting position until it came to a stop, got up then and ran off. I'd say if it was a human, your posterior would be out of bounds for quiet a while. It wasn't till I got home that I realised that the dog had the last laugh, there was a big dent on the front of the van and half the number plate missing.

Playing Pranks

Micheal Doogan and Hughie left me and Joe home from the Pier one night and I was just getting nice and cosy under the blankets and just about to drift off to sleep. Joe put an end to that when he jumps up from his bed, which was across from me and says, "I heard a noise outside". By the time we pulled on some clothes and went outside without putting any of the lights on, a quare sight greeted us. All the timber that was stacked up for a new roof for the house was piled across the gate, blocking us in, but the culprits were gone. It took us nearly an hour to get the lot stacked up where it had been left in preparation for going on the roof. But that wasn't all, there was a fancy bit of writing done on the road in a few places going past our house with white paint. We had a good idea who did it but we weren't a hundred per cent sure either. A couple of nights later I was talking to Hughie about it and he owned up that him and Doogan had done it. It was a spur of the moment thing that was a great laugh from their point of view. I was thinking to myself that there wasn't a lot that could be done at Hughes's own house in that regard. Hughie's father was very tidy and kept everything inside, leaving no room for mischief, and he had a good dog; so I said to Hughie, without letting him know what had been going through my mind.

Getting Revenge

We'd do a bit of blackguarding down at Doogan's house some nights, setting off a series off tit-for-tat actions. There was never any animosity involved. It was just a case of one trying to get one up on the other. I think it was the following weekend after getting a lift home from The Pier on the Saturday night, Doogan had got a car by this stage as he had got a job so he had a few punts to spare. Anyway, he left us home first, then Hughie, but unknown to him at the time, Hughie got his father's car and came up for us and off down and parked a good bit away before sneaking towards Doogan's place. There was a house being built on the same road as his. We spent an hour or two flat out carrying blocks, all the roof timbers, barrels, just about anything that could be moved and blocked up the whole road. We knew that they would not see it from their house because of a bend in the road. They would have no hope of copping on until they drove around the corner on their way to mass in the morning. Everything worked out grand. After mass, we had a habit of meeting up in Nial Rua's shop to discuss what topic was making the headlines, but not a sign of Doogan and we knew why. When we met up during the week not a thing was mentioned, same as the first night.

We never said a thing about what was done at our house. There were a lot of sleepless nights after that. A few weeks went by and nothing was happening but you still had to sleep with one eye open. I think it was a night during the week when I thought I heard a familiar noise of a car going past the house slowly, and then a noise of a door opening or closing. Again this would be in the early hours of the morning, so up we get and out the door like a shot. Didn't we spot Hughie and Doogan running around the corner; whatever they had planned it certainly wasn't going to work out this night. They jumped into the car and off down the road. We thought "There's no way they'll come back now, seeing they were caught red handed," but we were wrong. Lucky for us, we didn't just go off to bed again because half an hour later we heard the sound of the car again, mad rush out the door again but this time they just sat in the car with the doors locked and them laughing. They were okay. They were inside and could sit there all night if need be, there was nothing me or Joe could do. We tried rocking the car but sure that wasn't having any effect at all, just making them laugh more.

Then I got a bright idea. We happened to be in the middle of cleaning out the cow byres that day and we put most of the dung out in the fields, so there were heaps of dung in different

places around the field that we had left with a small dumper. Joe
went off and got two grapes from the cow byre. The boys would
not have been able to make out what we were up to. Although it
was a nice night, because of the darkness you could only make
out the outlines of the person. It was too late for them then
when we started landing big heaps of cow dung all over the
windscreen. They could not get out to clean the window so that
they might be able to see where they were going if they did try
to make a getaway, so they just sat there until we got tired of
piling dung on top of the car. They were well and truly manured
was one way to put it. Then it was our turn to sit on the fence
and laugh at them. If you had mobile phones then to be able to
take pictures, it would have been a very popular hit on YouTube
I would imagine.

After a while we got tired watching and went off into the house
thinking they'll have enough to do for the rest of the night
cleaning the car. As it turned out, when they left our house they
picked up a bucket from outside a house down the road and
stopped at a small river where they spent ages carrying buckets
of water up from the river trying to get the car cleaned. The unfortunate thing about this was that when the outside of the car
was cleaned, there was a worse problem to contend with. What
happened was that when throwing water over the windscreen
didn't it wash dung down into the air vents for the heating system, meaning that every time you turned on the heaters a foul
smell of cow dung came out. So that put the cap on it, putting
an end to the whole tit-for-tat ventures, as they have a nasty
habit of eventually getting out of hand and somebody has to pay
the price at the end of the day.

Boxing Clubs

Me and Joe started going to Dunfanaghy Boxing Club because
a lot of the boys we knew went there. As far as I know, Mickey
Durning was the man who got the ball rolling and started it

up. Steve McElhiny from Falcarragh was the first trainer. There was a Presbyterian minister who helped out with the training as well. Then Eddie Harkin came along and became the full-time trainer for years, and the amount of time he put into it, he should have got a medal long ago. There were others involved as well. It was great. The training was very hard and you'd lose buckets of sweat on the big heavy punch bags. The sparring was tough if you weren't used to it. Not that I did an awful lot for the time I was there, as I did not participate in any boxing tournaments for reasons that shall remain private.

Joe did alright, winning a few and losing a few. John and Martin, my younger brothers, boxed there as well later on, winning some and losing some. There was one stage later on where as part of our training we were going up and down Errigal as fast as you could a couple of times a week. It was a struggle getting as far as Dunfanaghy three nights a week because we had to depend on thumbing for lifts to get out there and back, until I managed to save enough to buy a boosted up Mini Clubman 1300GT from a fellow in Dunfanaghy. I couldn't afford to put tax or insurance on it so we travelled all the back roads to avoid the guards. That was fine until I crashed it one night trying to take a corner at high speed and went straight into a stone wall. There were three of us in the car, Me, Joe and Charlie Whorisky, who was in the back seat and ended up wedged upside down in the front, Joe half-way out the windscreen, and me jammed between the steering wheel that had turned inside out and the seat. The engine was nearly in where the gear stick was and the gearbox was sticking out the back of the car. We were lucky that none of us were killed.

Of course we had to go the doctors for a check up. That turned out to be a fairly rare setup. The doctor was not too happy about being wakened up out of his beauty sleep, but I did not realise at the time that Joe was suffering from concussion. As soon as the doctor got us inside, Joe started to act strangely. At first we did not pay too much heed as he was always at some sort of caper like that anyway, but once he started to dance on top of the table, climb up onto the presses or units and shout and rave without making any sense, we knew that something was amiss. I don't know what the doctor gave him or stuck in him but it seemed to have the desired effect fairly quickly.

A boxing club was started up in McCarthy's yard in Falcarragh. It was comical when it got going at first because there were people of all ages there, but then when things started to get a bit more serious it sorted out the men from the boys. I don't actually mean that in a bad way, it's just a figure of speech. We still kept going to the club in Dunfanaghy out of loyalty but in the end we opted for Falcarragh because of the handiness.

Michael McDermott from Creeslough, who is now a boxing referee on the amateur scene, was a very good trainer who did his best to show us how to defend and attack without getting hit, which is great if you take it in and retain it. It's hard to make a ballerina out of someone with two much lead in their feet. We had some great sparring that always ended up with the two of us covered in blood looking a bit more like a butcher going haywire in his shop than a nice friendly boxing ring. It was there that I did six and a half thousand skips without stopping. This wasn't done at a first attempt. The first time I did a hundred, I thought it was good, so you just kept trying to do more and more all the time. The first time I reached four thousand I thought that was it, there is no way I can pass that, but I did and I surprised myself. It took me exactly one hour on the dot. My wrists and ankles were numb, but try as I might I never surpassed that figure. Joe got up to four and a half when someone accidentally got in the way, putting an end to it, and one of my sisters won a skipping competition, beating the boys in the process, in the hall in Gortahork. She did five hundred without stopping.

An Old Green Beetle

I think the next car I got was a Volkswagen Beetle, an old green one that had seen many a better day, but it was a real workhorse because I used it for purposes that it was never meant for. We were putting in a found for a shed at home so I went to get the cement with my trusty old Beetle to Leo McGinley's hardware in Falcarragh. I got thirteen bags of cement into the car, and these were the big old hundred-weight bags. I had a few up on the bonnet. I can't remember exactly, but what I do remember is that the wheels were splayed out and a few boys had to push for all they were worth to get it moving and even at that it just barely made it out onto the main road at the side of the shop but kept chugging away until it started to pick up speed going down Falcarragh Hill. I had only a small portion of the windscreen that I could see out of because of the bags on the bonnet. I made it home alright but it would have made nice headlines in the local papers if the guards had caught me: 'Man uses Beetle as Dump Truck'?

We had the Beetle for one winter and there was plenty of snow so it was used as a sort of sled as well as everything else. We put some cement blocks into the front. With the engine in the back it needed them for a bit of weight so that the front wheels would grip a bit better, and away you go. There were more handbrake turns done with it in a week than there would have been in the whole of the All-Ireland rally. It may not have been as high-tech as we would have liked but it did the job for us all the same. My mother had as much of a liking for the snow as we had. If you heard the squeals and the laughing out of her when you'd take her for a spin and a few handbrake turns. We had a bonnet of an old car that we'd pull up to the top of the field that had a good steep slope and we'd set her off flying down. Sometimes she'd end up upside down with the bonnet on top of her and all you would hear was the cackles of her laughing.

Work on the Farm

I came from a large family, fifteen in all. Ten girls, Mary Bridget, Kathleen, Caroline, Elish, Sophia, Barbra, Angela, Dolores, Theresa, and Clair. The five boys were Michael, James, Joe, John, and Martin. I was the second eldest so I had a lot of responsibility because Michael was away most of the time. We lived on a small farm and so work never seemed to end; there was always something to be done.

Once we got Christmas over it was no time until spring was upon us, with all the birds starting to cause a fuss going about their business. We had to go to the bog and start paring the turf banks anytime after St. Patrick's Day. If there was heavy frost that winter it meant the sides of the banks had to be cleaned off as well, then open up the potato pit that had at least ten inches of clay covering it, just in case a real hard frost came. The worst frost I saw went in about six inches, so better safe than sorry. The seed for planting had to be picked for later on. The work was never-ending, ploughing, making drills, which wasn't one bit easy; it always proved to be tricky business setting the drillers in the correct position, the exact same with the plough. If it didn't turn the sod properly it made the following work that much harder. It's all very well if you have nice flat fields, but some of the places we were expected to go with the tractor was like going up the side of Errigal; you'd need a rock climber's safety harness by right. You wouldn't feel it until you were straight into the beginning of summer without realising it and everything just seemed to land at once. Cutting all the briars and bushes so the cows would not get their tits cut, spreading cow dung on the fields, spreading dung nicely along all the drills before planting the spuds, corn, some grass seed, all the other vegetables, lettuce, carrots, beetroot, parsnips, turnips, onions, and cabbage. Nothing exotic. The soil where all these had to be set had to be all dug or turned over by hand. The main man in the house would not let a tractor next or near the gardens because it would bake the soil too much. The hardest part of it was you could dig away as hard as you liked if you were in some sort of a hurry, but the finish line never seemed to get any closer. It was best to just plod away at a steady pace and ignore the blisters that would come up in a few different places on your hands.

The cows' calves would spend the summer months grazing on waste land that wasn't fenced up, or out on commonage, because what fields we had were used for planting, etc., so the animals were not allowed next or near them. In the fields where corn was to be set, or hay would be cut, all the stones had to be gathered. A few of us, girls and boys, would spend a good few hours walking up and down the fields filling buckets with small stones and making a pile alongside the fence where they would be used for filling into drains at some stage. Then my father would dig to let water away from where old drains would have blocked up by either collapsing or due to red iron ore in the water that turned into sludge. One summer we had a lot of carrots and onions set and we put Super Sward grass fertilizer on them out of curiosity. Unfortunately the weather turned very wet and rained nearly non-stop every day when they were nearly ready for pulling. I never saw carrots or onions as big in my life. The top of the carrot was nearly the same circumference as a saucer, with the onions as big as turnips. Ninety percent started to rot with the rain so we ended up having to dump three dumper loads of them up in the bog. What a waste.

The turf had to be turned and spread a little, then it had to be footed in an upright position. It depended on the weather; if it wasn't that good you would have to go through the footings a few times to move them around by keeping the wetter ones on the outside. When it came to the time when the turf was dry enough to be gathered, that was hard bloody work for the whole lot of us. The girls did not escape the hard work either. Mary Bridget, Kathleen, Caroline, Elish, Barbra, Angela and Delores would normally fill the turf barrows. My father, or

Michael, if he was unlucky enough to be at home from working in England, me, Joe and John would do the carting. Martin and Clair were the youngest and escaped most of the years when it was all hard labor. The turf banks were very long, so one person would wheel the barrow half-way, and then whoever else would take it the rest of the way. There were no sides on the barrows to make it easy to tip off where the stack was to be built. That also meant that if the sides were not built well enough when you were wobbling along trying to make it without stopping for a rest, the next thing that would happen was the wheel would hit a bump of heather and the barrow would tip to one side and the lot would fall off. You would mutter every curse under the sun, under your breath of course because that was something that wasn't done if you were anywhere within hearing distance of my father. It took a while to build all the turf back on the barrow and whoever was taking the other one half-way would get a rest.

At the end of the day, your arms would be nearly pulled out of their sockets. Sometimes I thought I looked like one of them monkeys with the bare ass and the big long arms down to the ground; I think they're called baboons. We found big lumps of butter while we were flat out cutting turf with the trusty oul slean. That's happened twice in my life so far. They were buried in the bog as a way of preserving the butter. It could have been there for sixty or a hundred years, who knows, but curiosity got the better of me so I couldn't resist the temptation and threw a lump of it into my mouth. It was a bit tasteless and like trying to eat a cardboard box. Way back in the olden days the cows were herded all through the hills during the summer and people would make little sod houses (Bóhogs) where they would make the butter and so on. Now the stuff that we found, eating it would be the last thing on your mind. It had dried up once the turf banks drained the water away and was a bit crumbly and pale in colour. They were interesting finds as it would make you think about the way people survived without the luxury of having a fridge to pop things into.

There was something that I used to see my mother doing during the summer and I never paid a lot of attention to it because I did not see what the big deal was, until I started thinking about it in later years. She would have lifted around a dozen eggs that a clocking hen would have been sitting on for a week or more and for whatever reason decided to get up and leave them. If they were got in time before they had a chance to get cold she would wrap them up inside woolly socks that she had knit herself and sit them carefully in a biscuit tin under the range where they would be kept at a nice even temperature the whole time. She would turn each egg numerous times during the day every day until eventually they would start to hatch. This was the equivalent of the incubator that is used for this purpose nowadays. You could lift and hold the egg gently while listening to the bird pecking away until the head would appear. You would be very lucky if all the eggs hatched because sometimes there'd be blanks because the eggs weren't fertilized, or, to put it another way, the rooster wasn't doing his job properly. She would also carry out this same operation if a duck decided to do the same dirty trick of leaving the nest. You find humans are capable of doing very much the same sort of thing to their young. As long as you copped if you saw the hen out walking about as if she hadn't a care in the world (again just like humans), they would have a good chance of making it under the range.

Harvest time was always very busy, weeding the vegetables and hoeing potatoes. The hay was the first to get the chop. It had to be turned and shook up a few times with the pitchforks, depending on the weather, before raking it into long lines and making small haycocks of it. After a while it was then made into slightly bigger ones to suit lifting with the tractor and hay lift if you had one. The wee grey T20 Ferguson diesel would not take a lot of weight without the front rising up in the air. Whoever was carrying a bit of weight about their bones would have to put it to good use by sitting on the bonnet when you were bringing the haycocks to where the haystacks were being built. Normally fairly close to the cow byres if you could help it because it was less work later on when the animals had to be fed inside.

It wouldn't be that long then when the corn had to be cut. That was mostly done by scythe with my father at the helm. Again there was always help from the neighbours. If you were wearing short sleeves when coming behind lifting and making sheaves your forearms would get all scratched and scourged. It would be irritated for a week after by the continuous rubbing of the corn as you lifted it. It was even worse if it was wet. If there was enough help, one or two would be making stuks behind you, like a conveyor belt as you went along. Then, weather permitting, it was another busy time gathering the corn in to build the stacks. There was a lot of pride involved in the building of the stacks. Barny and Phil Andy Ruaigh were the experts. A good pile of whin bushes had to be cut a few days beforehand for the found of the stack to keep the corn up off the ground so that it did not rot. There was another good reason for a good deep bed of whin bushes, and that was to help keep the rats at bay. Rats don't like the jags because they don't have eyelashes like other animals for protection. Whether it worked or not could be open for debate I'm sure, but we'll leave that for some brighter spark than I to ponder over.

There would be mighty craic on these days, debates on all sorts of topics. Charlie John Óg was an expert on the weather. He would rhyme off about millibars, troughs, cyclones and downpours as if it was second nature and he was always right. I would never hear anyone arguing about him being wrong. The young boys like us would never have too much to say apart from listening, which we were better off doing anyway.

Another two characters from just up the road a bit, if they happened to be around on those days, were brothers Mickey and Frank Mullany. They couldn't be beat when it came to telling stories. Their house was well known by all the local card players, especially coming near Christmas when the turkeys were in full flow, and the door was always open for visitors. Even a burglar would be welcome, because Mickey or Frank could make up a yarn that would turn the man to the priesthood after leaving again empty handed. The thing about being able to throw out a good yarn was that telling the truth wasn't compulsory, because if it was there would be very few stories going about and less craic and too much depression. Doors would never be closed anyway so if you saw them making a beeline for your door, you were guaranteed a laugh if nothing else. I remember sitting up at a wake one night and Frank was there among a few others who were just as good. The craic and the stories were getting better as the bottles of stout were doing the rounds. Each one getting taller than the next one. The night went past without anyone thinking about sleep or going home.

The smell of cow dung was never too far away. You'd be stuck in under a cow milking as hard as you could, you in a hurry to head off for school in the morning. Not that I had to do the milking too often in the mornings, more so in the evenings if you were doing your best to get off for a game of football. Next thing you would get an awful slap around the face with a tail that was covered in dung. You'd then get in a rage trying to get your own back by giving her a whack of a stick that would only make things worse because I would have forgotten to lift the bucket of milk. So not only would I be covered in dung but milk as well. There was another one of the cows you had to watch, because each time the bucket would be nearly full she would kick. If you were fast enough you could deflect the kick that then caused her to lift the hoof upwards and down into the full bucket of milk. A lot of cursing and swearing then trying to persuade the dammed thing to get her foot out without spilling all the milk.

These were regular enough occurrences. We had a cat one time that was very funny as it always knew when it was milking time. It would sit watching, waiting just behind the cow. Then as you were milking you would direct the spray of milk straight at it. It would sit with its mouth wide open and drink away as long as you kept spraying milk at it. And they say animals are stupid. The difference between then and now is that the cat now sits at the door of the fridge waiting for its daily fix.

When a cow was coming near calving time sometimes that meant sitting up all night. I remember me and Joe doing these all-nighters, because we didn't have any wild choice in the matter. If the cow started showing signs of calving around one or two in the morning and no one there to give it a helping hand, it could prove disastrous. If it was too big for the cow to deliver on its own it could smother easily enough. We'd be half lying on a pile of hay in the corner as cosy as you like because the heat from the animals would keep the place nice and warm. Then there was a bit of a competition on who could stay awake the longest. For all the times that we did this, I think we only ever had two calves that were born during the hours of darkness and both were in need of help. Once you got it to stand on its own feet you directed the calf to the mother's head and it would lick it clean. That's when they bonded. This was fine if you were going to let the calf suck on the cow, but if it was going to be milked, you would keep the calf away from the cow altogether, milk the cow and feed the calf separately. It was always better to play safe and sit up for a night rather than being sorry if something went wrong leaving you with a dead calf on your hands. I often thought that milking a cow would be great for anyone gearing up for the boxing ring, because if you had a bad tempered one like some of the ones that we had, you were trying to duck the tail and fend off the right hooves the whole time you were sitting in underneath them with the bucket.

One job that I always looked forward to was when it came to the time of year when the threshing mill started to come round the townland. It would go from farm to farm taking them out of face as they went along. You could always tell when it was in the area by the loud whirring sound it made, so the closer the sound came the excitement moved up a gear along with it. There were a good few stacks of corn in close proximity to our small farm. Paddy Eoin's, the Andy Ruai's, Johnny McLochainn, Phil Harkin, Joe, John, and Charlie John Óg, and there would be a good few of the neighbours going from house to house helping out. The big interest from our point of view was the rats. The stacks would be full of them, some more than others. If the stack was too close to drains or anything of that nature, it would guarantee a full house, and that's when the fun started. As soon as the thatch was taken off the stack and the mill set up and running you would see them making a run for freedom. We had a good dog that very few got past. I saw one big rat that managed to get a grip of the dog's nose and held on for all it was worth as the dog swung it in all directions before it came off and a bit of the nose as well. But there was no getting away. The dog had it killed in a flash.

Once the stack was near the bottom, it was all hands on deck, and some of the men would tie a cord around their trousers at the ankles for fear of the rats running up their legs. The thought of it would be enough to scare the living daylights out of anyone, especially us, because someone was sure to throw a dead rat at you at some stage. Then it was tea time and back to the house to feed a load of hungry men and sometimes girls. This would be one of the occasions when there would be a chance of goodies being in the house. I remember eating that much that I would be left with pains and a swollen belly. I'd be cursing myself for eating so much and think I'd never do that again as long as I'd live. There was always a bit of friendly rivalry going on as to who got the most or the best grain from their stacks, and sometimes the most or the biggest rats. That added to the fun of the whole occasion.

Phil Harken, who lived within shouting distance of our house, was a great man for watching sport on a Saturday. It didn't matter what work was going on, it would have to wait for some other day. If there was boxing on I would hear Phil shouting at the top of his voice so I'd be up like a shot. I watched all Barry

McGuigan's fights in Phil's, Tommy (Hitman) Hearns, Sugar Ray Leonard, (Marvellous) Marvin Hagler. I never missed any of these fights on TV while Phil was about.

My Brother Michael

My older brother Michael was away from home for years. He had done his stint with the cows and the chickens or rolling around in the straw with some girls from across the fields on threshing the corn day. I might have been very young but I could still see what all the carry-on was about. It wasn't all work and no play. But he knew what the hard work was all about. This was probably why he was in such a hurry to leave home. He had spent a couple of years in Australia chasing kangaroos, that's what he said anyway. But most of his time was in England and Scotland. I always looked forward to him coming home so that I might get a chance at driving whatever car he had home with him. Once he was home for a few weeks the engines would start to pile up around the place, because they couldn't last long with the abuse. There was no such thing as pulling off nice and easy. The wheels had to be spinning and clouds of smoke coming out of the tyres. It was always the same every weekend, a mad panic trying to find an old car with an engine that would start. It would be found somewhere, there was no doubt about that. It would be changed into a car on the Friday and get that much dog's abuse over the weekend that it would be about ready to pack it in, and if he could not come up with another one, it was back to picking out the best in a line of the bad ones. Some of the cars were in their death throes, with a lump of timber jammed across between the suspensions because they were collapsing inwards. The bodywork around the heads of the suspension was eaten away with rust.

During those days I don't think he ever had a license or insurance and I suppose not too many others around his age had anything on their cars either. I don't know how he managed to get away without getting caught by the Guards. I was with him many different times when he did get stopped at checkpoints, with baldy tyres and loads of other things wrong. There was one instance where he had to take me to the doctors because my tonsils were swollen up but he had a flat wheel and the spare was punctured as well. The car was a Toyota, a rare enough sort of a car in those days, but he found a wheel that was pumped up fairly hard that must have been off a Ford. He took the flat wheel off and tried to fit the new one onto it but there was a slight difference in lining up the holes so off he goes and comes back with a pickaxe and started to bang it into the holes on the rim to make them bigger. After about half an hour he had holes looking like big long slots and managed to get the wheel onto the car. It was a rare-looking sight but off we went anyway and because the wheel was so uneven the car was hopping up and down that much that you couldn't talk for fear of biting off your tongue. If you had milk in the car it would have turned into butter in no time at all.

As we were coming into the town the guards stopped us. One of them had a good look around the car, came round to Michael's side, took off his Garda hat, put his baldy head down to Michael and said, "There's far more grip on my head than there is on your tyres and what in under God is wrong with that wheel you have on? I never saw anything like that before in my whole life". The other guard was in stitches laughing, so with a straight, serious face Michael started and gave them a big story about the garage having to order a wheel from Japan and it would take three weeks before it would be here and the only reason he resorted to what he did was because it was an emergency taking me to the doctor. I thought I was for death with the whole spiel he gave them. I couldn't speak, so the guards told us to hurry on. So just imagine the weird sound of laughing as the car hopped away up the road. No doubt about it he would talk his way out of most things. I don't know if them excuses would work if you were stopped at a checkpoint now.

Cool Pete

I used to mate around with another fellow around this time. Everyone knew him as Cool Pete. He was a very entertaining character to say the least, and would have everyone in stitches laughing. I saw him getting into some arguments where he would just bamboozle all around him with big words. Now, to tell the truth, half of them were probably made up anyway but you had to pretend that you knew what he was talking about. Michael used to mate around with Cool Pete's older brother and a few other boys, so they would all end up in the Shamrock Bar until two or three in the morning with live bands. Me and Cool Pete would pass a few hours around the town late on the Saturday night hoping to see a fight or something along them lines as the crowd started to leave the Shamrock. It was normal enough to see some sort of scrimmage starting up over nothing, one man out in the middle of the road with his shirt pulled off in a rage and the tie still on.

Leaving that aside, we knew there was a good chance we'd get a lift home with them. One night the three of them had a good drink on them. They got a takeaway from the fish and chip shop and sat in the car and ate what they didn't empty out all over themselves. Between the drink and the feed they were soon fast asleep. However me and Pete soon came up with a plan on how to get home. Pete goes down head first at an angle in between the two front seats so that he would be able to work the clutch, brake and accelerator with his hands, and I lean in over the driver's seat so that I could reach the steering wheel and the gear stick. We got the car started after stalling a good few times and with a few jerky moves. We pulled off from outside the Shamrock Bar in the town. We took it nice and steady until we got turned up the Muckish Road. The three boys still never stirred, even though we were by now starting to act the eejit heading up past the hall in Falcarragh. Pete was jamming the throttle up and down, causing the car to bounce along like a kangaroo because we were still only in second gear. By the time we managed to progress as far as third there was a corner approaching and Pete had the boot to the board and him flat out laughing at the same time. Next thing we're in the corner and me turning the steering wheel making no difference whatsoever until we end up straddling a hedge and a drop on the other side. The fun and the laughing soon stopped and there was complete silence for a few minutes until we decided what best course of action to take to get us out of the predicament we were in.

We decided to try and wake up the boys. After a lot of shaking Michael half wakes up and says, "Jesus, I nearly smashed". It could not have worked out better if we planned it. Then we woke up the other two but we had to be careful getting out as the car was balancing on top of the hedge. So with some falling about, cursing and swearing the car ended up back out on the road and Michael drove home thinking about the close shave he had. Me and Cool Pete kept very quiet about what really happened for a long time after that.

PART III – LEAVING HOME

The first time I left home, I was in my early twenties. When I left it was to join my brother Joe and Hughie Harkin, who always had a box of matches in his pockets and would light a fire in every whin bush in the townland. We grew up not far from each other, a few hundred yards at most, here in the hills of Donegal. Hughie could make a very good story out of an uninspiring one, something he was adept at when he was in the early teen stages. He spent too much time hanging around with all the oul boys in the townland. They would meet up in certain houses different nights of the week telling old yarns and stories that if the lies were left out, there wouldn't be much meat left on the bones. This would mostly happen during the winter months, so when you picked up them habits, through no fault of your own, it would be hard not to use it to your advantage now and again. We could always make out when the truth was being stretched until it was well and truly blurred, but it all added to the craic and the fun anyway.

At the end of the day, leaving home for the first time was not something that I was looking forward to. When the time actually came, and me only going across the water you could say, I remember going to great lengths to make a fancy toolbox for my plastering tools. Looking back on it now you could do nothing but laugh. By the time we got as far as Heathrow Airport my precious toolbox was going around the conveyor belt in bits. All the nails did not prevent my tools from being scattered all over the place. It was a proper circus by the time we reached the Tube. They took a proper hand at me. As soon as we'd get on to one carriage, they'd jump out again just as the doors were about to close. I had palpitations a few times when I thought I wouldn't make it out behind them. Jesus was I glad to get out at the other end. There were beads of cold sweat on my forehead because I hadn't a clue where to go or what to do if I did happen to get lost.

King's Cross, London

The boys had a first floor bed-sit in King's Cross. The bathroom was down the hallway and was shared by a good few people from all walks of life. The building itself contained a lot of self-contained apartments. It belonged to a man from home who decided to seek fame and fortune when he was around sixteen years' old or thereabouts, and had ended up spending the biggest part of his life in London. He owned a lot of property in Spain, plus the whole big apartment block that our bed-sit was in. It was a place that was to open my eyes to the delights of living in King's Cross.

We were situated in a sort of a cul-de-sac, where our front window looked directly onto the street and the back looked out onto a little park. We were treated to some shows from our window that a lot of people pay big money to see, and there we were getting it all for free. It was mainly black taxi drivers who we would see bringing ladies who accept payment for services rendered. They would park outside our window to deliver their end of the agreement. Some of the ladies in question would be very pretty and some others you would have to put a bag over your own head in case it fell off theirs. I must say the fact that it was so entertaining made up for losing too much sleep, which was the least of our worries. There was never a dull moment. It was one incident after another. When you looked out the back window there was a bit of a green area and on the other side of that was a row of houses and one of them had a crowd of punk rockers, or maybe it was Goths; I'm not sure to be honest. You wouldn't really see them much during the day, but I suppose we weren't around that much during the day to see them anyway. They seemed to come out once it started to get dark. They took their dressing up very seriously, with all shades of dyed hair cut into all shapes and sizes, dressed all in black. I'm not sure what description they would have used for us when they saw us waving and shouting across at them when we would see the girls in a state of undress hanging out the window.

I remember another hilarious bit of taking the P that took place while staying there. It happened during the time that Prince Charles and Lady Di got married. The fellow living across the hallway was so excited about the whole thing he hung a big Union Jack out his window with a whole lot of smaller ones attached to strings. Of course the sight of it didn't exactly rock our boat, so Joe and Hughie managed to reach it after a bit of hokery pokery. Joe was that far out the window he was more or less standing on air, with Hughie holding onto him for all he was worth. It was no soft landing if you fell; it was a nice drop to the footpath. So with the help of a floor brush they managed to pull the whole shebang in our window. There was a bit of a debate then about what the best thing to do with it was, so it was decided there and then to turn the lot into cinders. So we set about the burning process without setting the whole place on fire. After that part of the operation was completed, the remains were left in a neat little pile outside his door with a few wee bits left to show what it was. That put an end to the flying of the butcher's apron outside our building.

A cousin of ours, Antony, moved in, then another two boys, Phil McHugh and Pat Bán, or Murphy as he was better known for a while. He was great at putting on a west of Ireland accent, so he would phone up other boys offering them jobs and hold a sort of an interview over the phone. What size were your hands and have you got your own wellies because we don't supply any, or how many bags of cement could they carry on a barrow, and tell them to be at a certain place to be picked up in the morning at five-thirty. Some copped on that it was a prank but there were others who didn't and were there at the meeting place to be picked up for work the following day or on the Monday.

Joe and Hughie had chanced their arm at carpentry with a sub-contractor from near home, and were bluffing their way along rightly the same as everyone else. They took me to look for work in through sites in the city because I did not have a clue where to go. We called into lots of jobs looking for a start, as you would say, until we were just about sick of hearing no, no, no. We called into one last renovation job in Chinatown. It's sandwiched between Soho and Leicester Square in London's West End. It was the second door once you turned into Chinatown and was, yes, a Chinese restaurant. All the workers were of Chinese or Vietnamese origin. Luck had it that they were in need of plasterers, so that's where we came in. Joe decided to come out to work along with me because at that stage he did not have too much experience at the plastering and he wanted to get the hang of it. That was leaving Hughie on his own at the carpentry. He did not mind too much anyway. Hughie had talent to spare. He went on to become a successful contractor at home. The thing about Hughie was that he only had to see a thing done once and it was in his head for good. He got himself out shuttering where the big money was. Although you had to work hard for it, rain, hail or snow.

'Borrowing' the Generator

There is one event that sticks out in my mind clearly when I think of Hughie. He phoned me up one evening and him in a foul mood. The contractor he was working for was messing him about big time, short paying him in his pay cheque and never sorting it out and being generally very crafty. When it was near finishing up time the concrete lorry was sure to land, so it meant two hours or more and not getting paid for it. This was a regular occurrence, so he said, "They're going to pay one way or another". Earlier that day he had hidden a brand new generator under some sheets of ply outside the fence next to a nice park near to the site. I think it was fairly near to the coast, about two and a half hours' drive, and he had to do that every morning and night. We got to a street adjacent to the park, left the van there and went for a stroll around the park to get our bearings. We were going to have to drag the generator the whole way across to one of the gates, but it was still daylight. To do that would have looked out of place for two rough-looking boys in working clothes out for a stroll. We were getting some strange looks from people. It was a typical English area, all prim and proper. We got the feeling that we stuck out like sore thumbs. We didn't have to wait too long before it started to get dark enough for the street lights to come on. Off we went on our mission and dragged our piece of equipment across to the gate. I had to babysit it while Hughie went off to get the van. It was only a small Astra van. I'm standing there trying to keep my mind occupied, but that's hard when there's nothing but shadows of all shapes and sizes surrounding you.

It was then I noticed the lights of this car driving slowly around the park. The road into the gateway where I stood was a dead end. I watched as the car turned into our road and pulled in about fifty meters from me, keeping the headlights on and shining in my direction. What was it but a bloody police car. I thought some do-gooder had reported the two suspicious-looking boys walking about through the park earlier, so I thought straight away that they must have been looking for us. This was why Hughie was taking so long to get back. If only we had mobile phones then. He had spotted them as well and had come to the exact same conclusion as me. There was only the one escape route for me now and that was over the perimeter fence, and that was about two meters in height. But the pressure was on. I don't know how I managed to climb up as there was no grip for your feet, but I ended up straddled on the top like some sort of cat burglar. The small problem facing me now was that it was pitch black on the other side. I wasn't able to see a thing. As far as I was concerned then there was no turning back so I jumped into the unknown and luckily for me I landed on my back in a massive clump of briars. It was like a fly stuck in a spider's web and me suspended off the ground.

I was lying there for what seemed like hours, wondering how the hell was I going to get out of this mess. I was thinking that Hughie had gone off and left me, and not a penny in my pocket. Well this is what you deserve for resorting to taking something that's not legally yours, but morally I'm helping a friend in need seeking recompense. Then I realised that I could hear a whistle every minute or so. First I thought it was some sort of bird, then I thought "Wait a minute, birds don't normally make a whistling noise like that". So I made a similar-type whistle back as an answer. After a while they began to get a little bit closer. "Hi, where are you?" I hear in a loud whisper. Boys oh boys was I glad to hear him as he trampled a path through the briers towards me with a plank of timber he found along the fence. After a struggle getting me untangled from the briars, I managed to get down. I had a few scratches alright but I wouldn't die because of it.

We came up with another plan that would go down well in any movie. He would go back the way he came, get the van and drive down past the patrol car, which was still sitting (twenty-five minutes must have passed by this stage) there with the lights on, nice and steady, do a three-point turn at the end of the cul-de-sac and then sit with the full headlights on facing the patrol car for a minute or two, just about enough time to get the generator into the back of the van as quick as we could. The idea behind this was that they would not be able to see anything with our lights shining at them, and they would think it was just someone having a little difficulty turning. As he was turning, I pulled the offending item out and opened the back door. He was out in a flash and into the back with it in three seconds. That's what we did until we jumped back into the van and as Hughie pulled off a wee bit too fast I didn't get time to turn around to get enough of a grip on it to be able to hold onto it. It was like slow motion watching it fly backwards and smash through the back window.

At that point there was no stopping. What a fecking thing to happen. If we needed any help from above it was now I thought as we passed the police car with half a generator sticking out through the back of the van. We were waiting for the police car to swing around with the squeal of burning rubber and flashing blue lights racing after us but it didn't happen and we drove on in silence until we got out of sight then pulled into a lay-by and tied a rope from the generator to the seat. You would think that we had expected something like this to happen, because there was a black bin liner bag and a roll of black masking tape lying in the back of the van as well. We had the window covered over in no time at all. Then it was boot to the board straight to London. An experience to be remembered but as Hughie says we wouldn't be doing it if we weren't owed it.

Conned out of Money

That reminds me of how I got conned for a few pounds one time by a smooth-talking conman. I was on my way back to England after being home for a week or two. I was on the boat from Larne to Holyhead when I got chatting to this fellow, which was fine, it shortened the journey. He told me he was over visiting relatives in Belfast and that he had meetings with refrigeration companies because of an invention he had come up with and got patented. He explained to me what it was all about. Now there I was expecting something dramatic, but it sounded like something children would come up with, coloured pins that you would stick onto food that would show you how long it was there. I was losing interest at this stage and feeling sorry for him when he asked me could I loan him a few pounds until he got back to London. He gave me his name, address and phone number, so I gave him a hundred pounds. Anyway, to make another long story a bit shorter, I rang the number he gave me a few weeks later but no good. When I checked out the address, sure that was pie in the sky as well, but I had to laugh because I knew that I was well and truly caught out.

Tottenham

In between times we moved from King's Cross to a house in Tottenham. There was me, Joe, Pat Bán and Phil McHugh. Hughie moved into a different house as there was a steady girlfriend on the scene, and so missed all the carnage. The way the sleeping arrangements worked out was because we were brothers. We had to sleep in the room with the double but bed sharing wasn't a big deal for us coming from a big family.

I remember the first night we could not get the heating to work and there were no bedclothes and I would get up in the middle of the night and start skipping to try and get warmed up. It was bloody freezing. It would have frozen the balls off a brass monkey. Everything was going good for a while then a few other boys who were coming over from home needed a place to stay. Patsy and John Bán joined the clan while they looked around for work. Patsy was mad for work but John wasn't too bothered until the funds began to dry up. Then the pressure was on. It wasn't long after that when a burglar visited uninvited and stole whatever money was around the place. We had a bag for the gym with sparring gloves and stuff like that in it, but that was emptied out and they used the bag for whatever they could take. They looked everywhere but missed the bump on the carpet in our room where Joe had three and a half thousand pounds hidden. A nice bit of money to get your hands on at the time. The police came around, but what could they do and they told us as much. Then after getting no satisfaction whatsoever from the owner – he just didn't want to know anything about it – the least we wanted was to get a few weeks' free rent to make up for what was lost. But as far as he was concerned it was our hard luck. After that things began to go slightly haywire in the house. We came to the conclusion that if he didn't care about us why should we care about him? It should work both ways.

Me and Joe would be working very late some nights plastering at the Chinese restaurant, so we were knackered by the time we got in, had a bite to eat if there was anything left and off to bed. Just as I was about to drift off to sleep one of these nights I thought I found something crawling over my face. Then it happened again, so I jumped up out of the bed and put on the light only to see a few mice running around on the bed. Joe shook them off and I flattened them with one of my boots, but I knew there was something strange because they were white and did not seem to want to run away. Next thing the door flies open and the other boys come in killing themselves laughing. They had got the mice from a pet shop and put them into our pillows. It was funny but not at the time.

I was up in my room when the other boys decided to play a trick on one of the lads, so they got him to stand up straight with his hands down by his side. There were a few rolls of brown paper, I don't know where they came from, but they wrapped miles of it around John, then miles of masking tape. There was that much around him that he couldn't move. They were then to carry him up to my room to play some sort of trick on me, but unknown to John the bath was being filled up for him, so they carried him up and then threw him into the bath. What a sight, and him shouting "I'm drowning, I'm drowning". Another unnamed person got the toilet brush that wasn't too clean either as the toilet was blocked up for a few days, and rubbed the paper from around his face, with the paper tearing up because of being in the water and him struggling around. The water was flowing out the door and down the stairs, which were carpeted. In the wrestling afterwards a radiator was half pulled off the wall in the hallway, so the whole carpet was like a sponge when you walked on it. We used to use the sitting room as a sparring room as well; the noise and shouting must have had the life scared out of the neighbours.

I was coming in from work one evening when a Greek woman living next door approached me saying that she did not want any trouble and her crying. I did not know what she was on about. Then she showed me notes that were put in her door. It turned out that she had a very good-looking daughter. One unnamed person took it upon himself to ask her out by putting a note in the door, but the mother got the wrong meaning from the note. So after apologies and explanations it was all sorted out, but that note scribbler never got seeing the daughter after all his trouble.

There was one night while still living in the house, just after I got the start in the National nightclub as a doorman. Phil had an old Vauxhall Cavalier that him and the rest of the boys would head off in. At the National one night, one of the doormen said to me "There's a few of your townies going mad outside". So I went to the door to see what the fuss was about, and what do I see but Phil with the shirt off and him dancing away like mad on the roof of the Cavalier. Now there would have been a fair bit of drink involved to say the least and not a policeman in sight, which was very rare. He would not give the keys to anyone and insisted on driving himself. He could only get one other foolhardy volunteer to go with him. By the time the rest got back to the house the car was parked half up on a metal fence directly outside the house with both sides of it all smashed and scored and part of the railings from outside a Wimpy fast food outlet stuck on it as well. It was a miracle that he even got that far, but that was one of many adventurous nights that started off from this house. Hughie bought an old Cavalier the same type as Phil's. He got it for half nothing, so the intention was to drive the whole way up to Holyhead or Stranraer and across on the night Ferry to get us home for the holidays. We'd never book a cabin that I remember; we'd scrounge around until we found an empty one. First in got the beds. Now if you'd lifted the bonnet and saw the state of the engine you wouldn't go around the corner never mind the whole way home; there was oil squirting out everywhere. It was filled to the lip with engine oil before we left and a few more times on the way But that car got us home and toured around for a couple of hard weeks driving and brought us back to London again.

Two unnamed boys came home from work one day and the only thing left to eat in the house was a loaf left in the press. Joe and Phil had been home before them and cut the loaf in half, took the middle out of it and put something you would not expect in your wildest dreams into it, and then glued it together. I was standing in the sitting room when the two boys came in and went to make a cup of tea and to put on some toast. All I could hear was "Ah Jesus Christ boys, ah Jesus Christ boys" so you can imagine that it must have been a pretty awful sight when he started to cut slices off the loaf.

There was another time when we managed to get all the clothes apart from the underpants off one of the boys and put him outside. The place was covered with snow and frost at the time as well. Me and Pat Bán were standing behind the door killing ourselves laughing while he was banging away at the door trying to get back in. Then it went quiet for a few minutes. The next thing this iron bar came flying straight through the door. It was pure luck that it never hit either of us. If it did it would have been a funeral matter rather than a laughing matter. He was let in fairly quick then. He told us that he found it in the garden next door.

At this stage the goings-on in the house were getting worse by the hour, never mind by the day. There was no point in having a lock on the door because it just got kicked in. Phil was the carpenter. That was a joke back then as he has come on a fair bit since that. He kept moving the lock up and down the door frame until there was nowhere left to put it.

You had to be careful and check your bed because you would never have a clue what was under the clothes. I came in one night to a bare room. They had thrown the lot, including the bed, out the window. I don't know how the house wasn't burned down because someone, I don't remember who, came in with fireworks, and not just little bangers but rockets, and started letting them off in the house and they would shoot up and stick in the ceiling. I was out somewhere. When I came back next day I was wondering what made the holes in the ceilings.

That was it. It was time to get out of the place so me and Joe got digs in a house not too far away owned by a couple from Mayo who had a few houses around the same area. There were a few rare boys in this house I can tell you. There were two brothers from Mayo who lived on the top floor. One of them never went out except to work. He had a big armchair sitting right in front of the TV and everything you could mention food-wise surrounded the chair. Once he came in from work and sat down he never had to move because everything was within arms reach except the toilet. There was another fellow from Derry on the ground floor who was double-jointed. He would put on his coat, twist his legs up underneath and walk around on his hands. You would swear he had no legs. He would often do this going into pubs. People would get up to offer him a seat on many occasions. He got into a fight with a ticket inspector on the underground one evening after he had a few drinks too many. It ended up with him losing one of his front teeth. The only thing that was bothering him then was how he was going to look when he went out because he saw himself as a bit of a ladies' man. We got some cotton wool and wood glue, mixed it up, and fitted in as best as we could (I was the dentist) to get him through the night. It wasn't such a bad job after all. I was the appointed dentist over the next couple of weeks until he had it repaired.

Buying a House

The wise thing to do was to buy a house. That's what the general consensus was among a lot of the Irish boys, and we were no different in that regard. So after getting in touch with a middle man, who supplied us with all the documentation that was needed, me and Joe went house-hunting without knowing anything about the legalities involved, or anything else for that matter.

After coming close to buying on five or six occasions after paying all the survey fees, solicitors, etc., it would fall through because the prices were going up so much that it would pay the seller to pull out and up the asking price (the exact same way things went here at home during the bubble boom). Frustration was setting in when the owner of the last house, which was supposed to be ours according to the estate agents, began looking for more money. So we had no option but to go along with the proposed hike in the price. As far as we were concerned this one wasn't going to be let go like the others. Maybe it was down to estate agents spotting our inexperience but they certainly took advantage of the fact, and so did the owner who I met on one of the visits to the house. He was from Pakistan, and the smell of curry and hot spices in the house would make your eyes water. The carpet and wallpaper was horrific to look at, all yellowish with red flowers. Definitely not in my league of tasteful decoration. He must have got the smell of easy money as well as the estate agents. He started his old sob story of getting more money and suggested that if we would give him a few thousand under the table, so to speak, he would go ahead with the sale. So we had to cross the palm of his hand with the few grand, then we had to buy all the junk in his house, even an old scooter that was parked in the hallway. Anyway contracts were exchanged and the house was ours. I nicknamed him Paddystani for his craftiness. He asked for one favour, which he had to get on signed paper. He said he would have to stay in the house for another week as his flights weren't arranged to fly home. Another week wasn't going to put us up or down.

The following week, a Saturday, the two of us landed at what was now our house to move into, but lo and behold, the door was only slightly opened for us by Paddystani. He told us that we could not move in yet as he still had not got his affairs in order. Then he invited us in (to our house!!) so he could explain that it could be a month or it could be six months and offered us a drink. He seemed to be on a bit of a bender, probably celebrating conning all the cash out of us. He showed me the piece of paper that I had signed. The mistake on my part was it did not state a leaving date, only to say when he got his papers, etc., sorted out, saying he would leave then. I said to him, "You want to stay in our house for as long as you want and we pay the mortgage??" He shrugged his shoulders and nodded. I went into a rage (up to that I was very placid and friendly) and said, "If you're not gone out of here by next Saturday I'm going to kill you and I meant every word of it". With a smile on his face, he said, "Oh! I'm not afraid of dying!!" With that I turned and walked out the door.

The following Saturday I landed at the door again but on my own this time (Joe had to go home for some reason or another). I was fully prepared to carry out the threat and do a life sentence. I had got keys in the estate agent's office and just opened the door without knocking. He was one lucky man, there wasn't a trace of him or his wife. He must have weighed up the consequence of staying when he sobered up, and thought to himself, life's not bad, I want to stay in this world for another while. He got the message that he had pushed the boundaries as far as he could on this time around. Sometimes ignorance can be bliss because you don't know the dangers, but on this occasion it was a costly hindrance.

Moving In

I moved whatever bits and pieces into the house and my sister Kathleen helped me to clean up and get rid of all the junk that we had to buy off the cute hoor. Getting rid of the smell of curry and making the place liveable was a fair task. We soon had tenants in to help pay the bills. They went from air hostesses, computer geeks, electricians, the odd cowboy, as well an Indian or two, which worked out fine for about two years. Then the ass fell out of the economy, interest rates went sky-high and left all house owners in negative equity.

We had some rare cases staying in the house at times. One fellow, a mature student, was one of the worst. His room had been repainted, replastered, new carpet, new furniture before he moved in. Well he was a walking disaster, he would fall going up the stairs, fall coming down the stairs. Sometimes you'd swear he wasn't the full shilling but he wouldn't be long proving you wrong on that one. When the college was closed for holidays I took him out labouring for me as he had laboured to plasterers before, so he told me. That was some learning experience that I could have done without; he could not see the difference between a watery bucket of plaster and a bucket that you would need a hammer and chisel to get the plaster out. There was just no telling him. When I'd rare up he'd just look at you as if you were stupid. It came to a head one day when he said to me that he should be getting the same money as I was making, so I told him the best thing you can do is go buy yourself some tools and go out plastering yourself. That's what he did and moved out of the house; God was I glad to see the back of him. When I went into his room, it was a sight to behold. There were coffee stains from the floor to the ceiling, and even on the ceiling, food caked into the carpet and the bed was in some stinking mess. Everything in the room had to be dumped. Renting rooms to strangers was no bed of roses I can tell you.

Three in a Bed

A couple that we knew well from home were staying in a room at the top of the house, so one morning when I was in the kitchen making myself a bite to eat, your man comes in and says, "Jesus! I had a strange experience last night". He said he was asleep when he found someone pushing him over in the bed. That was okay as he thought it was his girlfriend, until he realised that he was squeezed up against her as she was on the other side of him. When that thought registered in his brain he shot upright like a bolt of lightning to discover that it was another fellow from home who was staying in a room below. He got a fright and shooed your man out. What had happened was the fellow from the room below wasn't used to hard manual work and had got a job working in the tunnels. Sometimes he was on nights, then he would get changed to days. So with the mixing up of the times plus the tiredness he got up to go to the loo and sleepwalked into their room. He was the butt of a few jokes and plenty of slagging after that mishap. One of the scenarios discussed was what might have happened if he had climbed in the other side of the bed instead.

A Visit from a Burglar

A fellow was woken from his sleep in the middle of the night in his room on the ground floor, when he saw someone looking in his press using a lighted match. Thinking it was some of us, he said to turn on the light. Next thing he knew was your man told him to put his head under the pillow or he would blow his head off. He then asked if he kept any money or drugs and who was in the house. Your man explained to him from under the pillow who was in the house and that there were no drug users living in the house. He took fifty pounds before leaving, without going through the rest of the house. The following morning when we discovered what happened, we saw where he got in. It was a small opening at the top of the window that a cat would have trouble squeezing through. It was obvious that he must have put a child in first to open the door. I had to change the lock straight away as a set of door keys were missing.

Fireworks

Joe and Hughie had got their hands on one of them fireworks, the rocket type that goes up into the sky and makes a big bang. So between the three of us we came up with a bright idea. Rather than set it off pointing skywards, would it not be a better idea to set it off horizontally? Finding the best place was difficult until a suggestion was made about letting it off in the subway. We were beside an exit of the Tube Station. Down a flight of steps there was a long subway going across underneath the main road, four lanes of traffic wide. We had to wait a while as there were a few people in the way. As soon as the coast was clear the fuse was lit. Just as that was done this man walked past going in the same direction as our missile was pointed but he had got a glimpse of what we were doing. It started hissing like mad and your man with a look of terror in his face took off running as hard as he could go and the rocket took off a second or two after him. The last sight we had of it was it bouncing off the walls as it went past your man. We took off up the steps. By the time we reached the top we heard the bang echoing up after us. We crossed the road and went down another entrance out of curiosity. There was a cloud of smoke around but that was it. When we had time to think about what we had done we realised that it wasn't the wisest thing to do as it could have injured someone. So that put an end to them sort of pranks.

The Employment Agency

It would be a week or more before we were to start work with the Chinese as the job wasn't ready for us at that stage. I think it was the following day I bought The Standard newspaper. Someone told me that there were plenty of jobs advertised in it. The first number I phoned asked me how many plasterers there were. "Two," says I. He then gave me an address to go to for six am. I had fixed my toolbox by this stage so box and all we got there in time. But there were about twenty others standing around as well, which I could not figure out because I knew to look at them they were not all plasterers. It turned out it was a labour hire office. Next thing this buck in a suit comes out and shouts "Carpenters". A few men stepped forward. Same for electricians, painters, etc., until he calls for plasterers so we moved to join the other trades. "Oh, oh, no gangs," he says, and dismisses us like a couple of children looking for sweets and walks off. If he had known any better he wouldn't treat people like that, because the next he knew he was flat on his back on the ground. Joe had levelled him with a right hook. After being stunned for a few seconds he scrambled to his feet and made a mad rush to the door, leaving all his paperwork to blow away with the wind. Once inside he slammed it shut and bolted about twenty locks on it. It was certainly a strong door. I could safely say that we would not have been the first trying to get in uninvited. We spent a good few minutes doing our best trying to kick it in. There was a lot of squealing and shouting in the office.

At that stage we decided that the best thing to do was to run like hell before the police caught up with us because we knew they'd be sent for. I think it was the next day we got a job off the paper by ringing up, but we had to be careful and not make a mistake and ring up the same crowd that we gave the fright to in the office. It turned out to be a nice little job, an extension to an office. The man who owned the place had one of these real posh English accents and we could not understand a word he was saying. He got fed up when he couldn't even get through to us using sign language and us killing ourselves laughing. He got a lady who worked in the office to explain what he wanted done. It was fairly straightforward so it took us four days to finish it. He was happy enough. He gave us an extra fifty pounds without saying a word, which we were not expecting.

Shuttering Work

We were getting a bit tired of the plastering. Hughie told Joe about a big job. They were looking for shuttering carpenters, so off we go to the site armed with our new tool bags and hammers. We did our best to dirty and rough them up a bit, because if you went into a site with brand new tools, they would know straight away that you were a cowboy. But your man must have been fairly desperate, because he told us to start in the morning.

Shuttering carpenters always worked in pairs, so this was not going to suit us at all, the two of us being together not knowing what to do. Joe had done a bit of shuttering before, but I had never been in this sort of a site before, so I got a bright idea and I said to him that I could not start straight away as I had a job to finish and it would take me a few days. "That's fine," he says, "you start tomorrow" (pointing at Joe) "and you can start next Monday". It could not have worked out better if you had planned it. It meant Joe would get paired up, hopefully with an experienced man, which was exactly what happened. It was a man from Tyrone and he was sound, because he copped on straight away that Joe was only chancing his arm, and told him to look busy and stick close to him and he would be fine. They were doing staircases, one of the trickiest jobs that you could get on a shuttering job, so I'm told.

That was fine until Monday came, my baptismal day at the shuttering. I got paired of with a man from Mayo, who, once I told him that I would need a bit of help along the way, didn't want to know. He never spoke to me anyway, he just grunted. It was very basic stuff that we were doing, and all I needed to see was it done once. You did not have to be a brain surgeon. Your man had a beard and a dirty looking scar across his cheek. He looked the part and acted the part, so at the end of the second day the foreman gave me my walking papers. My partner just was not the type to give one a helping hand. It's a long road and I hope he remembers when he needs help some day and there's no one there to give it, because not only did he get me the sack but he got Joe sacked as well, so it was back to the plastering again for another while.

Plastering for the Chinese

When myself and Joe started work for the Chinese, not alone did we plaster the whole building, but we did all the carpentry work. We became right Jacks of all trades, but some would say masters of none (that's a joke). The Chinese had great time for us. They took us to a big swanky restaurant every day and nearly fed us to death. There was a casino or a gambling den underneath the building where we were doing all the work. We noticed that a policeman used to go down every now and again. I asked one of the boys what he was doing going into the casino because we knew it was illegal. I got a shock when he told us that he was in for his protection money. I must have had an unbelieving look on my face. He assured me that this was normal practice (another learning curve).

We must have been working on that job for eight months before it was completed. After that we did a similar amount of work renovating a shop for them. They asked us if we would be interested in traveling a bit to do another job for them. We said fine, sure it was work to us it didn't matter where it was at. They brought our tools to Kingston-upon-Thames where the job was. It was another restaurant. We would catch the first train in the morning and the last train home at night. We got paid extra for the overtime, otherwise we would not have done it. The restaurant was right on the corner of a very busy street. There was a large window that followed the corner right around. Our problem was that we would spend too much time watching the talent passing by. The Chinese must have copped on because we landed in one morning and the whole window was painted over on the inside with a white paint. That was easy enough to clean off if you wanted too. I asked them why they had done a thing like that. They said it was to stop people looking in; a lame enough excuse, so we thought. Well why don't we give them a good enough reason to look in. We'd be there a few days on our own without any of the Chinese coming near us, so we wrote along the window at about head height (well our head height) 'Sex Shop Opening Soon' in nice bold letters. It wasn't easy to do because you had to write it opposite to how you would normally write. We then made an arrow pointing downwards, where we cleaned a nice space along the bottom of the glass where I then placed some works of art that I made out of plaster strategically along the bottom of the window. That created a lot more interest than we expected, especially during lunch hour. One of the works of art was a fair bit bigger than the average life-sized model. If we could have taped some of the reactions, you would have made a pile of money selling it to TV producers. I don't know how many times there would be a few women standing giggling and laughing at our array of hardware without realising that we were standing inside looking out at them. The best part was when you would knock on the glass and see their faces turn all colours as it dawned on them that they were well and truly caught and made off like a shot. Some were not so easily spooked. They would just give you the fingers and wander off when they were good and ready. The word must have reached the Chinese about what was going on, because we came in one morning and the panes of glass were a shining example of how a window should be cleaned and all my artistic plaster ware in the bloody skip, putting an end to our piss-taking.

There was a big fish tank with a lot of exotic fish in it. I thought I was doing good by throwing a box of fish food into them before we went home. When we came in to work in the morning they were all belly up in the tank. I'm sure they thought we did it for badness in revenge for them putting a stop to our fun. On the last day at the job, when we had all our work finished, I climbed up a step ladder outside on the pavement to remove a cable for lights. I overstretched a bit too far, the ladder went one way and I went the other and landed with an awful clatter onto the hard concrete. A crowd gathered around me trying to help. I was completely winded.

It was then time to move on to other avenues of work. If the truth be told I think we were finding it hard to learn the Chinese lingo. During the whole time we were working in Chinatown, we never changed from our work clothes. We'd head off on the Tube and us covered from head to toe in bonding. You could nearly follow the trail from the job to the underground station. It was always a mad rush to get into a carriage, so anyone that happened to get squashed against us would be in a state when getting off. You'd get some distasteful looks from the boys in the pinstriped suits. There were plenty of occasions when we brought straight edges four meters long, buckets and whatnot onto the Tube without realising the hullabaloo or obstruction we were causing with people tripping and stumbling over our stuff. We looked a sight. That's why people would be afraid to say anything to you.

Jobs and Stories

From there we started doing work for a small English firm who did private renovation work around Bayswater, Kensington and Notting Hill areas. Every bloody job we did for them had its own interesting story to tell. One of the jobs was right in the middle of Soho. A big square block that had to be gutted from top to bottom. It was for some film director, I can't even remember his name now. The foreman on the job was married to the contractor's sister and that's the only reason he was there, because he knew nothing whatsoever about building and was far too quiet and mannerly to be running a job like this.

There were a few Indian carpenters, another fellow from Galway and a New Zealander. When the foreman went out for lunch we would screw up the door and go up onto the roof and fire tomatoes that we would take from a fruit and vegetable store next door. We fired them at any one unlucky enough to become a target. The favourite one was the couriers on the motorbikes when they would stop looking at their maps for directions. They'd be going stone mad, shouting all the names under the sun up at us.

Some of the streets were very narrow in around Soho. One day me and the kiwi fellow were on the way back from getting milk from a shop close to the job. A motorbike passed us. The driver pulled in up the street ahead of us and started giving us the fingers and shouted all sorts of obscenities. Little did he know that Joe was coming towards us with a three foot level in his hand. The boy on the motorbike took off, still shouting at us, when he got a mighty whack on top of his helmet with Joe's level. We had some laugh as he wobbled all over the road before making off like a rocket. We were back on the job about fifteen minutes when the police arrived with your man in a squad car. Me and Joe were up on the fourth floor looking down. A police inspector came up asking us questions. Of course we denied everything and your man would not come into the building to identify us so we never heard any more about it. It did not stop us from throwing tomatoes.

When that job started coming near to completion and close to Christmas the poor foreman lost control altogether. The kiwi fellow turned into a right tell-tit altogether, so we decided to give him a good fright. The building was four stories high and we had a pulley fixed on the top of the scaffold. which went up to the same height as the building. We caught him, held him down and tied the rope around his ankles, hoisted him up, and started pulling him up and down. He was squealing like a piglet going to the slaughter house. We'd pull him right up near the top and keep him there for a few minutes. We did not realise that we had an audience. There was an office building and a model agency across the road. There was nothing only women waving at the windows telling us to let him down, so we did, maybe a bit too quick. I think he shit his pants and him upside down. There would have been a bit of squelching on the way home.

We had to do a fair bit of plastering and some other work on a large apartment in a very wealthy area wealthy area just off Baker Street for the same contractor. It turned out it was originally two apartments that were owned by a very rich business man who had his mistress living in one, but it must be that she felt that it was not big enough. We worked away in one half while she lived in the other half divided by a large curtain. We were there for a week before we got a look at her. We didn't realise that she was there during the day but it turned out she'd spend most of the day in bed and was out all night. As we found out later she was Brazilian and what a stunner she was. We used to sit beside the curtain that separated the two areas when having our tea. There were four of us there because it was the only spot where you could sit down sort of comfortably. She must have overheard us going over the whole weekend's goings on. Who did who and who did what. You just would not want your mother to hear too much of it, that's for sure.

I was going out into the hallway later on in the day. We had sent the tools down in a small lift that we had attached to the scaffolding. Joe had gone up and down on the same contraption a few days previous, a dangerous stunt if there ever was one. Don't forget that we were up at least six storeys high and this thing wasn't meant to carry anything heavier than a bucket of mortar. Crazy stuff when you think about it.

So there I was turning the key in the lock when her door opened. To say I was speechless would be an understatement, she's standing there with a little piece of what I could only describe as a net curtain wrapped around her, and her smiling and she says, in a very seductive south American accent, "I listened to your conversation and I found it very interesting. How do you have energy to carry out your work? You must be very fit," says she. I did not know what to say, but I know what I was thinking and I think it was obvious to her as well by the way my tongue was hanging out. It was like the Kama Sutra flashing in front of my eyes. Next thing I hear the shouting from downstairs. Joe was wondering what was keeping me so I mumbled something to her as I stumbled backwards towards the top of the staircase. She must have thought it was a life or death situation when I had to run off like that. She never made another appearance after all the trouble she went to dressing up in a see-through curtain. It was another day or two before we noticed the two ladies eating the face off one another in the window directly across from us. Must tell a joke now – What would you call people from Lisbon? Lesbians! That's where they must have been from. The four of us would be glued to the glass looking at the action. They were that close it was like watching a film on TV. We were daft anyway. They knew that we were watching them all along, so they were doing it to wind us up, and getting a kick out of it themselves in the process. Most days until we were finished on the job we witnessed some form of naked goings on between the two of them. We were then to move on to another job for the same contractor, but Joe had to go home for three weeks or so to cut the turf. That was the plan we had made up anyway.

Snakes and Ladders

I then had a basement flat to plaster on my own. It was much harder trying to work on your own. It's double the bloody work. It was really hot weather, sun beating down every day. It took me two weeks to finish the flat. I was in on the Saturday morning finishing up bits and pieces. I would go out onto the street to wash my buckets and tools because there was a drain beside the footpath to dump the dirty water. You weren't supposed to do this by the way. I was stripped down to the waist and was fairly fit, even if I do say so myself. Each time I came out I noticed a girl across the street and she seemed to be watching over but thought *I'm* just imagining, but believe it or not over she comes and asks me if I could help her to move a table. Something clicked as my brain went into overdrive so I says, "Of course, I could never refuse a lady in distress" and that I would be over as soon as I got changed.

I could not go into anyone's house with plaster falling off me I said. She laughed and said there was no hurry in a rather posh accent. With buckets of testosterone flowing through my veins at that age, how could I possibly not be led into temptation? I put all my tools inside because I was finished anyway but I kept thinking "Am I reading this wrong?" After all, me coming from the hills, I was still a bit green if you know what I mean. I locked up and headed across the street towards her door. My head was racing that much that I still cannot remember whether I rang a bell or knocked on the door. As she opened the door the first thing she said was "What are you having to drink?"

I did not touch alcohol at all, but a bell started to jingle in my head, so I said, "I'll have a glass of wine please, but sure I'll move the table first for you". So she leads me in, explaining that she had a party last night and she was getting the house in order again. As my eyes scanned the place I could see no sign of a party having taken place. When she pointed out the table I started to get butterflies in my tummy. It was one of the tiniest coffee tables that you will find. I lifted it, took and placed it where she wanted it. She told me to plant myself on a seat (not exactly them words) as she went to get the wine. There were two big comfortable-looking chairs and a huge settee, so rather than sit on a chair I sat on the settee. I thought to myself "If I've got this right she's going to sit beside me, and if she sits on one of the big comfy chairs well it was nice thinking about it and there's no harm done".

She came around, handed me the glass of wine and sits down beside me. Well I don't know what came over me but I went completely blank and me sitting there holding a glass of wine that I did not know what to do with. I just could not think of one teeny weenie thing to say, only think of the lovely smell of her perfume. I could feel my face heating up. After what seemed like ages I turned my head and looked at her. She was looking at me over the top of the wine glass the way a cat looks at a mouse before it pounces. That's exactly what happened next. I don't know where the wine went and I didn't care either. That was about one thirty on the Saturday and I left around the same time the next day, Sunday. We were playing snakes and ladders. That's what I was always told to say if some nosy person asked too many questions.

It was on my way to the underground and me thinking that this only happens to someone else and I realised that we never even bothered with each other's names. As I went to go down the stairs because the escalator wasn't working after the first few steps my legs nearly buckled under me, weak as water, but I put it down to working too hard. I counted myself lucky when I got to my stop on the underground that the escalator was working. My tools were picked up by the van driver early on Monday morning and after all the years I worked in London I was never back on that street again. A bit strange – or is it?

Another Little Eye Opener

Another little bit of an eye opener happened to me while I was still a bit green around the ears (not worldly wise). I was on my way home from work one evening. I had a whole carriage to myself. Well that was until it reached the next stop. Two people got on, one a very attractive blonde girl who sat directly across from me, the other a young man who sat on the seat next to me. I wondered why he sat next to me, as the carriage was empty, but I figured out why soon enough. As the Tube started pulling off I had a good chance to have a look at the doll across from me as she seemed to be looking elsewhere, taking her in from the shoes up. Yeah it was a sight that would even make a monkey sit upright. The hemline was well up above the knee, leaving a lot more to admire than what you would normally be entitled to. I could feel myself blushing as she turned and caught me having a good look. She gave me a big smile so I smiled back. After studying my feet for what seemed like ages, I thought I'd sneak another look. Well holy jumping macaroni, I nearly choked, she uncrossed her legs at the same time and gave me a view that would give a rabbit palpitations. I could feel the redness return to my face as she caught me looking again, but she gave me another big smile.

Not the dirty look I was expecting. My face must have been a picture of pressurized torture as she repeated this move a number of times, knowing full well what she was doing. I looked at the fellow dressed in the suit next to me because I knew he could not have missed what was going on. Well the sweat was running off him and it wasn't because his tie was too tight, or the carriage being on fire. The only thing that could have cooled me down then was if I jumped into one of them round holes the Eskimos cut in the ice to catch fish. I got out at my stop with great difficulty and a picture of her smiling as she crossed and uncrossed her legs etched into my mind. Going commando wasn't a word that I was familiar with, but I copped on fairy quickly that it meant more than just soldiers playing war games.

Policemen

Talk about policemen. One morning we were going to work. It was ten minutes walk to King's Cross underground station where you got your travel ticket. Joe put money into the machine. It swallowed the money but did not give out a ticket. Joe had heavy steel toe capped boots on and started to kick the machine. Next thing there are two cops breathing down our necks. One of them says, "Why are you kicking the machine down there Pat?"(short for Paddy). Joe says, quick as lightening, "I can't lift my leg high enough to kick it up there," and made off like a shot and leaves me standing there with two cops who were anything but polite giving me an ear bashing. Me trying to explain that it wasn't me it was that other buck and I don't know who he is that kicked the bloody thing. They told me to remember why I was here in the first place. "Why?" says I, and he replies, "to dig drains and fill them in again". The first thing that came to my mind was, all the drains in the country wouldn't be fit to get rid of all your verbal diarrhoea. I was in no position to tell him to his face so I muttered all my obscenities under my breath, and thought "You're lined up nicely for a good kick in the nether regions". The odds of getting away were not great, so off I go safe in the knowledge that it was more than likely that us drain diggers, as he called us, were earning at least twice what they were earning, the pricks.

This little episode was the first in a list of encounters that would be described today as outright racism. On our way home from work in the evenings, our digs were about a ten-minute walk from the Tube station. I was always nervous when I was stepping from the train onto the platform for fear of slipping down between the train and the platform itself. Likewise, when you'd be standing waiting for the Tube to come along, it would get very crowded and again you'd get that nervous feeling that some head case might push you off just as the Tube came along. This had happened at Finsbury park underground, when a man who was not taking his medication for a mental illness pushed a man directly in front of the Tube, killing him instantly, because demons told him that he was evil and intended to kill him.

Chatting Up the Wrong Girl

I noticed this pretty-looking girl, I would guess that she was around twenty-two or so, at a bus stop. She must have been finishing work around the same time as ourselves. She'd always give a big smile as we passed her, and of course I'd give the big smile back. One evening I says to Joe "You go on ahead I'm going to have a craic with this one". So I stops anyway and started some chit chat. She was very friendly and wore nice classy clothes. I was thinking, "God I'm onto a good thing here". After a lengthy discussion, and me keeping an eye out for a bus, thinking "God this must be hers now," I think three came and went. She never even looked at them, never mind getting on one. I thought I was making that good an impression that she forgot all about going home, because by this stage I was in full flow. I asked her where she worked. She says, "Oh I work here." "Where?" I asked again. "Here," she repeated. It was then that it finally dawned on me what her occupation was.

Talk about feeling stupid. I said my goodbyes with a red face and left the pick-up point in a hurry. I did not want to interrupt any more of her business that I may have squandered. I told Joe when I got home that she had a boyfriend and wasn't interested. A good length of time passed before I told the truth about what really happened at the bus stop.

King of the Gypsies

Due to a keen interest in boxing and hard training we spent a lot of evenings in the local Islington boxing gym. You would get a good few professionals that came in for the sparring and another few just came in to help out by offering advice. We'd spend most Sundays in the local park underneath an old bridge sparring. Sounds mad but we got great enjoyment out of it. Joe had upwards of thirty fights with this same club, winning all but one if I remember correctly. Another friend, Josie, also had a good few fights with the same club, winning most if not all his fights. The Irish boys were well represented. A few of the trainers that we got on well with were originally from the West Indies, and they used to say, "You boys must come from a rough neighbourhood," not knowing that we came from out in country, so the term that they used to describe where we came from didn't fit into the picture at all.

The thing was, there were a lot of Irish travelers in the club as well, with some exceptionally good boxers, and then there were some very big men like grizzly bears that would spar all night without slowing down or showing signs of getting tired. One of the big boys, named Tom, came in one night looking as if he was run over by two trucks one after another. He had three of his front teeth missing, two black eyes and cuts everywhere. He told me he was after taking part in one of them King of the Gypsies battles. They had fought for an hour and a half and he came out the winner. He said, "You should see the other fellow," and went on to give me a list of the injuries your man received. All I could think was that he must have been in bad shape looking at the state of the man who came out on top.

Doorman at the National

Around this time we met up with Pat Doohan from Tory Island. He had been in London for a number of years at this stage and worked as a carpenter. He was doing quite well for himself; you could say he knew the ropes. I got a job as a doorman through Pat in the National, a huge Irish nightclub in Kilburn (which incidentally is now a mosque believe it or not). There was a big squad of doormen. I was used to two or three men on the doors back at home, so seeing so many in the one place gave me an idea of what lay ahead. Many's the rough night was there.

Pat was a good man to have on your side and was not afraid of being stuck in tight spots where the going was tough. There were a number of incidents that happened regularly outside the National that have stuck out in my mind and it tells you a lot about how Irish people were treated by the police. It was bad enough that we had to go over in the first place to find work in an environment that was in the main hostile if you happened to show in any way where your loyalties lay by the songs you sang or the bands you listened to or the pubs you frequented. The police used to deliberately pick fights with patrons leaving at closing time. I saw it happening right in front of me. A young fellow walked out not bothering anyone, but just because he staggered, they assumed he was drunk. The police were onto him straight away, wrestling him to the ground. Then other people would join in the shouting to let him go. Within a matter of minutes the whole of the Kilburn High Road in the vicinity of the National was flooded with police kitted out in full riot squad gear. Anyone that even dared look at them sideways was beaten into the paddy wagons. I saw one police woman beating one young fellow as hard as she could with a baton in an attempt to get him into a van, while at the same time her German

Shepard Alsatian had a grip of him by the upper leg, pulling him out. The police training college was a short distance away in Hendon and it was obvious that these nights were used as a training exercise.

But the good nights outweighed the bad ones. I mean there was an abundance of the opposite sex, and when you're a doorman with a bit of oul chat and plenty of red blood flowing through your veins, you couldn't but admire all the stunning females. Sure you couldn't help but indulge in what was on offer, provided there was an offer, even if it did get you into all sorts of unmentionable situations now and then.

During one particularly busy night a girl came up to me asking me where the toilets were. She was clearly in a very distressed state but drunk as a lord. At the same time as I began to give her directions to the toilets she says, "Excuse me," and just sat down right there in front of me and all the other people milling around and proceeded to do an almighty endless pee on the carpet. This was done without taking her pants half down, at least that's if she was wearing any, or lifting her dress. If a man had caught her by the heels and pulled her around, she would have made a great carpet cleaner; I might have been able to patent my newly-developed rug cleaner. A few of the other doormen who saw the whole carry on were buckled over, nearly peeing themselves with the laughing. She jumps up when she's finished, shakes herself and disappears into the crowd with a big wet patch over the back of her fairly short dress. Hope she didn't put it on a radiator to dry out because the pong would be lethal.

Another night it was packed to the rafters. I think the capacity was about fifteen hundred. But as long as people were prepared to pay at the door it was a case of just squeeze them in. On these sort of nights it would not surprise you what rather strange happenings you could stumble upon. The toilets had to be checked out at the end of the night in case there was someone sleeping that could be left there all night. It happened more than a few times. This time in the ladies' toilets one of the cubicles was locked so it was obvious there was someone asleep inside. One of the doormen got a helping hand to climb up where he could see there was a girl sitting on the pot asleep. He lowered himself down inside and opened the door.

Another of the doormen, who was from Derry, had a few ash-trays stacked in his hand. They were piled up with ash and ciga-rette butts. He asked me to keep a lookout for a minute in case the manager came along. If he got a sniff of anything you'd be sacked on the spot. The poor girl was so drunk sitting on the pot with her pants down at her ankles. Two of the doormen lifted her up. She could have been getting a lift into a taxi for all she knew. Then your man starts nice as you like he emptied the contents of each ashtray into her knickers before pulling them up, followed by her trousers. You can just imagine the mess that would greet her eyes when she sobered up in the morning.

On the nights when there were concerts being played by up-and-coming bands, some who later went on to become world famous, it was a great opportunity to make some money. The first time that I found myself in a situation where I could make a few pounds was pure luck. It all depended on what exit door you were told to keep an eye on. There were all sorts of tricks used by customers trying to get in free. One or two would pay in and then try and let their mates in one of the exit doors if it was not being watched. I was on my way to the National walk-ing up Kilburn High Road chatting to this West Indian fellow who happened to be going in the same direction. He asked me where I was working. I told him where and that it was Simply Red that was on that night. He says, "You try and get on a door and I'll line up a few customers and you get ten pounds per person that gets in and five for me". We shook hands on it (it was no accident that he got talking to me in the first place I realised afterwards). After a while I opened the door to have a look around and saw him with about ten people so I gave him a wave. He came over and handed me my money. I let them in and closed the door and not a word said. Five minutes later it was repeated again except there were about twenty this time. It was done a few more times before other customers who were turned away from the main door copped on what was happening.

I had the door open at one stage just grabbing money from all directions and people piling in on top of each other in such a way that I had trouble getting the door closed. All my pockets were stuffed with notes. When I had a quick look out again there was a queue formed up along the pavement, but I could not let any more in, even though I was getting all sorts of very tempting promises. Just as I was trying to close the door again who comes down the steps only the manager who was a bad tempered so and so. He eyeballed me and says, "What's going on here?" I told him that I had to put a fellow out who was causing trouble and when I opened the door to put him out a whole load of people tried to force their way in. What made it even more convincing was the fact that people were now banging at the door trying to be let in. He was happy enough with that explanation and asked me if I needed another man here to help me so I agreed that it would be safer to have the extra man just in case. It would be hard to get a closer shave than that, fair play to Mick Hucknall and Simply Red for putting an extra bit of lining in my pockets. I think I got around four hundred and fifty quid. Not bad for half an hour's work.

A Few Bob on the Side

The next opportunity I got to make a few bob on the side was not as profitable because I had to share with another doorman. The manager had brought in a squad from an agency so I was partnered up with a Greek fellow on a door. He was sound enough but did not have much experience of this type of work. A similar type of situation arose except that there was no one lining the customers up outside this time. It was working fine until a bit of a brawl broke out and I ended up in the middle of it. The other doorman was useless when it came to throwing a few punches so it put an end to the profit-making venture for that night anyway.

I was called out to the main door where there was a bit of a comedy going on. The head doorman, who was part of the agency package, was a big Englishman who looked the part, wearing a white suit. He was shouting orders at other doormen as if he was in the army. That was fine until a scrap started and mayhem broke out. It took a while before we got things under control again. There was a couple of torn shirts and a few scratches to laugh about. Then in the middle of the inquiry someone asked "Where's the white suit?"

When we managed to find out what happened or what started the hullabaloo the laughing started. It seems someone waiting to pay at the pay booth took exception to his loud-mouthed ordering them to hurry up and belted him and the bouncer was last seen running out the door. He never came back for his money and was neither seen nor heard of again. It proved that you can never go by looks. He certainly looked and acted like he was the real deal but we should have known. Who goes to work at a concert or in a nightclub wearing a white suit?

Going to the Church

The other regular doormen working there kept asking me to go to church with them on Sunday. I was thinking they didn't act like they were too holy, but looks can be deceiving. I just thought that they were all very religious and fair play to them. Little did I know. So rather than go sparring one Sunday Pat says, "C'mon, we'll go to the church". Me thinking to myself, "I've already been to mass, no need to go twice," but I agreed anyway.

Off we go down to Hammersmith on the Tube. I asked Pat if he had been here before. He answered yes but did not elaborate so it was left at that. On leaving Hammersmith underground station we must have walked about twenty minutes when we stopped outside this pub with loads of people milling around outside. Pat's leading the way and heads in towards the door. I says, "Is this it?". "Yes," he says without giving any more information. So I follow on inside. It was certainly far bigger inside than it looked from the outside and was heaving with people, a mixture of all nationalities. Men and woman in equal proportions, mostly Australians. Well boys a boys was I in for a shock and a treat.

We pushed our way right to the front of the stage, where all the other doormen from the National were, as well as loads of women I vaguely knew, and some I knew quite well. Most I had never seen before, nor they me, but this was what they were referring to as the Church. Well damn it how could I have been so stupid? They were a holy-looking bunch all right. I was no sooner settled in through them when the whistles and the shouts hailed the first attraction as she made her way out onto the stage, the likes you would see gracing the pages of certain magazines frequently purchased by men with a keen interest in photography.

This fit-looking babe, not in the least bit nervous, starts dancing around the edge of the stage and losing her clothes in the process. I was really getting into the swing of things by this stage, joining in the chorus of "Get them off!" and me leaning over the stage as far as I could to get the best view possible, you understand?

As she strides around the stage she looks at me a few times and smiles. Of course I smile back thinking "God, she must like me". Third time around she comes right over to me and ties a little white ribbon around my little finger and starts to tug on the ribbon to get me up on stage with her. Well my bravery soon went out the window I can tell you. There was some roaring and shouting for me to go up. Before I could argue the boys caught me and just threw me like a sack of spuds right up onto the middle of the stage. You just cannot imagine what it was like. About six or eight hundred shouting and egging her on to strip me, and vice versa. She went through a whole routine. I must say I enjoyed getting half smothered between two sun-kissed mammaries. There was more, but this was getting too hot for me as I back-pedalled out of playing a more active role in this public display of titillating affection. It took me a long time to live that down.

It was a mad place. Just about anything was allowed as long as you were brave enough to go up on stage and strut your stuff. One of the most vile acts was this wee skinny Welsh man came on and him dressed like Superman. He pranced around for a while then brought a table onto the stage then stripped the lot off. He got up and lay down on his back on the table and then bent his two rubbery legs up around his neck. What does he do then? He holds a mike to his dumping area and starts to fart to the beat of the music. Then they pick a girl from the crowd, bring her kicking and screaming up onto the stage where the buck interviews her, she has to tell her name and country of origin, likes, dislikes, then Superman lays back again on the table, puts his legs behind his head, starts doing what he does to the music again, all of a sudden the unsuspecting girl's face is held down barely touching his ass and he continually lets rip in her face. The length of time they held her face in that position it would not be possible for her to hold her breath that long without filling her lungs with poisonous gas from his rotten hole. Ugh.

Then there was another competition where a man and woman from every country present would come up on stage. The women would have to discard their tops and anything underneath so that one of the lucky lads would have to measure the boobs to see which country's females had the most voluptuous pair. Talk about over-the-top groping. When you volunteered to go up in the first place you had to be game for whatever was to be your fate. The winning lady then had the privilege of measuring all the men's pride and joy in whatever shape or form. The noise in the place would resemble Croke Park at an All-Ireland final.

Then it was the turn of those that thought they could tell jokes. Now you had to be brave to do this or just plain off your head, because if the crowd thought the jokes were not up to scratch or just stupid, you had to be fast to get off the stage before you got yourself killed. Everyone would start firing all the beer cans at the would-be comedian. The stage would fill up in a matter of seconds. I saw one New Zealander, a real giant of a man, but in this case size didn't really make any difference as he found out. He got an awful going-over. His jokes were pure shite anyway so in a way he deserved all he got. I saw a beer pack with three full cans bouncing off his head. He had to be pulled off because there was an unwritten rule that you only stopped firing once the person left the stage. So that was only some of the goings on, the rest belongs up on the high shelf with the naughty magazines.

On the Door at The Gresham

It turned out to be a bit of an addiction. No, not the church, I mean working in nightclubs. The next one was in The Gresham in Holloway Road. I got Joe the start there as well. After a short while we got other Donegal boys that we knew as dependable to work there. Me, Joe, Blondie John, and Tory Pat (who always found money lying somewhere, his eyes were continuously scanning the ground).

Josie Jack Ban had one too many one night in a pub that everyone used to meet up in and fell asleep. Someone, we'll not mention their name, decided that he had a great idea and went and got a razor and shaved off half his eyebrow and half his moustache then stuck two big chips with red sauce up his nose. Someone else took a picture. It was not a pretty sight.

You would get all sorts in The Gresham. Martin Jim and a friend of his came in one night. James Logue from Downings. I thought to myself "There's going to be some bit of bother with them two here tonight". As the night progressed Blondie John comes over to me and says someone is after pouring a pint down over a few people from the balcony. So we ran up thinking we might catch whoever did it. As we reached half-way up the stairs we met Martin Jim, who told us that he had come up to see who was responsible for doing it. We could not find a culprit or a witness. It was Martin's mate and his girlfriend who had got the soaking. It was a few years later before I found out what really happened. As Martin Jim explained to me himself, Martin's mate had got himself a woman and was being very romantic. The drink was playing its part as well so Martin decided "This is no good," and went upstairs and deliberately poured the pint down over the two of them to cool their ardour. That's what he was after doing when me and Blondie John met him on the staircase and him pretending that he was looking for the culprit.

There was some nights when you could hardly keep your eyes open because of the smoke; they'd be nearly burned out of your head. No mention of smoking bans then. I suppose it was just like in any other nightclub when you think of all the weird things that can happen in front of your eyes. There was always someone trying to come up with some new tricks as a way of getting drunk. The weirdest was getting a small shot glass half-filled with whisky or a spirit of some kind. It would be placed or fitted tight against your eye, then tilt your head backwards letting the spirit circle around the eye as you blinked. Seemingly the alcohol worked its way into the bloodstream quicker this way. It seemed to work, but it's not something that I personally would have a go at and I wouldn't advise anyone else to play Russian roulette with your eyeball in this way either.

We spotted a man in his late teens or early twenties lying on the floor in noddy noddy land. It wasn't the best place to lie down for forty winks. We managed to prop him up on a seat next to the wall. As we were making our way through the crowd what did we come upon but another fellow that had decided to go for a sleep on the floor right in front of the stage. So up with him as well. The only suitable place we could find was beside the first fellow so we propped the two up against one another, then started yapping to some customers who had commented about the two boys being so drunk. One of the girls I was talking to suddenly opened her mouth wide and pointed over at where we had left the two boys. I looked over at them. Oh my God what was happening was the two started to wake up with one thinking the other was a woman and locked lips and were really getting stuck in with the whole tongue down the throat stuff. Maybe it was the stubble that did the trick.

All of a sudden both sort of took a jump backwards, and sat staring at one another, before the most sober of the two took off as if there was a bull after him. It would not be the place to start moralizing about what should or shouldn't happen. The whole door working thing was a great way of educating a person. It would teach you how to read people, who you thought were likely to be troublemakers, steal drink, or rob handbags. A girl comes out crying telling us that someone was after stealing her handbag. She had gone out for a dance when she thought of it, went back to get it and it was gone. Joe took off like a shot towards the toilets and came out a few minutes later with this fellow in a headlock and him struggling like mad. He had caught your man in the process of stuffing the empty handbag out the toilet window. He got a well-deserved roughing up on the way to the door. It turned out the girl had quite a bit of money in it. That's why she was so upset about losing it. All was returned to her and she went home happy.

Two fellows that I know started chatting up these two girls who were at the bar waiting to get a drink. The boys bought a drink for the two ladies and were then asked to join them at their table. Everything was going great until a third fellow that they knew joined them but he soon fell asleep once he sat down as he had been on the beer all day. The two girls went out for a dance, which suited the boys as they wouldn't be too hot on the dance floor anyway. The third fellow woke up and he did not look well at all. Before the boys could do anything, your man reached for the nearest handbag. It must have looked like a bucket to him because he nice as you like stuck his head in and puked his insides into it, then left it back on the seat. That put an end to any idea of the lads getting a shift. Knowing they couldn't face the two girls on their return, they bolted for the door, leaving your man who had gone back to sleep to face the music on his own. A few girls came in who were regulars who I knew fairly well. One of them was celebrating her birthday that night so she invited me and anyone that I wanted to bring along to a party she was having. They were intending to leave early to get things arranged. I soon gathered up a dodgy enough crew for the job. Once we got all the customers out, it must have been around three-thirty. Me, Josie, Pat Ban and Phil Mc Hugh set off for the house where the girls were staying in Tottenham. By the time we got there we had to step over a few bodies to get in the door. There was a fair crowd but they were mostly strangers to us. Once the drinking started up again among the fresh recruits the dancing and leaping about started with renewed energy. There were piles of food available so between the dancing, eating and the drinking it was becoming a recipe for disaster as far as I was concerned, knowing the boys involved.

It was around five when some of the girls decided that it was time for the birthday cake and the candles. By this stage some of the boys had the idea in their heads that they were still in The Gresham but did not know why all the free food was available. The first thing I saw happening that was going to change the course of the night's partying was Phil with a chocolate bun in his hand and I knew by the look of him that he had no intention of eating it. Next I saw it whizzing past and hitting Pat Ban on the head. He had no idea who threw it but lifted this big cream bun off the table and fired it at Josie. It was a good aim, whether he meant it or not. It splattered right on the back of his head. This is where it got out of hand. Some of the girls were coming down the stairs singing happy birthday with a cake the size of a cartwheel with twenty-one candles all nicely lit up. In the meantime Josie, well steamed, was scraping the remains of the cream bun off the back of his head, looking around at the same time, trying to focus on something from the pile of food that was still sitting on the tables to throw back. Meanwhile the other boys were buckled over laughing as the girls came past with the cake not knowing anything about what was after happening. All Josie could see was this big cake right in front of him and the next thing he did was to grab it with both hands and threw it at the boys that were laughing. Between girls squealing and the buns flying in all directions, it was some sight.

I felt sorry for the birthday girl herself as she never even got to blow out the candles. It would be one birthday that she was unlikely to forget in a hurry. When Josie went back home after a good few years, he bought the Rake's Bar in the town, and renamed it Biddy Jack's and bought the Anchor Bar that he renamed Flynn's Bar after a good friend of his who passed away. This was just one of his business transactions, not bad for a boy who left school with little or no education.

The Guilford Four

The Guildford Four – Paul Hill, Gerry Conlon, Paddy Armstrong and Carole Richardson – were released from prison. Some time afterwards they came into the Gresham and of course we made sure they did not have to pay. I went up to the band playing in the ballroom and asked them to read out a request congratulating them on their release. After a while, on not hearing it read out I asked them what the problem was. He said that the manager would not allow it, so then I asked him what his problem was. He said it was too political. I said, "Of course it's political. That's why they spent the best years of their lives being abused in a British prison". I felt like strangling him. This was the same man who laid on free bashes at Christmas for the local Holloway Road police officers, bosses, wives, and girlfriends.

Paul Hill and Gerry Conlon were there quite a number of times after that. Niall Quinn, who played soccer for Ireland and Tony Adams, the England captain, who was nicknamed The Donkey, used to call in now and again. Frankie (mad) Frazer, a notorious East End gangster who spent forty-two years of his life in twenty different prisons, was also a visitor. There were loads of others that look familiar when you would see them going in past.

One night I was standing out at the door. It must have been around two-thirty when Josie comes out with this fellow who had a few drinks too many. He left him standing against the wall outside the door then turned around and started to talk to me. Next thing, we see a policeman and woman one on each side of your man, walking him past the door. Josie says to me "There is no need for that," so we went out around the cor-ner to see what was happening. We could have swore that we saw the policeman tossing a coin. It must have been to chose whether to leave him or take him in. Josie told them to leave him alone, that he was doing no harm. At this stage your man realised that he was being held and did not know what the hell was happening. He started wrestling in an attempt to get away. Immediately the sirens were blaring and like at the National they were all over the place (minus the riot gear). By this time the other doormen, as well as the owner's wife, were protesting about how they were treating him. I don't know how but he ended up in a rubbish skip with at least six police men on top of him beating the living daylights out of him. Before managing to bundle him head over heels into the back of the wagon, one of the policemen came right up to the owner's wife and shouted at her that if she did not fuck off that she would go into the van as well.

Another time Blondie John was addicted to one-night stands, and God were some of them rough. One night this black girl came in and John got talking to her. Whatever he was saying to her made her laugh and she fell in love immediately, he was so charming. He had never been with a black girl before so he was in no mood to let a chance like this go. He asks me if I could cover for him if he slipped away. "Of course," says I, "isn't that what friends are for?" "Don't tell anyone". The reason for the secrecy was that when the man above was distributing the good looks among the girls, this poor girl missed the queue altogether. But that wasn't going to stop our John.

As soon as I got the two of them out an exit door I went straight away and told all the other doormen. Next day he filled me in on the whole craic, but he was worried about seeing her again as he did not want her getting too attached. He wanted me to warn him if I saw her coming in again. The following weekend a few of us were standing around the main entrance keeping an eye out for your wan and didn't I spot her in the queue. Unbeknownst to John we had it made up that once we saw her coming to the door rather than warn him, we were going to make a big show and escort her in telling her that John had told every one of us that as long as she was his woman she would never have to queue up or have to pay in again. So that's what we did, amid all the cheering and clapping, and left her standing beside John and told him that he did not have to worry about taking the tickets, that one of us would take over now. If you saw the look of thunder on his face. He was pure red and beads of sweat starting to appear on his forehead.

I'm sure when he reads this it will bring back fond memories. Between all the hard work he spent every minute he could on the sun bed and looking at himself in the mirror. He just could not see that there was a likeness between him and a giant burger. That's a joke of course. He's a fine specimen of a man.

Never a Boring Moment

There was never a boring moment. Every spare minute was used up for something, whether it was good or bad, depending on your point of view. We used to go and poke fun and do our best to rile the guards with the big furry beaver hats at the gates of Buckingham Palace. They got ten out of ten for being so daft to stand there all day without moving. We insulted them in every way we could think of. I remember at one point asking what did they do when they had to go to the toilet, did they just shit their pants and change later? But they refused point blank to take the bait and never moved. I can sure as hell think of what they might like to do with us given the chance.

We used to go Hyde park some Sundays because there were always women around, mainly tourists. Americans, Australians and boy did we have some fun in the process. One sunny summer's Sunday two women, an Australian and an English girl, brought us for a romantic trip up the river Thames. They paid for everything, but me and John were completely knackered from the night before so in between falling asleep and snoring we would go into these fits of laughing that we could not control about things that happened the night before. Obviously we could not tell them about it. I would like to know what was going through their heads when this was happening. The boat we were on pulled in beside an old sailing ship called the Cutty Sark. They wanted to go inside to see what it was like. The two of us sat on a bench and said we would wait for them. Once they went inside, John looked at me and I looked at him. Just like that we jumped up and made off running in the direction off a signpost for a train station and us laughing like maniacs. We had to wait half an hour for a train and in the meantime we were thinking what if the two women decided to head for the train as well. The last five minutes before it came were nervous moments. We breathed a sigh of relief as it left the station with us the only passengers on board.

Gandhi, who was always smiling just like Jack Nicholson in that film One Flew Over the Cuckoo's Nest, was very deceiving for anyone that thought he might be a walkover because he was tall, but a bit on the skinny side. I saw him in a few scraps and he would remind you of a very good darts player. He was very accurate, getting the bull's eye every time. Then there was Barry, who had a habit of putting his foot in it. If for instance Barry was chatting up a member of the opposite sex he would spend nearly all night talking instead of getting more or less to the point using a shorter bus route. We were discussing this one night and he said, "Right that's it. I'm going to try your technique," which was just out and out filthy chat.

After watching this very well put-together German girl who came up to me enquiring about the music that was being played in the club that night, little did I know that he was timing me. It took me a less number of minutes than you have fingers on one hand before reaching an intimate stage, where really you should have a contract signed and the bridal suite booked at the Savoy before you could get yourself into such a position. It was the flirting and the challenge, which meant once conquered interest waned. Barry tries this very upfront approach with a different girl and of course I'm standing nearby watching like a hawk. You could see straight away that it wasn't working. She gave him an awful telling off and what he said about her after you could not print it. I nearly died laughing and him cursing me up and down. It was never that easy, as he said himself.

He got off with this other girl one night, so the two of them sneaked out the back door of the disco. He gave me the nod so I would cover for him in case he was missed. The next morning about 10am he phoned and all I could hear was him killing himself laughing. He says, "You're not going to believe what's after happening; I had a great night," he says. So next I got a rundown on all the details, very juicy indeed. I was envious until he told me what happened when he woke up in the morning. He said she was out for the count so he just wanted to get out before she woke up. So he got dressed as quick as he could and off out the door just as a taxi was passing. He waved it down. When he got as far as his own place he put his hand in his pocket to pay the taxi driver and realized he only had a tenner left on him. It was enough for his fare, but the thing was he had nearly two hundred when he went into her house. It was only when he got inside and he started to search his pockets that he copped on what happened. He had thought the trousers had been a bit tight alright. It began to slowly dawn on him that he had squeezed into her trousers by mistake. "The bitch. She had the last laugh," he said. "I can't even remember where she lives but I don't care. It was well worth it."

A Death in Australia

I had read of a case involving a young couple and their family from Belfast who had emigrated to Australia to get away from the mayhem and strife of everyday life in the North at that time. They were out for a night's fun with some friends and ended up in a nightclub. Didn't it turn out that there was a rugby team inside as well and some of their members were ex-British soldiers who had served in the North, so once they heard his Belfast accent a confrontation occurred. It resulted in him being killed. There were loads of reliable witnesses to say that he was the innocent party. When the case went to court the judge dismissed the case against the defendants, despite there being ample evidence for a conviction. A petition was started to get a retrial. The family wanted people to write to the Australian and British Embassies. I took it upon myself to do what I could to help in that regard. I knew someone who at that time worked in an office for the crown prosecution service, so this person printed out all the leaflets outlining the case with the addresses of the relevant embassies and easy-to-follow instructions on what to do.

It was very handy and I never got around to thanking Her Majesty for the use of her time, paper and ink. The response was very good. You would get a lot of interest once you got a few minutes to explain what it was about. There are always people who are more than willing to support a good cause. As I had started doing the odd night in some other nightclubs it was a great opportunity for me to hand out the leaflets to customers. The odd person who refused to accept them would have a change of mind as soon as a bit of gentle persuasion came into play. In some circumstances, depending on attitude, which was rare, one in two hundred or there about, they could find themselves barred. Two men did not want to take them off me one night, but I sort of put it into their pockets. About ten minutes later one of the men came out again and started shaking my hand. Didn't it turn out that he was an uncle of the man that was killed so I gained great satisfaction from that chance encounter, plus the fact that there was more to come.

I had barely sat down one evening after coming in from work when the phone rang. It was the editor of the Irish Post, because I had also been writing to that paper. He asked me if he could forward a letter that the paper had received addressed for me. "No problem," said I.

It could have been a day or two later before the letter landed in my letterbox. When I opened the letter wasn't it from the same young man's family in Belfast thanking me for what I had been doing. To say that I had got satisfaction from that letter would be an understatement.

Me and Barry Plastering

Me and Barry worked a lot together plastering on all sorts of jobs, big and small. We got a start on a big job in Welwyn Garden City. It belonged to some big pharmaceutical company so there was no shortage of money. It was about an hour's drive outside London and the plastering contractor that we got the job with was Irish. He was a sound man to work for.

There were some mad happenings on that site. There would have been up on a hundred people on the job at any one time, and not one would say anything to us because they thought we weren't half right in the head. Most Mondays we came in late with cuts, bruises or black eyes of some sort. It was a very big site, spread out over a wide area with a nice canteen and showers if you wanted to use them. Me and Barry would run everywhere flat out. It was always a race, whether it was to the toilet, canteen or out the gate, then do a hundred press ups, before we'd lay into one another hammering away as hard as you could, without hitting on the face if at all possible.

That was the deal, so you can understand why no one ever said anything to us. Barry was trying to put on weight. He would have a dozen eggs and two full chickens with him every day. When we'd go into the canteen we would sit at a table that we had sort of claimed as our own with the other plasterers, a few Italians and plastic paddies; by the way, in most cases the plastics were more Irish than we were ourselves. He would sit down, spread out his grub, then hold up one egg at a time, break them and let them drop into his mouth. Sometimes he'd break them into a pint glass full of milk, hold it up and swallow it down with raw egg stuck around his mouth. This used to make a lot of people nearly puke. Then he would eat a full chicken, by just holding it up and chewing away at it. He ate half his mixture at breakfast time and the rest at lunch.

Towards the end of the job things were going a bit haywire. A couple of steel fixers that I saw on the job had an attitude problem. One of them who spent most of his time gawking at strippers at the nearest pub got a bit brave one day during an exchange about what soldiers were really up to in the six counties. It all started while we were sitting in the canteen when it came out over the news that the Birmingham Six had been released. Well your man started ranting, saying that they should be kept inside.

Immediately I challenged him outside for a square go but the wind left his sails and he started making excuses about why it bothered him so much, letting it slip that his cousin, a soldier, had lost a leg in a bomb blast. I don't know, did he expect sympathy from me or what? But after the history lesson he got with me telling him that if he looked a bit further than reading the propaganda next to page three in the tabloids, he would understand the whole situation better looking at it from my side of the fence, I'll bet he wished he had stayed at the pub and stared starry-eyed at the strippers who were depriving him of his earnings.

Myself and Barry were standing in the queue another day when I spotted this boy up in front still wearing his helmet. It was a bit unusual as everyone took off their helmets before they came in because it was so hot. It might have been because he was very loud and mouthy that I took an interest in him. He was half turned around when I saw what was written in black writing on his helmet, which was white so it was hard to miss. 'Fuck the Pope'. That was like waving a red flag at a bull. I took off that hard to get to your man I sent tables, chairs and people in all directions before grabbing your man and swinging him to the ground and half strangling him before pulling the helmet off and telling him to read what was written on it.

He got such a fright that he was hardly able to speak never mind read, and me roaring like a psychopath at him the whole time. I pulled him out the door where he denied that it was his. "You were wearing it and that's enough for me so don't give me any shite," I said as I stood over him beside a water barrel until he had every bit of the writing cleaned off the now-gleaming helmet. I went in then, cursing like mad, but not one made eye contact so I got my food and sat down across from Barry who had a smile back to the two ears. He then winked at me before he started to wind up one of the Italian boys sitting at our table by saying that he had seen him wearing the same helmet earlier on.

On our way to the job one morning, I was driving a Land Rover that Joe had bought a week before. The damn thing started to heat up so I pulled in and lifted the bonnet. Whatever I was at I nearly got my knuckles chopped off with the radiator fan when I tried to pull a water pipe up that had loosened off. Between the time I stopped and lifted the bonnet the police had pulled in without me seeing them. As I turned around to ask Barry to look for something to use as a bandage to cover up my bleeding knuckles, I nearly bumped into a policeman who once he saw the blood forgot to ask me for my tax or insurance details (I had none of course). Instead he started to give me directions to the nearest hospital. I thanked him for his help and I jumped in and off we headed, not in the direction we wanted to go but in the direction of the hospital, laughing as we went because there wasn't a thing on the Land Rover. My knuckles were not half as bad as they looked. We ended up being a bit late for work as we had trouble getting our bearings after getting stuck on one-way traffic systems.

Towards the finishing time my arm was getting very sore and had swollen quiet a bit. By the time I got home on that particular evening, my arm had ballooned up looking more like a leg of an elephant and when Anne Marie saw it was off to the Whittington Hospital just off the Holloway road with no ifs or buts. I could not believe it when they got a bed for me within a matter of minutes and got me yoked up to drips and pipes. I did not realise how serious things were until the doctor told me that if I had left it any later that I could have lost an arm. It was cellulitis.

The fan in front of any vehicle is full of all sorts of germs with all the flies and insects that get plastered on the blades, so by getting cut with the blades as I did can be dangerous, as I found out. I spent one full week in that hospital bed, but the craic wasn't bad at all because I knew a lot of the Irish girls who were nurses there, through them going into the Gresham and the Archway Tavern. I was very well looked after to say the least and was in no real hurry to get out of the place.

Me, Mother and Wife

Tara and Fionn. Ahh, isn't that nice

Myself and Herself

Posing for family photo

Mother, myself, Pete and Auntie Kathleen

The Woods Family

Lucky Day

Doormen in Gresham London,
Me, Joe, Blondie John, Josie and Gandhi

Working in Dublin - Johnny, James, David, Ivan, Victor and Joe

*Picture I took at first gathering of
Maze escapees at reunion in Letterkenny*

Commemoration Gaoth Dobhair,
first left row Martin and middle right row Joe

Symbol of freedom

Hughie, me and Joe in London

Travelling in style in Manhattan

Getting advice from father on how to ride a motorbike

Uncle Jack, Teresa and myself

A Foreman from Galway

There was a foreman plasterer on the job from Galway whose name was Joe and his eyesight wasn't the best. We kept a good eye on him as he did his rounds on the site, letting everyone know that he was around. It did not matter much to us anyway because if we saw him coming in our direction, we would hide in case he had more work for us. As soon as he moved on to where some of the other plasterers were working, you would soon see him sneaking away as if no one could see him, before disappearing out the gate at lunch time. Five minutes later we'd be nearly touching his bumper going down the motorway. We often passed him on the way home and he never copped on. There was one Monday that we came in kinda late with the intention of sneaking off at the earliest opportunity. There was no sign of the foreman so on our way to the canteen at lunchtime we decided to head for the car instead. But didn't we bump into the man we were doing our best to avoid. He just shook his head and said, "Well there's no point in being late twice in the one day, so keep going".

We had an English fellow labouring for us for a while. He was a very honest, good, clean-living type of a boy. He would have been ten years older than Barry but he always called him young fellow. He'd be in the middle of mixing a big bath of bonding with a shovel with a hole cut out of the centre of it to make it easier to use. Every time he stopped to talk in the middle of mixing Barry would shout to talk and mix at the same time. He would jump down off the scaffold and pretend to be mixing alongside your man with his imaginary shovel showing him how he should be doing it and the sweat would be running of your man trying to keep in time with the strokes as Barry went faster and faster, saying "Hi young fellow, you're slowing down". He would tell your man some mad stories. One of them was about plastering back at home. He would say "Hi young fellow, we have to burn stones in a big fire from early in the morning till late at night, then start crushing them into dust with a sledge. It's handy over here, you just get it from the shop in bags".

When your man left to go to New Zealand Barry brought in another young fellow, his cousin, who was just after coming over from home and needed a bit of work so he was happy enough to mix plaster for us for a while. The weather was very hot at the time so we'd get a big bottle of soft drink to quench the thirst. The other thing was the toilet was a good distance across the site from where we were working and Barry was under pressure to go for a leak. Rather than go that distance he finished what was left in the bottle and did his pee in it, then hid it in behind some pipes out of the way, but near to where his cousin was mixing the plaster. So me and Barry were plastering and yapping away when the next thing we see is your man coming down the stairs four at a time half-puking, cursing and swearing like a madman. We realised straight away what had happened. He had been busy mixing away and did not see Barry doing the business in the bottle and went for a drink ten minutes later, even though Barry had hid it in behind some plumbing pipes. He thought that it was hid so that he wouldn't get it. Not realising anything unusual about it, he took a big slug out of the bottle. Once the warm liquid hit the back of his throat it was a bit late to be thinking about the salty taste. He then thought that Barry had done it for badness and was threatening to jack in the job, which would have left us in a tight spot. After a lot of persuading and all the rest he worked away, but it didn't stop him being called piss breath every time he came near us after that.

When that job was near finished and it was time to move on, I think we got a start with Michael Roarty, a tunnelling contractor from near me at home. It was night shifts, not what we had in mind, but we thought we'll give it a try anyway. Something tells me that it must have been coming quite near to Christmas because there was lots of snow and frost at the time. The job was in Waterloo Train Station.

Before starting work the first move to be made was us having to attend a lecture on security. So we were shepherded into a large conference room. There was this buck there looking extremely important, or so he thought, telling us to take a seat as if he was talking to children, and then proceeded to tell who he was, a former head of some police unit in Scotland Yard, in a tone that meant we should be impressed. That was followed by a question that really impressed us. Did we know who the IRA were? I found it very hard to keep a straight face. This was a room full of mostly Irishmen remember. He went on talking to us as if he had some sort of inside information that he really shouldn't be sharing with us. He said that their main aim was to kill as many innocent people as possible. "Why give warnings then?" I asked. "Wouldn't it be easier to bomb cities without warnings like the RAF did to Dresden when they left it in smithereens during the Second World War?"

"But that was a war," he said. I didn't care whether I was sacked before I started work or not so I thought the best thing to do here was to keep asking him really stupid questions. This seemingly intelligent man went on to answer every daft question put to him in detail. I asked him if I found a bomb should I lift it, put it in a dustbin and put the lid on it so that it wouldn't do any damage if it went off? It proved one thing - that he knew as much about the IRA, security and bombs as we knew about tunnelling and that was sweet F-all. But as luck would have it when we did get a wee scout around to show us the ropes, there was very little work for us to do anyway.

The first bit that had to be done was when the foreman came and told us that a three foot tunnel had to be made to connect two shafts. Michael landed then and handed us two pneumatic drills. I think they were called German jiggers. He says to us "Don't worry a bit, just make sure you look busy if anyone happens to comes along". Well no one ever came along so we never did anything much as we were too busy now keeping an eye and having the craic with the ladies as they were on their way towards the exit doors of the station. The last trains would be about 12.30 or 1am, so they'd be overflowing with office workers on their way home. A lot of them a bit tipsy from one too many at the wine bar.

We had a generator outside the main entrance that we kept going. It was supposed to power the jiggers that we were to be working with but were inside gathering dust. Every so often if you were inside, you would have to go out and turn it off because of the fumes. This was the excuse that we had to be in the right place at the right time. There were a lot of down and outs sleeping around Waterloo Station. One freezing cold night I went out to switch off the compressor, but wasn't there this poor woman who was down on her luck standing leaning over it because of the heat. She was drinking from a bottle of whiskey that was half empty or maybe it was half full (figure that one out), so I hadn't the heart to switch off the compressor. She would wake up now and again when the cigarette she was smoking would smoulder away until it started to burn her fingers.

It was hard to keep an eye on everything. While me and Barry were winding up and having the craic with any ladies who seemed to be in a good mood and who were silly enough to stop and get dragged into a conversation that was only going to lead in one direction, we began to notice that as they went past the woman heating herself at our compressor they would keep turning around and staring back, some with shock and horror and some would burst out laughing. As she was on the opposite side of the generator to us, we could not see anything unusual. I thought to myself, "There's something strange going on here". So I decided to go and have a look.

Well it was a sight for sore eyes. The down and out woman, because of the effect of the whiskey and fumes combined had fallen asleep half-standing/ half-leaning over the generator. She was standing right in front of the exhaust. She had peed in her navy blue tracksuit bottoms that she had on. So with the weight and the shaking from the exhaust, her trousers had slid down to her ankles and everything was left exposed to the elements. It wasn't funny, but what could you do but laugh. We went back inside as quick as we could. You would not know what people might think if they saw us standing looking at the poor woman in that state. After all this unfortunate woman was someone's daughter and possibly someone's mother. We still had the problem of turning off our machine. After a while most of the throng of people had disappeared out into the night. Barry eventually headed over to turn it off but just before he reached it, didn't it just run out of diesel.

When we'd leave for home around seven in the morning there was always this middle-aged man with a big long white beard and he always slept standing up. His beard would be frozen and covered with ice. We often bought him coffee or a sandwich from a mobile sandwich shop that would be setting up as we were leaving. Around the corner on the right-hand side of the door, every morning without fail you would see two purple feet sticking out from under a frozen blanket that covered a dirty old mattress. For all the time we were there we never saw them moving. Whether it was a man or woman, we'd say the same thing every morning as we passed this sorrowful sight, there is no way that that person could be alive. But lo and behold, going in to work every night, the mattress was there but always empty and the occupant nowhere to be seen.

Barry could not come in for a few nights, so you'd be fed up on your own. I went away wandering around the job. It was huge as it was part of the same line as the Channel Tunnel. I got the nice smell of fried bacon in the air so before long I came on a canteen. It must have been around break time as the place was nearly full. I queued up and got a coffee and a bacon sandwich, seeing that was in my head since I got the whiff of it in the air earlier, and sat down. I was in the process of taking my first bite when I hear this voice loud enough for me and most of the men at the tables where I was after planting myself to hear, saying,

"I'll bet you're not as big a man now as you are when you're standing with all your hard men beside you at the door of the Gresham".

I looked in the direction of the voice with a chunk of the sandwich hanging out of my mouth and recognised this thick-looking gobshite that I had put out of the Gresham for being a nuisance and causing trouble. My immediate reaction was to throw my coffee and the rest of the sandwich at him, followed by the table and chair. He thought because I was on my own that I'd be afraid and that he'd somehow have the upper hand. After throwing that lot at him, all the other lads he was sitting with jumped and scrambled back out of the way, leaving him on his own among the upturned chairs. I challenged him outside for a square go. You never saw a man turn into what could only be described as a shrivelled up penis so quick. He put his tail between his legs then alright and refused to budge an inch. I went off outside then because I knew he would have to go back to work sometime and there was only one door and that's where I was going to wait.

When he did come out about ten minutes later he had his head down and his hard hat on, hoping that if he bumped into me I might not recognise him. But I did. I grabbed him by the shoulder and I pulled him over to one side. Before I got a word out he was apologising for his loud mouth actions and that he was only joking. I had calmed down a bit by then so we shook hands and it wasn't mentioned again.

If I was Running Short of Plastering Work

If I was running a bit short of plastering work, or more to the point getting fed up with it, it could be a year or two between plastering jobs. But I would give Michael a ring to see if there was anything going. The next job he sent me to was in Stonebridge Park not too far from Kilburn. I was there at half-six in the

morning, starting time was at seven. There were two men there,
a lead miner – the man in charge that knew what he was doing
– and the other man a bit like me but more experienced. He told
me what the story was. Out we go after getting changed into
the working gear and the wellington boots. I soon realised why
I had to wear these. They were in the middle of sinking a shaft.
It works opposite to building a house, where each block you put
on, the higher you go. In this case the blocks were called segments, if I remember correctly, and as you dug down you fitted
them in and bolted them together. I learned this afterwards,
not before, and it all sounds very nice and straightforward on
a piece off paper, yes, but in reality for me, it was drizzling
rain and every step you took you had to hold on to your wellies
because with the suction your foot would just come straight
out. The mud was already nearly up to the top of your wellies.
I was there most of the time looking like a bullock bogged in a
swamp.

There was very little talk going on. It was shouting and roaring.
I never saw the like of it before in my life. I thought first that
maybe the clown thought I was deaf. The other fellow looked
like he was afraid of his life. You would think the miner boy
was some sort of a man-eater. He was covered in muck from
head to toe and we had barely started. If the lead man said jump
your man jumped. He started shouting at me to do something
or get something. I wasn't used to that shite and I had no intention of getting used to it either. My temper got the better of me
and I ploughed over towards him and stuck my straightened
fingers in to his stomach and said, "Don't you ever F-ing shout
at me like that again".

Well he got some fright. It was fairly obvious that he wasn't used
to anyone answering him back. That was it. He never opened
his mouth to me the rest of the day. Even when he was laying
on his back nearly getting swamped in glue-like muck trying
to fit the segments, rather than ask me for a spanner, pliers or
nail bar, he would just stick out the hand. If it wasn't the right

tool, he would stick the hand out again. We had one tea break from seven in the morning until half seven in the evening and it was just gulp it down without a word spoken and out the door again. There is no need to ask what it was like the second day as I never went back to find out, in case I might bury him alive.

Myself and Joe spent a few weeks working in an old tunnel that ran across underneath the River Thames. It must have been about a mile long and you had to climb down a metal ladder fixed to the side of the shaft. It was a services tunnel for an electricity cable that lay in a channel full of water that kept circulating to keep it cool. There were two channels with an aisle along the middle, with just enough room for two people to pass one another.

One of the channels was a spare so that when there were repairs to be carried out on one, the power was switched to the other. One of the permanent staff had a bicycle for going from one end to the other. It looked like something that was down since the Second World War. A hard limescale tended to build up around the cable, much the same as what you find building up inside a kettle if it's in an area where the water is hard. The problem was that with the build-up around the cable, it caused it to heat up, so it was our job along with a few others to chisel it off.

The foreman was a real panicky sort of a fellow that was under pressure even when he was asleep. Joe had been given a van to drive us to work. There was another fellow from Creeslough that we would pick up near Holloway road in the morning as well. We'll call him the Yapper because he never shut up. He had the foreman driven mad as he would do absolutely nothing for him apart from entertaining us with all sorts of stories and the tea breaks getting longer and longer with Yapper winking and nodding his head in the direction of the foreman. As the foreman hammered away at the limescale and the sweat running down his face, it was very hot and humid. That didn't help anyone under pressure.

The air in the place never seemed to circulate, as there was a musty smell the whole time. There was a time or two when Yapper had wound the poor foreman up so much that I thought he was on the brink of committing hari-kari. He would go into a mad rage where you could not understand a word he was saying and Yapper still would not back down or shut up. When we finished up there after a hilarious couple of weeks, we were then sent out to the coast, to Ramsgate, a very busy harbour town.

Ramsgate

It was a new sewerage tunnel, as the old one couldn't cope with all the shit flying through. We got digs there easy enough as we intended to stay there during the week. It was a massive big house with seven of us altogether. Three of the boys were from Armagh and I never saw men without a pick of meat on them who could shift so many pints of Guinness and get up for work the next day with not a bother on them.

Three of us shared a big room, me, Joe and a man from Meath. Every single night he drank at least a dozen pints of Guinness. You would hear him coming staggering in most nights, but there was one night in particular that causes me to have the odd horrible dream even to this day.

I was in a deep sleep when I thought I could smell this suffocating stench. It got that bad that it woke me up. When I opened my eyes I got the fright of my life. There, two inches from my face, was this big hairy ass where the rotten smell was coming from. He must have farted as I was taking my breath in. I was still half asleep and things were in a bit of slow motion. He was that drunk he thought he was in the toilet. Even though I knew in my head that he was about to flood the place where my clothes were thrown over the back of a chair, it was only when he turned around towards me with his todger in his hand and my head directly in the line of fire, that I did move.

If I did not wake up from my slumber as early as I did, I would have gotten a hot shower all over my head and that would have resulted in him getting his balls kicked that far up his scrotum, he'd be as well to get a sex change. Anyway I let a roar out of me you'd think an elephant just stood on my foot and I shoved him at the same time towards the door. He was hard enough to move as he was a fairly big brute of a boy. I then managed to direct him backways into a small toilet, where he sort of collapsed. It's a wonder with the weight of him landing on the toilet that it didn't smash into smithereens. I left him sitting on the pot where he fell asleep straight away. He was snoring away like a happy hippo when we did get up, so we left him there to sleep it off. A comely maiden, who just happened to be very easy on the eye, came in to do the cleaning around ten most days so God only knows what sort of a sight would have confronted her when she came on your man.

Our job there was concreting a channel along the centre of the tunnel and to leave it as smooth as possible, which was not one bit easy I can tell you. The tunnel itself was about fourteen feet in diameter, so the concrete had to slope upwards to meet the round on both sides. Getting it to stay where you wanted it to stay was a story in itself. A dumper would bring the concrete through the tunnel to where we needed it, but the worst thing about this was the exhaust fumes. Some days it was that bad your eyes would be burned out of you. I saw the health and safety officer walking through one day when it was bad but all he did was to get his own arse out by climbing up the ladder as quick as he could. By right there should have been fans blowing air along to keep the fumes moving but it was obvious that the safety man's back pocket was being looked after, so as not to cause problems, except for us having to breathe in carbon monoxide all day.

Every evening we would train by doing all sorts of exercises or going out running. I made a point of doing a hundred press ups once I came in the door from work. That was how I started my workout. We were there two weeks when an English man working on the job who was from the area told us about a gym that we should try out. We did just that. It was funny because it was full of posers kitted out in the finest gym gear, all-year tans and muscles to match. It was obvious that steroids were part and parcel of the training regime. We were nearly pure white with being in out of the sun all day and we wore old t-shirts with holes in them that had seen better days. That aside, most were friendly and helpful. There was this one woman body builder who trained there that I got talking to. The reason being, I saw her using a leg press machine as if there was no weights on it. When she was finished I sneaked a try on it just to see what sort of weight she was using. I couldn't even move the dammed thing, so I moved away as discreetly as I could without anyone seeing the embarrassed look on my face. She was a very attractive lady, but the muscles and glossy lipstick just did not seem to match up properly in my mind. It turned out she did bouncing at a nightclub right on the beachfront. Needless to say we paid a visit at her request. All I'll say is that it was a very interesting place.

Martin Jim

Martin Jim is another soul I just have to mention. He was a pure headcase; that would be the sort of title I would bestow on him. Maybe he still is to a certain degree. Well whatever the case may be, you would have to make your own mind up after meeting him. He could be mistaken for a bit of a saint if you let the guard down.

There was one night before any of us left home Martin Jim and Burger John were heading for Letterkenny to try their luck with the ladies. John was driving, and somewhere along the road there were two women thumbing a lift. Martin says, "Jesus, give them women a lift," but for pure badness he drove on past and Martin shouting and roaring to stop. John was killing himself laughing. Then he said to Martin, "I'll turn back if you take off all your clothes". "Right," says Martin and off with the lot and John swings around and passes them by. He went for a bit so that they would not cop on that it was the same car, turned around again and them killing themselves laughing. Martin was getting stuck as he tried to take off his trousers without taking the shoes off first. He just about gets them off as John pulls up beside them. Martin jumps out with only his shoes and socks on. "Come on, jump in there's plenty of room for you". They were standing there in shock for a minute, before making off running as fast as their high heels would let them, with Martin in hot pursuit. I don't think you could imagine a more comical sight in your whole life. One of them had an umbrella and she was taking lumps out of him with it before he decided to retreat to the safety of the car. To add to that it had started to rain so he was wet as well as sore. I think they ended up in the Grill Night Cub and spent the whole night laughing. John told me the whole story in detail, and tells me over again every time I meet up with him.

Martin used to work on and off with Duffy and Carr, labour hire contractors in London, whenever it suited him. He was sent to a job one morning where he was told by the foreman to go up and paint the roof. There was a parapet wall surrounding the top so it was not too dangerous. Unless you were Martin Jim of course.

This was a five-story building and all the scaffolding had been taken down the previous week, so Martin started. After a while he was getting a bit fed up. An idea pops up in his head. Off he goes and gets a sweeping brush then proceeds to empty the five gallon drum of paint and starts to brush it but he wasn't able to keep up with the runaway paint as it starts to nun down over the finished walls. He just throws the brush on top of the mess and heads off home.

As he was going out the front door he looked up and started to laugh. There were big streaks of dark grey running down the recently painted brilliant white walls. That's only one story. There are many more every bit as good as that one but which he can tell himself. It would not be in my best interest to divulge any more than that without permission of course.

A Nightclub in Chiswick

Me, Joe and Barry worked in another nightclub in Chiswick, West London. Although it was Irish-owned, ninety per cent of the customers would have been English. Thursday nights were always guaranteed to be dodgy. In a strange sort of way they were my favourite because it would be full of soldiers.

It would be fair to say that I wasn't suffering from any sort of inferiority complex when confronting them or their threats. As a matter of fact I took great pleasure and enjoyment out of battering the heads off them any chance I got and I have to say I got plenty. Nearly all of them were just back from or going to the six counties during that time, and being Irish you were considered fair game to most of them. I often got called a Fenian bastard, along with a plethora of other choice words. Those that did all the shouting did so only when the numbers were stacked in their favour or when they were well out of striking distance. They weren't half the hard men without their mates or their weapons.

Of course there were times when I was shitting myself leading up to an encounter. That was natural enough, you wouldn't be human otherwise, but as soon as the fists started to fly the butterflies disappeared. With me being fit and sober I knew I could go toe to toe with the best of them. I'd intentionally get involved in debates with some of them if they had the IQ to understand what I was saying to them. Quite a few agreed that they had no business being in Ireland in the first place, but explained they mostly came from economic black spots and were likely to end up in trouble with the law, so they chose to join the army to escape the unemployment queues. The usual shite sob stories that you were expected to swallow to put you off asking them any awkward questions that they had difficulty answering.

The Scottish soldiers were the ones who had a chip on their shoulder and got thick straight away. I'd just say, "If you're so proud of your Scottish heritage and your flag, why are you out fighting for someone else's queen and country, not to mention their flag?". They'd lose the rag then because they found it very hard to justify to me why they were doing it, other than being used.

One Thursday night I was collecting money at the door. It was a sort of loose arrangement and there were no strict guidelines; the money was all going into a money box where I could have abused the system (it could have been one for me and two for the box). It was all cash so none of it would have been going through the books. I suppose you could say there was a certain amount of trust involved. Barry came rushing out and shouted "You better come in quick. The manager is having an argument with a nasty looking piece of work and his mates are getting rowdy as well". So I closed up the door and went inside only to see this boy with a bottle above his head about to level the manager. I grabbed it and got my arm around his neck at the same time but he was strong as a horse. It was like me on the back of a bucking bronco. Drinks and people going all over the place. Out of the corner of my eye I saw Barry jumping like a kangaroo in the middle of your man's mates and them trying to murder him. In the meantime I was doing my best to choke the living daylights out of the bucking bronco. By the time we managed to get the war zone moved out to the door I had your man throttled and I flung him out the door in a heap.

I could feel the blood trickling down over my ear. I was getting hit from all angles. It would be hard to see who was doing the damage as a few bottles came flying in and bounced off the walls around us. The next thing I saw was the boy I thought I had choked back on his feet sneaking into the doorway as quick as a snake. He gave Barry a kick straight in the nether regions while Barry was in the middle of a wrestle, throwing one of them out the door. After a few minutes Barry was buckled up with the pain. I don't know how, but I managed to slam the doors shut and by God was I glad.

We looked a bit like male strip-o-grams; the dickey bow and the collar was nearly all that was left of our shirts. The end up of it was, after eventually getting the place cleared I had to take Barry to the hospital on the way home. He was in some pain by the time we got into the hospital and as luck would have it a tall, stunning, dark-skinned lady doctor was on duty. She beckoned us to follow her into a room. I was making all sorts of suggestions as to what she was going to do and all Barry could do was groan. She tried to get him to stand up straight but he couldn't. He was sort of bent up like one of those bananas that the EU banned because there was too much of a bend in them.

After a few pulls and tugs, she had his trousers down around his ankle. While she was hunkered down on one knee she got his thingamajig out with one hand and started to feel around with the other. It was so funny I could not help but burst out laughing. She gave him the all-clear along with some strong painkillers to help him along. He was calling me all the names under the sun on the way out saying that he was never as embarrassed in his whole life, not because he had to drop his trousers but because there was no life in his oar if you know what I mean. We've had some laughs thinking about that visit to the hospital.

The Quieter, Tougher Boys

It was the quieter, tougher-looking boys who stayed in the background that you had to keep both eyes on at all times. It was without doubt one of the highest adrenaline-rushing places I worked in while in London, a nightclub close to Chiswick Roundabout west London. One night in particular turned out to be scary enough. I was standing out at the door when a lady came out and asked me to come inside that there was a fight going on and someone getting beat up. In head first I go and grab this skinhead of about thirty-five who seemed to be doing a fair bit of damage as bodies were flying in all directions. I got him in a headlock and dragged him outside. It only took a matter of seconds as he was off balance and I kept him that way. Once I let go of him, I closed up one side of the double doors and stood outside. What I did not say there was that I fired him out the door with a good shove and now he had got back to his feet again. Before I knew it he had a knife out and was circling me and his eyes mad in his head. I couldn't try and get in the door in case he got me in the back so I had to face up him. Whatever came into his head, maybe he thought I wasn't worth it, he proceeded to put the knife back into his pocket.

This was my chance. I gave him the nicest one-two you ever saw. He was knocked out cold in two seconds. He hit his head an almighty crack on the ground. I was sure he was a goner, to put it lightly, but what I did not know was that there was a whole gang inside. These were no sixteen-year-old teenagers. They were all between twenty-five and thirty-five. There was another exit door at the side. By this time the DJ had finished up and people were making their way out, which included his mates. He had got to his feet and looked a sight, his face covered in blood. When he spotted his mates he got brave again and made a lunge at me, but I just booted him out again. They just looked at him without saying a word. They went over to a car, opened the boot and brought out baseball bats and headed for me. There were seven or eight of them. Where the doorway was situated there was an alcove about a meter in length. I had a hold of each side of the door and was kicking like mad. I was getting hit on the arms and such when one of them, who was a nasty looking piece of work, managed to reach in and grab me by the shoulder.

I was wearing a black leather jacket. He had such a grip and was that strong that it took all my strength to prevent myself from being pulled outside. Meanwhile another one was trying to jump over the top to hit me in the face. I saw a knife the length of a bread knife streaking upwards past my chin. At that point to this day I don't know where I got the power from. I pulled away and left your man with a lump of my leather jacket in his hand. I turned and went through the first door and banged it closed after me but they smashed it in. The same was done to the second door.

When I met a woman drinking from a pint bottle I grabbed it, turned around and made smithereens of it on the first head through the door. I found myself beside a table full of these bottles and by God I let them have it. I was on that much of a high at this stage that I had the strength of half a dozen men. Even so, one who was crazed out of his head still managed to get through the barrage of bottles and made a swing at my head with a fire extinguisher. I ducked and he levelled a customer that just happened to be in the wrong place at the wrong time. It was like a scene from the Wild West. The rest of the gang outside smashed all the huge tinted plate glass windows in the place before they all made a getaway in two cars. Some of the customers got the registration number of one of the cars and gave it to the police when they landed half an hour later. One thing's for sure, you wouldn't suffer from constipation after nights like that.

After all the ructions night after night I had no intention of going back, but by the following Thursday I was feeling brave again. Who's there waiting for me when I get in the door but a police superintendent who was right down to earth, something I did not expect. He went on to inform me that the registration number we had got from one of the cars was false, and that I was a very lucky man to be alive. It turned out that the previous weekend the same gang had gone into the local snooker club and after an altercation with staff returned with a double barrelled shotgun and blasted all the lights in the place. He told me to keep a good lookout in the next few weeks in case they came back.

As the night wore on, with me trying to keep an eye on every car coming in, I'd think one minute "That's it I'm finishing here tonight", then the next minute I'd think "Sure it's not that bad". Until the head barman comes up to me and says there's a man at the bar and he's refusing to pay for drinks that he's just ordered. I followed him to where the barman could point him out to me. When he nodded his head in the direction of the bar, I thought "My god what am I getting myself into?". He was the biggest, nastiest-looking skinhead I'd seen around the place since the last big battle. They say everything comes in threes. There he was, and him standing laughing with a pint in his hand, more or less saying, "Here I am. What are you going to do?"

The first thing I did when I got close to him was grab the glass in case he intended to use it and asked him to pay for his drink. Then he says to me, "Do you know who I am?" He then went on in a menacing manner to tell me he was head of security at the British Embassy. "Where, when, and how I don't care," I says straight back. He makes himself even bigger and then asks me outside for a square go.

I couldn't back out, even though I was sure I was going to get a severe hiding. He led the way out through the door with his mates and a whole load of the customers coming behind. He swung round and tried to hit me with a haymaker. I was expecting something like that to happen anyway and was able to duck just in time. I felt the draught that came from his fist when it whizzed past, barely missing the top of my head. I don't know whether it was pure instinct, or just madness, but I got stuck into him like a wild animal. I had him battered all over the place, before he eventually went down face first. I jumped on his back, grabbed him by the two ears and proceeded to pound his face off the pavement because I thought it was a fluke that he was down in the first place and I sure as hell wasn't going to give him a chance to get up again. After I thought he had enough I got up off him. It took him a while before he staggered to his feet. His face was in some mess, a bit like a scene from a horror movie, but he wasn't for giving up that easy so he launched himself at me again.

I knew that I had the upper hand at this stage so I lined him up nicely and gave him a lovely one-two that knocked him out stone cold. There was a very big crowed watching the fight. I was surprised that none of his mates got stuck into me, but not one said a thing as I made my way inside again. I got myself all cleaned up and was happy to have got off without getting a scrape. Anyway, that made up my mind for me, that was to be my last weekend working there and in many ways I was lucky to have got out of the bloody place in one piece.

On One of my Regular Trips Home

In between all these exciting times, and on one of my regular trips home me and a few boys would head for Letterkenny. The nightlife was a bit more challenging as there were loads of very attractive girls. That's not saying that there weren't any attractive girls at home. It's just that most of them had other fish to follow, or there was too much competition.

They came from all the surrounding counties to Letterkenny; sure what am I talking about, you'd even get the odd one from Timbuktu. Anyway I managed to meet a lovely wee wan from Derry who stopped me in my tracks when I spied her and became infatuated by her ample bosoms. She knew she was on to a good thing, me being a Donegal man and all that, so she asked me to marry her on the second night. I just couldn't refuse. I felt very intimidated because you see she had a few of her brothers with her as backup. When she put her proposal and dowry on the table, it's the God's honest truth, after that I knew that my perks as a doorman would be somewhat limited or would have to come to an end, because if you want to get or remain married, you have to turn your back on all those tempestuous, man-hungry females. You could say we were a courting couple for couple of years before deciding to tie the knot, but that's another story.

Praying for the Queen

I was at mass in the church closest to where we stayed in London one Sunday. It must have been fairly close to Christmas and the priest was asking the congregation to offer up their prayers for all sorts of different intentions, but when he asked us to pray for the Queen, I thought "This has gone far enough" and I started getting the hiccups. A confrontation then was inevitable.

When the mass was over he was at the back of the church shaking hands with people as they left the church. I waited until I got a chance to ask him what exactly did he mean when he asked me to pray for the Queen. He was a bit shocked, but I said that I did not pray a lot and when I did, I did not want them wasted on a British monarch or her siblings' intentions and as an Irishman I felt I had to make that clear to him and as seventy per cent of those attending the church were Irish or of Irish extraction, he would have to be more sensitive in future about what he asked of us. I also let him know that she did not contribute to the church collection. The priest himself was English, which may have had a slight bearing on his thinking. Now whether he took my advice or not is another story, but it would certainly have provided him with food for thought, which was my intention.

Pre-marriage Courses

We had to attend pre-marriage courses one or two evenings a week. I would rush in from work and then walk up the road. It was only a few minutes away, but each time we went, with just the two of us and the priest sitting directly in front of us, I would start falling asleep and Anne Marie would keep digging her elbow into me trying to keep me awake, sometimes to no avail. I would start to snore. The priest was the same one who I had been raring up on about praying for the Queen, so he would not have been in the least bit impressed with me. We got through the courses without any major hiccups, but if I was asked anything about what had been said to me during these courses, I'd have to be honest and say I don't have a clue.

Talking about getting married, wait till you hear this for a story. My sister Mary Bridget decided to go down the marrying route. This was way before I had any intention of pursuing that as an idea of the way forward myself. She asked me to be the best man, as I was the best man about. I agreed without bothering to even think of what that entailed. As far as I knew you just had to be there for a few pictures and so on. The grand day was upon us and off we headed to the church and up to the front seat. Fr McGlynn was the parish priest at the time and was known to not take kindly to any messing about, although he had a liking for the odd wee half himself and could be quiet contrary.

Anyway the bride comes up the aisle and everything was going smoothly with them going through the marrying part when Michael says to me, "Right it's time to take the ring up because they're waiting for it." I says, "What are you talking about, sure I have no ring". Then he says, "What the hell are you on about? The best man always has the ring?" I started laughing because I thought he was trying to wind me up until I looked up at Fr McGlynn and there he was glaring down at me. Then I noticed that everyone else was looking at me as well.

I sat where I was at with a big red face while my mother and Joe raced off to try and find the missing ring. What a handling. When they got to the house it was locked up and they had no keys but lo and behold there was a small opening on top of one of the windows that was left open and Joe managed to squeeze in and got the ring, which was left on top of the mantelpiece. I think we spent half an hour sitting twiddling our thumbs. If you could have seen the looks I was getting. Not only that, the look from the priest nearly turned me into stone because as far as he was concerned, I had done it on purpose. But I sure as hell learned a lesson and did not repeat the same mistake again.

Snow a No-show

Myself and herself were in London and talk of a wedding on the horizon began to cause me undue stress. We decided to go to Austria for a short holiday, because the thought of real snow, and, more than that, deep snow, was appealing. But when we got there, there was no sign of all the snow we were expecting to see. Just plenty of sunlight. Once we got over the shock, we were not to be one bit disappointed. It was roasting hot and getting a tan was an option. We had a nice log cabin all to ourselves up on a hillside. It was nice and cool inside, but you couldn't stay indoors just because the weather wasn't what we were expecting. So we hired out two bikes and went touring all around the place.

It was spotlessly clean everywhere you went. People were courteous but not overly friendly. Someone told us we should get a cable car and go up the mountains where you'll get all the snow you want. We did and saw Hitler's nest on the way up, a place nearly impossible to get to. But the funny thing was, we were in shorts and t-shirts right at the top of the mountains with snow drifts that were up to eight feet deep and it wasn't cold. We had a snowball fight with some others who were on the cable car. It was something else.

Another day we went cycling in the forest and of course I had to do a bit of showing off skidding on the gravel road. One of my manoeuvres did not work out quite right and I ended up with an L-shaped back wheel. I tried straightening it but to no avail, so I ended up having to carry the bloody thing for over three miles and pay for it when I got to the hire shop. It would have been cheaper to have bought the bike in the first place, when he handed me the bill with a big smile on his face and me having to smile back and utter my apologies for causing the damage in the first place.

Stag Nights

As the wedding date started to come closer the more nervous I became. It had a fair bit to do with the marrying part, but it also had a whole lot more to do with mates, friends or whatever you want to call them. I told them that there was no way I was having a stag party, because I had taken part in a stag party for one of the doormen who I worked with a short while previous to this, and he ended up walking through Willesden Green with not a stitch on him. The plan was for the police to arrest him, hopefully for indecent exposure, but not one of them Bobby hats was to be seen the whole time that he was wandering around naked. If it was now he would surely end up on YouTube, Bebo or a similar site.

He eventually made his way into a 7-Eleven shop looking for something to cover himself up. There were two girls working in the shop, one Indian, and the other Caribbean. They were a bit shocked at first but when we explained what was going on, they thought it was funny but strange. I told one of the girls that it was customary to do this. That in Ireland you had no choice. The groom-to-be had to be paraded up and down through his own town so that everyone could get a good look at him and make up their own minds about his worth. He ended up coming out of the 7-Eleven with his tackle in a cup, the only thing he

181

could lay his hands on to cover his packed lunch, or more to the point his compressed lunch.

Me and Barry were working together at the time and as happened on more than a few occasions we could sometimes be under severe pressure during the day, especially if we had plastered on more than enough and it began drying out too fast. In the middle of this he'd suddenly start laughing away to himself. I'd ask him what was so funny, but he wouldn't tell me. This got me thinking that something was afoot. Whatever it was, I got a sixth sense that made me very uneasy. This was the night that something was going to happen. Once I got to the house and in the door I said to Anne Marie, "C'mon we're going out as quick as we can". So I got showered and changed in the blink of an eye. She was dolled up anyway so out the door like Speedy Gonzalez, and straight into the underground, which was only a hop, skip and a jump away from the house and headed for Leicester Square. We went to the cinema, then to some pubs. We got back about half-one in the morning. I was that nervous that I would not let Anne Marie put on a light in the house. Our room was at the top. We were in for about five minutes when I heard the noise of cars outside. As I sneaked a look out the window, there were two cars and I could hear voices saying "There's no lights, they can't be back yet".

It turned out that they had it all planned, even hiring a camcorder (not a mobile phone in sight and the camcorders were scarce enough back then) and a male stripper to put the hat on it. God only knows what that was about and I'm glad that I didn't hang around long enough to find out. It had all the ingredients for one dodgy stag night, something I had no intention of having myself because I was on a good few and I knew what could happen when things got out of hand. It's great when someone else is the victim, but when it came to my turn, I have no problem in saying that I was a coward and I'm proud of it. I never slept a wink the whole night. I was terrified. So the next morning I had my mind made up. We headed for Heathrow airport and off home to safety. I heard later that they had come back a number of times, got fed up, and went off to some nightclub in Tottenham where they ended up fighting. I suppose they had to get rid of their frustrations in some way and that was as good a way as any on the night, considering that their carefully laid plans went haywire. Some of the boys did not take it too well, and let me know in no uncertain terms that they were not happy, but that they were still going to get me even on the wedding day. Nothing was to be ruled out. I was going blank, as I could not concentrate on anything but what they could still do to me. I did give them all a good going over when it came to my turn to make a speech, so because of that I had to leave the reception early. We sat out along the road in a lay by for about two hours before sneaking back to the hotel and into the big fancy bedroom.

Honeymoon in Mombasa

We had decided to spend the honeymoon in Mombasa in Kenya, because an Indian girl who worked with Anne Marie had relatives there and had spent a lot of time on visits herself. According to her it had to be seen to be believed. We went and spent three weeks there. It had its good and bad points like everywhere, but it would have been the nearest thing to paradise that I would have come across in my little trips. The hotel that we were staying in was right on the beach, pure white sand and the clearest blue water I have ever seen. We met an older English couple who were very friendly and I'll tell you how we got talking to them. After some confusion about rooms and who was lucky or quick enough to pick a room facing the beach, it turned out good enough for us as we had gorgeous gardens outside our window with the beach on the other side, so no complaints about the view.

We got our stuff sorted out in the hotel in a hurry, as we were mad to get onto the beach and into the water. It was like something you would see on a postcard. There were steps leading down towards the beach, with a small stream, and a small bridge, with very green grass – not like what we have at home, the blades of grass were about half an inch wide – and all the palm trees. There were some people sitting around eating co-conut that had fallen off the palm trees, but later on we saw a Kenyan man who was working as a gardener and handyman climb up the tree with his bare feet and a big blade on his back that he used to chop down the coconuts. Down he would come just as fast as he went up. He would then make a hole so that you could drink the white milk from inside. Once that was done, he would chop it in half and like a flash he would have the inside cut up in nice little slices, and boy were they nice. Ten times better than the ones we get at home.

As we made our way towards the sand, chewing away, Anne Marie was about two yards in front of me, when I heard this big clump. There on the ground between us was this big brute of a snake about four foot long. It had fallen down from a palm tree. We didn't have time to move with the fright. As we watched it disappear into the long grass, I looked to one side where this couple were sunning themselves. They had seen what had hap-pened and were smiling. I didn't think it was a laughing mat-ter, until he explained that these snakes were not poisonous. I could see the funny side of it then. They told us that the exact same thing had happened to them. It turned out that the bloody snakes were everywhere. We went out for a bit of a splash in the water, which was nice and warm, but I nearly choked when I saw two snakes, one after the other. I know it's hard to run when you're up to your waist in water, but I think I got out of the water faster than a jet ski and left Anne Marie behind. That's a brave Donegal man for you. It turned out that they could give a nasty bite but wouldn't bother you as long as you kept out of their way.

We sat down with the English couple at one of those tables with the big umbrella over it, because we wanted to stay in the shade for a while. The waiter left cups and a bowl with packets of sugar sitting on the table before going to get coffee that we had ordered. We started to talk about the fright we got with the snakes and started laughing. Bloody hell the next thing a monkey jumped down off the roof onto our umbrella, swung down onto the table and took a fistful of the packets of sugar from the bowl. It happened so fast that there was nothing you could do but watch in amazement as the little runt swung back up onto the roof and sat looking down at us, then started to tear the corner neatly of each packet, holding it up and nice as you like poured the sugar into its mouth and shook each packet to make sure that there was nothing left behind, throwing the empty packets cheekily down at us. That wasn't the end of it. We realised then that we weren't the only victims of the cheeky monkeys. A whole group of them had come in from the trees and swooped on every table that people were sitting at, at the exact same time. It would make you wonder who were the real monkeys, us or them?

Once we got wise to all the goings on we were able to relax a bit more and think more adventurously, so we were advised to go on safari. Eventually about twelve of us squeezed into a rickety old Toyota minibus leaving from the hotel early one morning and headed off out into the middle of nowhere. We were going to stay in these small huts for a night, but on the way we passed through a few spread-out villages with an awful lot of small children running around. Before we left that morning the driver told us to buy some sweets from this stall so we did as he had suggested. I realised now what for. The children must have known that we were going to pass by, and they swarmed all over the minibus. The driver warned us to keep the windows nearly closed, just leaving enough room to throw out sweets. Well what a hullabaloo that caused. If you saw the clamour for the sweets. I asked the driver was this the normal thing that happened when tourists passed, and he said yes. When I asked about the damage to their teeth he just shrugged. It left a bad feeling; it was no different than throwing breadcrumbs to birds.

We were then herded into jeeps that had seen better days. We were in the standing-up position in the back with the English couple and a Dutch couple who were sound but did not speak too much English. We drove around for a good while before we saw some elephants. The driver took us too close for comfort at one stage. One big daddy of an elephant must have felt we were invading his territory, because he started to roar and made a run for us. There was the driver flat out in reverse and him not knowing what he might bang into. Big daddy lost interest after his sprint and turned back again. Off we go again looking for more wild animals. We came on a good few giraffes, and a few lions that completely ignored us, even though they started to scratch themselves on the side of the jeep and then wandered off, as if they were well used to daft humans looking at them.
Our next stop was a small village of huts, some big, some small. We got off to have a look around and I saw what I thought was a big boulder moving. It was a huge tortoise and I got to sit on its back purely out of curiosity. It made the same difference to it as if a fly had just landed on it. It would never make a taxi. At thirty feet per hour it would be a bit on the slow side. We were told that it was a hundred and twenty-five years old; whether or not it was I don't know.

They put on a show of native dancing that went on for ages, I can't remember rightly but I think I had a go myself as it would be unusual for me not to have a go. After that we had to sample some of their traditional food, mostly meat thrown on top of a fire of small branches and let roast away for ages. It was different but very nice even though it was a bit on the tough side. Driving around on an open-backed jeep was a good place to swallow dust if that makes you happy. The driver was on the radio a lot, getting directions as to where we might see something of interest.

The next scene we came on was vultures pulling the insides out of a wildebeest and them too fat to fly. God but were they dirty looking brutes. When we got back to the camp there was a big spread of all kinds of fruit under the sun. There was all sorts of lumps of meat, some big bones and some small bones, with meat that fell off when you tried to lift it. I was wary at first because I was thinking, "Is it monkey, hippo, or maybe another human?", as some of the bones looked like a person's arm. But do you know this, arm, monkey or giraffe, I ate my fill and boy was it good.

After gorging myself nearly to death, like the vultures we saw earlier except I didn't have to try and fly, I sort of half-rolled into our little hut. Managing to sleep was another problem. Between the cold and thinking about what might stick its head in the door, closing your eyes was the last thing on your mind. We were all glad to be on the way back the following day to the comfort of our hotel. Although when I say hotel, don't compare it to one at home. The sleeping end of it was very basic. It was like a cell in a prison. There was only cold water. The same went for the shower. When we got back to our room we just lay on the bed we were that tired. It felt like we were in the Hilton. Next there was banging on the door. It was the English couple and them in tears. Their safe had been opened and all their money and valuables gone. We had decided to put ours in a safe in the reception area where a few guards seemed to be wandering about at all times. We went down to the reception with them, where the guards had two young fellows who were crying and frightened out of their lives.

They were being forced to make a confession, there in front of us. In the end up, the English couple told them to let them go, it was obvious that it wasn't them. It was more likely to have been one of the guards themselves. We gave them five hundred sterling because they did not have a penny left and the hotel management wouldn't accept responsibility or give them anything.

I had an idea so I went and got my key and tried it on a few other doors. I called the manager. When he saw what one key could do, he was shocked. He went around trying doors himself just to make sure. It was no big consolation to us that he was going to have them changed because with the pace of things it would be another year before they would get around to it.

We decided to go on one last trip before going home, so we went off on an old rickety minibus to a sort of factory, except it had no roof on it, or indeed it didn't have anything in it apart from people sitting on the ground with lumps of wood being held between their feet and them hammering away with a number of strangely shaped wood chisels. They seemed to be a very happy bunch and were laughing away. I thought "We're a funny look-ing crowd to them so why shouldn't they be laughing". I was curious as to how they were able to carve the perfect shape of a lion, zebra, monkey, or any of the various figures that they had piled up. They had no drawings, no markings, nothing; only a lump of wood and primitive tools. I came to the conclusion that it was practice, practice, and more practice, but I did find out why they were all laughing away.

This old boy signalled for me to come over. I thought, here we go again, because everyone wanted to sell you their crafts. He kept looking around as if he was hiding something. Well he sure was. I had to go down on one knee beside him. Then he started to clear his pile of crafts and pulled out this big bag that he had hidden. He stuck in his hand and pulled out this big fistful of grass and stuck it under my nose. The smell was that foul I nearly choked. He wanted the equivalent of around fifty cents. I declined the offer but I did buy some other bits and pieces which I still have.

When we returned to London we did go and visit the English couple on their farm. They brought us out for a meal and treated us like big shots, and in case I forget they did repay us the money that we loaned them, when they were left penniless by thieves.

Return to London

When we got back to London after the honeymoon there was a message about a small job that someone wanted done. I phoned the number up and a fellow with a real cockney accent answered saying that he had got my number off some builder that I must have done a bit of work for before. He explained what he wanted done. He gave me the address and I was there around eight in the morning.

It was a rough enough part of town, but this place sort of stood out on its own because there were security gates and high walls. The gates opened and I went in and was greeted by two dodgy looking boys in suits. They brought me inside, where I was greeted by another dodgier looking boy with a lot of gold hanging off him and rings on every finger. He asked me if I wanted a cup of coffee. I thought I'd better take it in case I don't get the chance again. Someone said to me one time that you should never say no to a cup of tea as they might not be so forthcoming next time.

He chatted away until I finished my coffee, before showing me exactly what it was that he wanted done. It wasn't a big job. He had closed up one door and opened up another with a dividing partition, all within a kitchen which was huge. It had to be skimmed. I asked him did he want a price. He says don't worry I just want it done, then said, "I'm off out for a while," leaving me in the house on my own.

There was no shortage of wealth by looking around. I set about my work and while waiting for it to dry I decided to have a wee nosy around. The first door I opened, I was just about to pop my head in to see what was inside when I froze on the spot. This Rottweiler dog as big as a calf with its teeth bare, drooling at the thought of taking a lump out of me and it about ready to pounce. I slammed the door that hard I nearly took the handle off it. That put any idea out of my head about having a snoop around the place. I made myself a cup of tea and ate the few sandwiches I had with me. After giving the few bits another rub of the trowel, as they were starting to go off nicely, I went to go outside and was about to open the door, when I spotted the same bullock of a dog standing outside the door looking in at me. It sort of dawned on me then why gold chain man had no problem about going off leaving a stranger in his house. I'd say the same boy would be having a good laugh at my expense, knowing fine well what might happen in his absence. After finishing the job I had to sit twiddling my thumbs for ages before he returned, smiling of course and wondering if I had met Bruno? I saw him and that was enough for me. For all I knew he could have had cameras installed watching my every move, but who cares, he was sound. He gave me an extra hundred pounds on top of what I asked for.

Burger John

I then got a few days with an agency to keep the ball rolling until something better came along. That took about two weeks, which resulted in me starting a nice big job at the Intercontinental Hotel at Hyde Park Corner, for an English contractor who I had done a few small bits of work for some time ago, not really expecting to hear from him again. I was in need of a labourer so Blondie John, the big burger look-alike, volunteered his services. I think it was a Tuesday that we started work. They were refurbishing it section by section. One squad were in gutting it out and another squad of carpenters were straight in doing a first fix. Electricians and plumbers followed. Then it was our turn.

On most jobs all trades were in at the same time doing their bit, which was very disorganised to say the least. The first week was great, everything went according to plan. Burger John lost about a stone in weight. Now the second week was an entirely different story. To get to where we were working we had to go up the fire escape stairs. Whether it was curiosity or accidental we ended up walking through a corridor that we obviously had no business being in. There were trays sitting outside some of the rooms untouched. They weren't like that for long. We robbed all the fancy biscuits, cakes and sweets. This became the norm every morning. We got to know a lot of the lady staff members who would hoover the corridors or clean the rooms and others who brought food or whatever was ordered to the rooms. It got to the stage then that we had all these girls coming at different times with bottles of wine and boxes of sweets. We were well looked after from then on that was for sure.

There was a receptionist's desk on each floor. We got to know this girl on one of the desks. She used to laugh her head off at the mad stuff that we would tell her; not all of it was true but it had the desired affect. We'd see these absolute stunners walking past. Burger John would be dribbling at the mouth. Sheila, which was her actual name, told us they were escorts. Neither of us knew what that meant so she had to spell it out for us. One day we saw two of these stunners go into a room that this well-dressed old boy was staying in. We had seen him go in or out on a good few occasions, you'd know he was wealthy as sin. The secretary told us that he had a suite rented permanently. After a while we made it our business to go over to the door. We even had the cheek to put our ears as close as possible. Well what a racket. They must have had him tied up and were whipping the hell out of him or else they were beating him with a shillelagh. How could anyone, sane or not, concentrate on work in an environment like this?

It was downhill from there on. I noticed that the burger man was getting overly friendly with a girl from the West Indies. It came to a head one day when I was plastering a ceiling. Burger John asked me if I had enough mixed. I said I thought so but it turned out I was a bit short so I shouts for him to mix some more, but could I get an answer?

Off I went looking for him. I spotted the cleaning trolley outside a room so I thought "He's in there". As I got closer, I could hear a rare bit of giggling and laughing. What confronted me on entering that room is going to stay with me for a while. She's perched on the edge of the big fancy bed with him on his knees behind her giving her a massage. You wouldn't mind but he hadn't even the decency to take of his dirty big boots. I left them to it 'cos there was no point in saying that I need a bucket of plaster quick. Mixing a bucket of plaster or...?

Another day we were up on the eighth floor working away and he would take these mad fits of laughing every few minutes. "Jesus," I thought to myself, "what the hell is he at?" It was only when I needed my bucket of water changed as it was getting too dirty for using on the plaster. Out he goes and then he calls me and says, "Look down and tell me what you see". I leaned out over the railing and looked down. I could see one of the exits out of Hyde Park underground station with a few people coming out. Next thing he threw the dirty water down over them. I could do nothing but jump back in out of sight. Then the two of us nearly died bloody laughing. I went to have another sneaky look over but by this time there were about twenty people and them all looking up. The first few must have been part of a larger group. Next thing Burger John squeezes past with a larger bucket of pure filthy water and threw it down over them. You could see the whole pavement around them, which was parched dry with the heat, going all blackish as the water hit it.

I shouted to John to get out of here as fast as we could. We gathered up the tools. It was the fastest I ever saw him moving. We put them into a small locker that was used as a secure hiding place and went down the exit stairs four or more at a time. I think we fell down half of them with all the laughing. The next day when we went in the contractor himself was there waiting for us. He was not a happy chap. He asked me had we thrown water out. I said that was ridiculous to think that because we had only been in at work for two hours because we had to go and price another job. He thought someone else must have got into where we had been working. He told us that he had to pay dry cleaning expenses for six people who came into the hotel to complain. He apologised for thinking it was us. It must have been the big innocent looking gobs on the two of us that did the trick.

Later on the same day when we were coming back from a stroll through the corridors, I spotted this brand new Hoover. I thought "That's handy," because I needed a new one as my own had seen better days. Sure a big outfit like this would never miss a little thing like this. That was the line of thinking that I decided to follow so as to convince myself that I was doing nothing wrong. I took it along to where we where working where I put it into a rubbish bag. When we got finished up later on and put the tools away, me, John and my disguised bag of rubbish went down on the service lift to the basement where the skip for all the rubbish was parked. We made our way out from the lift area. Who did we meet but the contractor and he started to ask how things were going and so on. Me being so smart I walked the few steps to the skip and threw my bag of rubbish into it. After some more chit chat me and John started to walk up toward the exit as if we were going home.

What happened next you could not make it up if you tried. We met a skip lorry coming down the incline to the underground car park where the skip was situated. "I don't believe this," I thought, and turned back to get my new Hoover before he lifted the bloody thing. Wasn't the contractor still standing beside the skip talking to one of the hotel managers. All I could do was watch from a discreet distance as the lorry driver did his job and drove out with my new Hoover still in the skip that was now on the back of his lorry, and that was the last I saw of it. I could have stabbed Blondie John on the way home if I had anything to stab him with because he laughed and took the piss at me the whole way.

The following day the contractor asked me if I could do him a favour. They had a burst water pipe in the ceiling of a ground floor restaurant, which had to be taken down and had to be re-plastered as quickly as possible. It was an emergency so I was in no position to refuse him even though it meant we would have to work late. When we did get started on it, after it was all plaster boarded like new.

There were these big windows that went from floor level to ceiling in height. It was a bit of a coincidence that the under-ground exit from the Tube station that John had been dumping the water down at was directly outside our window so I knew it was only a matter of time before the shit hit the fan again. I'm there troweling away as hard as I could at the ceiling, as it was drying a bit too fast for comfort, but there was a strange silence, like if there's children around and it's just too quiet; you know that they are up to something. As this thought is floating around in my head I heard the laugh but it was more like some-one choking. I looked around and went into a fit of laughing. Burger John was standing bent over at the window, the scaffold was about a meter and a half off the ground, with his trou-sers down at his ankles and his ass nearly up against the glass. What was the crowning moment was the big crowd of Japanese tourists outside and them all killing themselves laughing and taking pictures of a newly discovered moon! John's oversized posterior. I haven't a clue how we never got raced out of that place. About a week later he needed work done on a hotel in High Wycombe, miles outside London, so he gave us his work van to use. The first morning we left at four-thirty and got to the job at two-thirty. There was a stage where we drove through a small town about three times, we just kept going around in circles. It was the same then on the way home. You could not stop laughing, from John peeing out the window to us sitting in this posh English country pub roaring our heads off pretending to be some sort of psychopaths (he wasn't pretending) and John having a big conversation into one of the handsets of the first mobile phones that came out. It had the big square box part as big as a suitcase but that was missing and him shouting into the phone about how many men he was after sacking and he was in trouble now because he was after buying two hundred new vans and he had no one to drive them.

He was at the same craic another day when we were on our way home in heavy traffic and him hanging out the window talking to some imaginary person on the phone. I would be laughing that much that I couldn't see where I was going half the time. When we suddenly came flying onto a very big roundabout (Chiswick Roundabout) where I managed to cause a bit of a pile up but managed to avoid getting hit myself, and all he could do was laugh. Because of his antics I kept going around the roundabout and turned off at the next exit, not caring what direction we were going because there were a few cars banged into each other all because of my driving. The more distance we got between them and us the better. It wasn't that long after that John went up to Leeds where his brother was working as a building contractor. Whatever was up there and whatever happened, believe it or not he stayed and worked.

England Crashes

When the whole economy in England crashed and interest rates went sky-high, people were losing their jobs and then their homes that they had bought as investments. It was a terrible time for everyone; it did not matter what colour you were or what country you were from. We managed to keep working and stuck it out for another few years until things began to prosper again. In the meantime my brother Joe moved home for a few months, where he bought a small farm and did a bit of plastering with Martin, a younger brother, before going back to London for another while to tie up some unfinished business. Martin had spent a few months plastering in London with me and Pat Kelly but got homesick. He had a fine doll at home whose schoolbag he used to carry, so was afraid of his life that she might get someone else to do it for her and went home to keep an eye on her. As a matter of fact they're married now.

In the meantime we were stuck in London and most of the other Irish boys that we knew headed off to greener pastures. For those who, like us, stayed it was fairly lonely. In that time I did a lot of work to the house. Re-plastered, re-wired, re-plumbed, new windows and doors. What a waste of time, I would have been as well to put all the money that was spent into a bucket and burned it, not unlike what our government decided to do with Irish taxpayers' money when they started pouring it into the abyss that was Anglo Irish bank, without ever having a hope of a return on what we were told was an investment. But I suppose that's life. If you make a decision in the middle of the night, you win some, you lose some.

Working for the Nuns

I remember getting a phone call from this builder from Meath who I had done bits and pieces for before. He wanted me to go and look at a bit of work in a convent in Hammersmith. This vision of domineering nuns who ruled with an iron rod kept coming into my head as I went for a look the following day. It turned out not too bad. There was a fair bit of plastering to be done. Personally speaking I had more than enough work to keep paying the bills so I stuck on an extra digit or two on the price, not expecting to be hearing from him again. A few days went by before he got back in touch and wanted me to start as soon as possible.

I had a fellow from Armagh labouring to me at the time. He was mad as a hatter, had a stutter, and to complicate matters even more was a bit deaf, with a big mop of long hair seventies-style. Now the first day I went to look at the job, there wasn't a sinner around because it was a Saturday as far as I remember. But we got in to start on a Tuesday and the place was heaving with female students. Your man from Armagh was stuttering that bad, I had to hit him a clout on the back same as you would do if you were choking. That was bad enough until we met another fellow who was to show us where everything was and to give us any help that was required. All of a sudden, my mate gets into an almighty stutter, grabs your man by the arm and points at it for me to look at. I went into shock myself when I laid eyes on what he was getting so annoyed about. There in big bold lettering tattooed on his arm was the letters UVF.

First thing I thought was there must be a mistake, a man with this sort of tattoo working in a convent, it just did not add up. At that point he knew he was in a tight spot and started to give an explanation of his own free will as to how he got it. We are all guilty of making the odd mistake in our lives, so he was given the benefit of the doubt along with some advice about getting it removed if he did not want to get into any trouble over it. He was appreciative and turned out not a bad fellow at all, apart from the fact that he believed that humans evolved from monkeys. If that's the case then, why are there still monkeys around or did humans form some sort of perverse intimate relationships with the monkey population to get the ball rolling? I'm sorry, but I just don't buy the whole monkey business of where we originated from.

I never thought that it could be a scary place to work, but some of these girl students were not one bit shy or innocent with some of the suggestions that were thrown in our direction. The nuns were continually patrolling. If and when a group would start to hanging around where we were working the nuns would shoo them away. There was one male teacher, he could have been a sports teacher, I wasn't sure, but it was so funny watching what was going on. He was a good-looking fellow and the girls would follow him around everywhere asking him silly questions as an excuse just to get talking to him. There were a few hilarious moments with the labourer, between him saying things that he shouldn't say, and doing things that he shouldn't do, with being a bit hard of hearing. He thought he was whispering and me having to try and cover up for him then. We were in and out in a week. I did learn something: all is not what it seems to be looking at it from the outside.

I didn't have a clue nor did it cross my mind about it being a school. That's how clued in I am to convents and teaching. I had an idea that there would be a few nuns about but that was it. The reality was quiet different. The nuns who were there, and were teaching some of the students, were very pleasant and wearing normal clothing. Everything was going very well for us until they wanted this emergency job done. It was a Friday and it had to be completed over the weekend. It was a big parti-tion, eighteen foot high and they were using four by fours for uprights that were soaked with being left lying out in the rain. They didn't use any noggins whatsoever, which was not a good idea I thought to myself, but it was none of my business so I said nothing. I skimmed it as soon as they got the plasterboard on, and came in on the Monday to see the foreman and a good few well-suited gentlemen looking at the wall as I approached and saw the state of the wall that was warped in all directions.

The foreman decided to act the big man and blamed me for the mess. I don't know why I didn't flatten him on the spot, but instead I explained how I saw it being constructed, wet timber and no noggins and that if he could not understand what hap-pened after being in charge of putting it up I said, "Well my friend, you're in the wrong line of work if you didn't know that soaking wet timber will warp like a dog's hind leg when drying out in the heat".

Talk about a man squirming when caught in a tight spot. The lot had to be taken down and put up properly the next time, nice dry timber and plenty of noggins, and I plastered it the sec-ond time, and got paid twice, so all's well that ends well.

Other London Stories

One of the lads, a man from Wexford who worked with us in London, was a mighty worker and could turn his hand to anything. As well as being a real prankster David Jordan was the title given to him when he was born so we'll stick with it. He had a liking for going on the odd tear now and again.

This is one story about him. The two of us were to screed floors in this house for Pat Kelly and had a lorry load of screed ordered. Everything was in place for an early start the following morning. I was woken at 4am in the morning when the phone started ringing. It was him apologising because he could not make it for work in the morning. "God did something happen?" says I. "No," says he, "but I have a problem. I'm in Wexford."

Well I was ripping mad. I felt like calling him a few undesirable names as you would imagine in these circumstances, but I didn't, mainly because I was still half asleep. He had gone on the tear and whatever got into his head he made for Heathrow where he got his flight home. As soon as he began to sober up he realised the predicament he was in, or, more to the point, he had left me in. But all was well when he came back the following week and we never mentioned the pressure me and Pat were under screeding the floors ourselves. He ended up working with us at this same renovation job in Dublin. On another occasion while we were still in on a job in London, he had brought his travel bag with him as he intended going straight to Heathrow after work and getting a flight home. Without him knowing it, I had placed a few bricks and a few top shelf magazines in his bag and off he goes.

I got a call next day explaining what happened when the customs started to search his bag. He could not believe it when he saw what was being taken out. They had a good laugh and told him to enjoy the rest of his holiday. He told me to watch out because revenge would be very sweet, and he was right, for every time I caught him, he got me back twice.

Working with Pat Kelly

Pat got another job where the two of us did the plastering; it was for a wealthy Greek man who owned a few jewellers shops, so you can imagine the nice posh house. There was a fair bit of carpentry work to be done as well so Pat got this carpenter he knew from home to help out. He turned out to be an interesting kind of a boy. He classed himself as a sort of a wild man of the hills who liked to think he could live off the land by eating wild berries, plants and all types of wildlife. If some of the stories he was telling me were to be believed, a film should have been made about him instead of Robinson Crusoe. He had these big pair of hands that he said himself were handy for killing wild animals. When at home, he lived on his own in the middle of nowhere with not a sinner next or near him. As it turned out he was fond of a drop of the strong stuff as well, which I did not know at the time until one day me and Pat had to go and finish a small bit of work on another job. Leaving your man on his own in the house, we had our small job nearly finished when Pat got a phone call telling him to come back to the house quick. What happened was that your man had stumbled upon the drinks' cabinet and could not resist the temptation of a slug or two.

The owner and his wife had come home from work, which was fine until she went into their bedroom. The decor was all cream and white with two dirty big boots of your man sticking out from under the bedclothes and him sound asleep cradling an empty whiskey bottle. They were not at all pleased about this sort of unprofessional behavior. When Pat went back and got your man up from his slumber, they began to see the funny side of the whole thing. They even gave him a drink to try and sober him up a wee bit, which to all intent and purposes had the opposite effect. He had to be bundled unceremoniously out of the house and head first into the van.

I ended up plastering this doctor's surgery in Earls Court and, come to think of it, it was for Pat Kelly as well. There were some peculiar happenings going on every day on this job. I'd be there very early in the morning around 6am or thereabouts. There was scaffolding up on the front of the building right on the footpath, so I would sit on a box watching the world go by. It was a very busy area not far from the underground station, so there was always loads of people around from seven am onwards. I was sitting on my box waiting for the plumber, who was from Kerry, to open up as he was trusted with the key. He was a real header. Me and him used to get up to some wild carry ons. Anyway, a white box van stopped directly across in front of me. The driver leaned out and started shouting at me "You're a bit early Paddy, haven't you got a bed to go to?" and then drove off before I had any time to react and him giving me the fingers as well.

I jumped up and away running flat out after the van but I hadn't a hope in hell of catching it so I turned back and me like a raging bull and sat down on my box again thinking of all the unsavoury things that I would have done if I caught the so and so. I must have been sitting down no more than ten minutes when the same buck appeared again shouting and giving me the fingers. I couldn't believe that he had the neck to do the same thing again and me being so stupid that I was caught on the hop for the second time. As he took off didn't I spot a brick behind one of the scaffold legs and I made a dive for it. As I did that wasn't there a postman walking away from a door after delivering mail and he saw me going for the brick and running in his direction. He thought I was going to murder him with it. If you saw the terrified expression on his face. He tried to jump out of the way, but instead jumped straight into my path with me crashing into him and going head over heels over the top of him with letters going in all directions. What a sight. As I got up again the van had stopped at traffic lights. As I came within striking distance the lights changed to green and he made off again. I fired the brick in his direction anyway, knowing that it would have been pure luck if I got it. I got something alright, the tail lights of a bus that I never even saw. I had to run like hell in the opposite direction passing both the plumber and the job going round a few side streets before returning to the job.

If it had have been the Olympics I would have got the gold medal no problem. When I told the plumber why I had to run past him at top speed, he had some laugh. I kept a small stockpile of ammunition hidden close to where I would sit in the morning just in case the driver intended to reappear, but I never saw him again after he had done his bit for his country.

Missing Underwear

Myself and the plumber were sitting drinking a cup of coffee in under the scaffold when this hot-looking lady walks past without noticing us. She was carrying a plastic bag, which she placed very discreetly inside a bin. The plumber says, "That was a wee bit suspicious looking. I think that could be worth checking out".

He wandered over to the bin looking a bit suspicious himself as he pretended to throw something in, and took the plastic bag out at the same time and over to where we sat for a closer inspection. The first thing that came out was an empty wine bottle, nothing exciting about that. But you could not say the same about the next item that was carefully removed and held up for close scrutiny, a nice sexy G-string. So that put our minds on overdrive. We checked for wear and tear with no evidence of anything untoward. We came to the conclusion that seeing that it was a very hot day, she had decided to go into work early on to take advantage of any slight breeze that might arise, or if she had to go the loo, it could be done in double quick time.

What we did next was to get a big sheet of eight by four ply, fixed it to the scaffold, tacked the offending item onto it, then in big letters wrote if the owner did not reclaim them within twenty-four hours they were then going to be auctioned off to the highest bidder. This was a very busy street and it was creating a lot of interest. The laughs we had were just non-stop. There was a pedestrian crossing beside the job so the traffic was constantly stopping. Then you would see people burst out laughing when they would spot our advertising board. I was standing out on the pavement having a look to see if there were any more additions that could be done to spice it up even more when this car pulled in beside me. It turned out to be a lady looking for directions so I was down on one knee trying to point her in the direction she wanted to go, but I was laughing that much she asked me in a posh voice what I was laughing at. I just pointed at our board, and she says, "Oh my God, what's that?" and I went into a fit of laughing. I looked over at the plumber and there was these two big bodybuilders the size of two dump trucks talking to him and he was in stitches laughing as well. "That's great," I thought "we're all having the giggles over some lady's missing underwear".

The two dump trucks went off up the street about their business. When I regained my composer, as the man says, I gave the lady proper directions and sent her off laughing as well. The plumber was still going into fits. "What did them two big boys say about the carry on?" I said. They thought I was laughing at them and were saying what they would do to me and me on my knees. I cannot bring myself to say what their intentions were but as luck would have it they were after leaving a gym just across the street that catered for a mostly gay clientele. So that was me off in a rage again and away up the road looking for the two of them, but not a trace could I see of them anywhere. What a stroke of luck that was for me when I think of it. They would have probably pulled the legs and arms off me first before stuffing me upside down in a bin.

The Foreman from Mayo

The foreman on the job was from Co. Mayo and a fairly stout boy he was too. I got on fine with him so that was a plus and the other thing was that he was a wild man for the ladies. Nothing wrong with that you might say. The thing was he would go from one end of the scales to the other in terms of looks and size. That could be explained by the mood he was in when he was out on the town. He could be the most vulgar and insulting man on the planet when it came to corresponding with the opposite sex. The other side of the coin then was that he could be the dressiest and most decent fellow any woman could possibly meet and would have no bother in charming even the most stubborn birds down off their perch.

I was down in the basement working when he comes down in a rush and says come on up here till you see what I'm after having a look at. There were only the three of us on the job so up the stairs we go to the top floor where there was a window looking out into the garden of the house that was backing on to ours. Their garden came right up to within two meters or so of our job. "Have a look out there," he says. Me and the plumber nearly jammed ourselves in the window to get a look at what was getting the foreman into such a sweat. There, with not a care in the world, was this lovely lady lying on a big towel wearing nothing but a pair of sunglasses. Her garden was surrounded by a high wall and a higher hedge, so this was the only spot that she could be seen from, and what a picturesque view. It was obvious that she did not know that there were prying eyes studying the plants and flowers in her garden.

The plumber threw a few small bits of plaster into the hedge to try and get her up, which didn't work too well as she had a radio with a bit of music going He threw a big lump into the hedge that would wake someone up from being in a coma. She turned the music off, got up, strolled around the garden peering through the hedge in a few places and lay down again. I think she must have copped on because we were killing ourselves laughing. She would have to be deaf not to hear it. She got up shortly afterwards and went inside so we went back to our work.

A few hours later the foreman had gone off to get a few bags of bonding for me. Me and the plumber were sitting having our tea on the pavement and commenting on nearly everyone that passed, when a woman stopped and asked if she could have a look around. We both jumped up at the same time to show her around with me getting the upper hand because I was a good bit taller than him, so I sort of smothered him out of it, giving him the fingers in the process, without her seeing of course. I showed her all around. She told me she intended doing some work on her house and would be interested in getting a price. She also said that she was a film producer and was off to South Africa at the weekend to concentrate on some films that she was working on. We made our way upstairs looking and commenting on the work in each room until we got to the top room, which took in the whole floor. It had an en suite. Well this is very nice she said as she looked out the window that we had been stuck in earlier in the day and pointed her finger. That's my house there with the nice garden. There I was caught hook, line and sinker. This was the naked woman that we were having the grand view of earlier and she was letting me know that she was well aware of where the laughing and the chips in the hedge came from. I'd say my face was as red as a fire brigade. She had a very contented smile, just like winning a game of cards, that went back to her two ears as she made her way back down, telling me that she would be in touch as soon as she got back from her trip to South Africa. I'd say she would have some laugh to herself as soon as she went around the corner, and there was us thinking we were being cute. She was after letting us know in a very simple but nice way, you had your fun don't push your luck. She was one cool operator.

Looking at things from a happy sort of an angle, we were doing well enough, a comfortable lifestyle, going out to different night-clubs on a fairly regular basis, an active social life you could say, that everyone should make the most of without going silly or turning into a right blooming clouster in the process. Life is short enough, looking back, and if you still had a few pounds for the odd feed at the restaurant, not forgetting a well-deserved holiday now and again, you'd be doing grand.

Speaking of which, we had one booked in eighty-two when Donegal won the All-Ireland, so there was a choice to be made. It was going to be the football or the holiday. It was a bit sickening for me because as far as I could make out, every Donegal person in London was heading for Croke Park and I was heading for Greece. But sure what more could a man want, you would think, than sun, sand, sea and sunburn.

I remember us lying on a very crowded beach and me completely ignoring all the tanned, topless talent, with only one thing occupying my thoughts. How did the game go? Next thing I see is this fellow making his way through the bodies wearing a tee that said Donegal All-Ireland Champions. I shouted to him and he made his way towards me telling me the good news, he was at the game and left as soon as it was over, which was only a few hours previous, and flew out here. His girlfriend worked in the travel industry, which was why he had everything fall into place so easily. He was from Gaoth Dobhair.

A Birthday Dinner

One night I took herself out to this restaurant for a bite to eat as it was her birthday. I had spotted this big castle-type building with turrets sticking up on the corners when I'd be on my way to and from work at top end of Highgate Hill. It looked like a nice restaurant and always seemed to be fairly busy. I booked it over the phone. It was a Saturday evening, and we made our way in where we were seated, had our meal, which was very nice, and everything seemed to be grand. But the restaurant itself was very quiet. This did not add up at all because there were lots of cars parked along the road as well as the car park itself. It was dark when we came out, apart from the streetlight. We made our way around to where the car was at the back, started the car and switched on the headlights. Well you would not believe it. There were men running in all directions through the trees. I switched the lights off again and says, "Did you see what I just saw?" She started to laugh and said, "Was that rabbits?". I waited a few minutes before turning the lights on again and by God she wasn't far wrong when she asked was it rabbits?

They certainly seemed to be doing what rabbits generally do, going from burrow to burrow. I had to close up her jaw because it was hanging open. I can only describe it as a free-for-all. Groups huddled here, men running there, some hiding behind trees; it was a sight to behold is the only way I could describe it. It was a bit like a rugby match in the dark. It all started to dawn on me then why cars were parked all over the place. It was beside Hampstead Heath, which is well known for its homosexual after-dusk capers.

Speaking of restaurants, we were in this joint in Leicester Square one night when who do I see sitting a few tables across from us but Gerry Fitt, who I would assume was in the company of some Tory party chums. This was shortly after he was awarded the title of Lord Fitt. It was a decision that irked a lot of people, me included. So when I saw him going to the gents I decided to pay a visit too. It was a chance to deliver my message in person. I do not know whether the man had a stutter or whether he developed one there and then. I relayed my displeasure to him, clearly stating that accepting such a title after him being involved in civil rights marches and so on was something to be ashamed of. While not intentionally wanting to spoil his meal or the fun he was having with his Hooray Henry pals, I wished him all the best in the future with his new-found friends and made my way back to my table, feeling contented with myself for how I had managed to convey my message of discontent in the best Queen's English I could muster.

A Derry Baby

The next natural step for us to be thinking about was babies. So when the boss in the house (wife) decided the time was right to go down that road, me being me it had to be an Irish baby. So Tara was eventually born in Derry, an eye opener for any man I can tell you, but the best wee bundle that anyone could ask for. The first squawk that came out of her sounded like Fr Jack shouting "Drink! drink!" in an episode of Father Ted, except that it was "Books! books!" It turned out after the nappy stage it was books instead of a dummy, moving on then it was books instead of a pillow, books at breakfast, books at bedtime and it's still books, except that they are now the thickness of a concrete block and just as heavy. Not to worry though, she is able to rattle out any amount of tunes on the fiddle, or to them posh hoity-toity ones with the noses turned to the heavens I think you would say "playing the violin". We stayed at home for a year so that I could do a little bit of work to the house. I got most of what I wanted to do concerning changes and repairs done but there was slightly more work than I had anticipated for the time I had allotted to do it, so the finishing touches were put on hold for a while.

An Old Vauxhall Cavalier

I had an old Vauxhall Cavalier diesel to do me for the time I was at home. If the truth be told it was a good enough car that had been well looked after by the previous owners but there was one problem that I could not get sorted out anywhere after trying all the bloody garages in the place. It was something to do with dodgy electronics. The car had a habit of conking out when you needed it most.

One day I was picking up a wheel from this other man who did a bit of repair work and I mentioned it to him while he was in underneath this brand new car with a lump hammer giving it lilty. He came out and smiled when he saw me looking at the big lump hammer. "Every man should have one of these," he said with a laugh and the fag sticking out the side of his mouth. He walked over to an old scrapped car, lifted the bonnet and came out with a condenser box, and then he took one out of my car and when he tried to stick it in, it wouldn't fit because it had a few extra terminals on it.

Normally if a thing didn't fit that was it, but what did he do? He broke off the few extra ones and said, "That should do the trick," and stuck it in to where it was supposed to go and believe it or not my car never let me down again.

Another funny thing happened to me with that same car. One day the boss (wife) in the house sends me to the town for a bit of shopping. I got parked nicely outside the shop and went in, got what I was told to get, and put two bags of shopping into the back seat of the car. I saw someone else I knew across the street and went over for a chat. After we finished our bit of scandalizing just like two old women, I went off home. I went to take my shopping out but there was nothing to take out. I looked and I searched but no shopping was to be found. Well I scratched my head and cursed the thief up and down that had stolen my shopping when I had gone across the street for the chat. That was the only chance anyone would have got to do it I thought.

Anne Marie was putting doubts in my head when she'd say maybe you left it on the boot or in the shop. But I remembered quite clearly leaving it on the back seat. So I went the whole way back to the shop just to please her. I went in anyway and said to Eddie, the manager "You didn't happen to see a couple of bags of groceries walking around?" trying to be funny. He burst out laughing and said a woman came into the shop with two bags of shopping that she had found in the back of her car. I did not know whether to laugh with Eddie at myself, or cringe with embarrassment. I think I did both. If it was a drunk man that did it at least he would have the drink as an excuse, but me I had none apart from this, that it was the same car and the same color so it could even happen to you.

Going Back to London

When we eventually went back to London, it was very hard to settle in. You just had no freedom. Before I ever left home, I could not wait to get away from the depressing monotony of the turf, the potatoes, the milking, boiling corn for feeding cows that were in calf, cutting cabbages and chopping turnips on frosty mornings or evenings for feeding, cleaning out the cow dung from the byres, putting molasses on hay and straw to give the animals a boost during winter time when they were being kept inside, and looking at the same hills, the same fields, the same people.

But it's only when you are away stuck in an unfriendly city that you realise what you had at home and why you are now missing what you disliked about it in the first place. You can take the man out of the hills, but you can't take the hills out of the man. We weren't back in London that long when we were driving around the North Circular, a road similar to the M50 around Dublin. There were three lanes but because of road works they were all moving at much the same stop/start speed. I was in the outside lane driving a scrappy little red Mini Metro. I'm always checking in my rear view mirrors so I noticed this car right up nearly touching my bumper. But I thought to myself, there is no point in me going to all the hassle of moving lanes just to let him past 'cos he's going nowhere in a hurry anyway.

After driving for another hundred yards or so. I noticed the car behind moved into the middle lane and came up alongside my passenger side. Anne Marie had the window down because it was hot and stuffy with Tara in the back, she needed a bit of air (not fresh). Your man started giving the fingers and all sorts of signs, then pulled forward and pulled in front of me, whacking the wing of our car and nearly knocking Tara out of her seat in the process. I started blowing the horn so he started to stand on the brakes to try and get me to run into him. He wasn't going to get away; I was raging at this stage and was going to stick to him like shit to a blanket.

Eventually he pulled across the lanes onto the verge over and jumped out, I was out a bit quicker and got to his car where he was shouting and threatening me because there was a dirty score on his car and nothing on mine. He was a West Indian man minus the dreadlocks. He got some shock when he felt my fist connecting with the side of his jaw and went head over heels over the boot lid of his car. He was like a cat landing on his feet. That was the one and only shot I got at him. Because as I made the second tear at him he took off like Linford Christie sprinting at the Olympics, around and around the car after him (not sure if it was me after him, or him after me). I kept telling him the whole time what I was going to do with him when I caught him. A bit of reverse psychology is always good in situations like this. It ended in a stalemate with me on one side of the car and him on the other. He drove off after a while because he knew he wasn't going to get anything off me and likewise I hadn't a hope in hell of getting anything off him, or so he thought. When he drove off what did I spot on the grass only a nice expensive watch, which was some consolation for messing up the day.

Joe and Theresa (brother and sister) were still in the house keeping a good place open for us when we decided to go back to living as city dwellers to earn another few pounds. Joe told us he was watching TV in the sitting room one evening after coming home from work when he got up to go and make a cup of tea, because there was a good film about to start and he wanted to watch it. Just as he was going out through the door the whole ceiling fell down, in one huge slab. We had taken down the same old lath and plaster ceilings on some jobs that we had done for people before and it is one of the dirtiest, filthiest jobs that you could wish to do. Pure black dust that's so fine it spreads right through the whole place, so you can just picture the bloody mess in the house after that. It puts into perspective the cost that's involved in owning a house rather than renting.

Brand New Chimneys

It reminded me of one we did for a lady in Camden town, who was a clothes designer by trade, and some well known actresses and stars of the stage were among her customers. That's what we heard through the grapevine. Initially she had wanted two chimneys re-plastered. Looking up at them from the ground it looked like the plaster was all falling off so we worked out a price to repair them. Then she showed us this small bedroom, where part of the ceiling was ready to fall down, so the best thing to do in that situation was to pull the lot down. So another price for that. We had it worked out that it would take about a week to give us enough time to compensate for any unforeseen problems.

The price was not a problem. She gave us a key to let ourselves in. We had scaffolding erected, etc., but when we went up to have a closer look at the chimneys the plaster work was in perfect condition; it was just paint peeling off, so we gave it a good scraping, then mixed up some strong cement and water and painted both of them. Half an hour's work and hey presto – two brand new chimneys and it wasn't 10am yet.

If it was now we could have featured on some of those cowboy builders being exposed programs that you see on TV. We had the ceiling down, new plasterboard skimmed and all tidied up by four-thirty. It was a week later before we got paid but she was delighted with the whole job, apart from the fact that she withheld twenty pounds for dry cleaning because in the rush to get finished we forgot to tape up around a wardrobe that was full of clothes. Silly mistake on our part. If you got four or five jobs like that you could take the rest of the year off.

Renovating Old Houses

We rented a flat off an older English couple. In fact she was from Ukraine. They had met while both working in South Africa. She was a doctor and he worked as an engineer. When they returned home to England he had started to renovate old houses, so it was a stroke of good luck for me when he found out that I was a plasterer. He asked me to go and price a big job that he was about to start. When we went to look at the job, it was a four-story terraced building still full of furniture and all the knick-knacks associated with years of hoarding. No doubt they had plenty of cash stashed away as the man says. I ended up doing all his plastering work for him after that. He was very tight with his prices, but you had to play him at his own game. A bit of reverse psychology, give him a good high price and then let him haggle you down a bit to where he thought he had one up on you. Then that was both of us happy as Larry.

He was getting a fair lump of it back again in rent anyway so he could not complain too much about having his bread buttered on both sides if you want to put it like that. He brought me to have a look at this other job that he was thinking of doing, a complete renovation, to get a second opinion. It was a large building with about ten large apartments in it and was lying unoccupied for some time. He had the keys so in we go. It was his first time to see the inside as well. It was a bit weird because whoever had lived in some of them had seemingly just walked out the door, leaving everything behind them. Of course I started scrounging around. I found pictures that were obviously taken in the apartment by the then occupants who, judging by their appearance, were in their twenties and proved to be very easy to look at, the ladies that is, until some of them showed them injecting each other with what had all the hallmarks of heroin. I immediately dropped everything that I had picked up earlier with the full intention of taking home with me, once I had focused my mind on what must have been going on. It was only then that I started to really see what was lying around, needles and all sorts of drug paraphernalia lay strewn around the place.

All I could think about at that minute was how to get out without tripping over something and sticking a dirty infected needle in myself. Both of us got out as swiftly as possible, and I didn't set foot in it again until it was completely gutted and all ready for plastering. When I got home I gave myself some scrubbing I can tell you, just in case a bug of some sort saw a good opportunity for a bite and hopped onto me. Mike got some house clearance crowd to clean the place out. I worked for a further two years before deciding to return home for good.

John in London

John (my brother) had damaged his back through his work as a roofer and come over to London for an operation on his back. While waiting for this to take place he did a bit of door work through some friends of ours to pass the time. We were sitting in the sitting room one evening and John had a very bad dose of the flu coming on so was wondering what he could take for a cure. Someone says a hot whiskey, so off out he goes and buys a bottle.

Anyway we heard him coming in and going into the kitchen. After a few minutes he sticks his head in the door and asks "How hot does it have to be?" "God," I thought, "that's a funny question". Something made me jump up and out to the kitchen. Didn't he have the whiskey poured into a saucepan and it starting to bubble on the gas. Jesus, what a fright!! He could have burned the bloody house down. I turned it off as quick as I could. He would have been as well to put petrol in the saucepan.

After getting over the shock of how a hot whiskey should really be made, he drank the lot, and started talking non-stop until he slid off the seat and we carried him into his room and left him lying on the bed. It did not cure the flu, but I don't think he ever drank whiskey again.

I knew it was time to head for the green grass of home and leave negative equity and all that went with it for the British exchequer to sort out. There was just too much marmalade on the whole damn mortgage carry on for me to get my head around. I wanted to be where people knew one another and spoke to one another. I was tired of the blank stare and the never-ending rush. At the end of the day there is no place like home.

Part IV – Back in Ireland

A Russian Story

This is another story that I have to tell, possibly at the expense of some of my own gallivanting around the place, but in my opinion it was too interesting to leave out. It took me quite a while to extract all this information. I felt like a dentist at times to be honest; there was this inbuilt iron curtain secrecy to contend with. It sounds simple, but it was far from it as I was doing this without anyone realising what I was up to; ask a few questions today, let another day or two go past, and ask some more. After I had put it all together and told them what I had done they were surprised but excited that anyone would be interested in their lives enough to write a story about it, and they gave me their blessing.

17th Feb 2001. Three men, Ivan, married with two daughters, was a former medical director of a five-hundred-plus-bed hospital who spent upwards on five years in the Russian army, where he first gained his experience in the medical profession; Victor, also married with two children, a boy and a girl, who worked in a technical unit in a space station in Kazakhstan and also owned a small pub; and Iurii, a former soldier who worked in an orthopaedic hospital as a doctor was also married with one boy and one girl.

All three were friends for many years. They would have long discussions planning on what steps they could take to try to better their lives, and more importantly the lives of their families. They held many barbeques in the local forest during the summer months. Normally this was a get-together, or booze up for the husbands or the men folk of the village. After all it was a very male-dominated society, as were most of the eastern block countries before the breakdown of the Soviet Union. The forests were full of wild pigs so they'd go out and shoot a wild boar or two, which would then be spit-roasted. The wives made the homemade bread nice and fresh nice in ovens that were specially made for this use only. Then there was the matter of strong vodka that they had brewed themselves, a lethal concoction similar to very good poiteen that's made here. And as those in the know know, poiteen has to go through the still three times to get the real deal.

Most learned the tricks of the trade while serving in the army. It was a very macho environment and it was compulsory to serve a minimum of two years or so. If you got out of it for some reason or another, women would not look on it very favourably because it could only mean two things!! You suffered from an illness or you were gay. The latter was a complete no no. They would steal barley and yeast from the barracks where they had their own bakery so they had no problem in that regard. They would have a crude still set up that could be dismantled fairly quickly, just in case any of the officers came along and caught them in the act. It would mean a week in solitary confinement if caught, unless you could bribe your way out of it, so naturally a good watch would be kept while the whole operation was in progress. I'm not altogether sure how they disguised the smell, because if it's anything like the smell of poiteen being made, it's a foul enough stink. I was in close vicinity to one years ago that was functioning at full capacity. The person in charge looked like they were baptized in a tub of the stuff and it was that strong you would smell it a mile away. That caper was all very well, but a safe place had to be got to store it as well. You would never guess even if your life depended on it where the hiding place was. Right under the noses of their superiors.

The fire extinguishers were situated at different points throughout the barracks. One strategically placed here and there that had been opened up and cleaned out all ready for the big pour. You couldn't beat that with a big stick.

They eventually decided that enough was enough, they had heard too many stories of the freedom people had in the west. The men decided to pack their bags, leaving their homes in Moldova, a small country in Eastern Europe, to try and find work and maybe a better life in England, or so they thought. It did not turn out quite as they had planned, but they had no regrets.

This is part of their story intermingling with our adventures and where our paths cross, at least what and where I remember. The time had arrived for them to depart. It was 9 pm. There was ice and the snow was about three feet deep and the wind so sharp it could cut straight through you. We never really get a taste of the bitter cold that you get in Eastern Europe. They described the sky as being full of stars, something that we do not see much of any more because of light pollution. It was a very emotional scene, and also an exiting opportunity for those concerned; children, mothers, fathers were all in tears wishing them well as they said their goodbyes. Really it was a trip into the unknown for all concerned.

They left for the capital Kishinev by truck. Once there they had to catch a train to St Petersburg, 700 miles north of Moscow, a long, cold journey. They had to go through the Ukraine and Belarus before reaching St. Petersburg, where they boarded another train to Russian territory called Kaliningrad. This train travelled through Latvia and Lithuania, where following instructions they were to get off. While waiting with a mixture of anticipation and anxiety for the train at St. Petersburg station, they were met by a member of the Russian Mafia at a pre-arranged spot, who provided them with Latvian passports and documentation in exchange for a sum of money, which was quiet a substantial amount in Russian terms at that time.

Once on the train, you had no choice but to stay on. You were not able to leave because you were traveling from one Russian city to another, which meant the doors stayed locked. The reason being you had to travel through independent states like Latvia or Lithuania. But there is a price on everything when corruption is rife (The brown envelope was not invented here in Ireland). By once again giving the guard who was minding the doors a hefty bribe, they were let off in Vilnius, the capital of Lithuania. The reason for getting off in Vilnius was the fact that they were told the customs would not scrutinise the Latvian passport too closely, but luck was not going to be so free flowing. Iurii was given away by his nerves as his hands started to shake whilst handing his passport to the customs officer. "This is not your passport," the customs officer said, eying him coldly. Both Ivan and Victor knew that something wasn't right because they could see the customs officer scrutinising his passport as they checked through with theirs. Once they came through the customs check, they had to climb a long flight of stairs, at the top of which was a foot bridge, where they had a good vantage point as they stopped to look back to see their friend being led roughly away.

As it happens, when Iurii handed his passport to the officer, the officer ran it though the computer and the person named on the passport was being hunted by Interpol, so all the protesting he did from there on did not do him any good. He even showed them his genuine passport that he had hidden in the lining of his heavy jacket but the immigration officers did not know at that stage which one was genuine and which one was false. It had been discussed between them before they had set out on their journey; that if one or more got caught the others would carry on regardless, and so they stuck to this agreement.

The Lithuanian custom officials could not be bribed as easily as the Russian or Moldavian officers could, as they earned a lot more money than their counterparts. Meanwhile Ivan and Victor made their way to a travel agent to purchase flights to London via Dublin. Getting tickets did not turn out to be an easy affair either as both of them were only carrying US dollars, which to Russians were like gold dust. The travel agent would only accept Lithuanian currency. This was around 8am and they now had to find a bank in which to change their money. This took a considerable amount of time. They were never told that there might be a problem about exchanging currency. They assumed that the dollar would take them the whole way. They eventually managed to get their tickets, after a bit of a debate that was nearly turning into an argument. They had a choice, either to go via Copenhagen that day and pay 500 dollars, or wait and go the following day for 400 dollars, so they opted for the cheaper option. This meant there was plenty of time to take stock of things and find out what the next step would be. The airport was half an hour away by bus, so they looked around and got directions to where they would catch the next one. On their arrival Victor's nerves started to give him bother so he took to drinking whiskey and espresso out of fear of getting caught. The stress of the whole situation led to him drinking a full bottle of whiskey to try and calm his nerves, after which he was still stone cold sober.

It was a long wait until their flight at 5am the following day. There weren't any problems on boarding or disembarking. Once in Copenhagen they had another two-hour wait for their flights to Dublin, where they observed their fellow travelers. One difference they did notice was a lot of these passengers were very attractive young women. Each one had the potential to be a supermodel, who, they later informed me, would most likely be involved in the sex trade. Where, they did not know. Thankfully for them there were no problems at Dublin airport either. No real scrutiny apart from one little scare. They had got friendly with a Latvian man on the flight. The three had been walking together approaching the arrivals desk where you had to show your passport as you walked past when they heard the shout. Your man beckoning to come back. All three went back and the officer took the passport of the genuine Latvian and gave him a telling off because his was a bit grubby looking, reached for Victor's and said, "This is a real passport," meaning new and clean (Unbeknownst to him the grubby one was the real one and the nice shiny new ones were fake). They just followed the crowd and eventually managed to get on the airport express and were relived to be going in the direction of the city and were dropped off at O'Connell Street at around 11pm.

They remember the date well, it was the 23rd of February. The rain was coming down in bucketfuls, which did not make any part of O' Connell Street look very inviting. Worse still, they did not know where to go. One of the things that stuck in their minds as the plane was coming in over Dublin was the amazing sight of Dublin city. It was a mass of lights. Back home they only had electricity for two hours per day, sometimes in the morning and sometimes at night. There was always panic when the power came on, children trying to do their homework, adults trying to do housework; you had to make the most of the little time that was available. You just had to be content and accept what you were able to get done at home or at work. This was a fact of life in most of the Eastern European countries that were just emerging from the shackles of communism, but things were rapidly changing.

They had in their possession a telephone number which they were given for a man in London who they managed to ring before leaving the airport and he gave them a contact number in the city centre. A man who worked in a restaurant near Trinity College but would not finish up until 1am. When they did manage to find a phone that wasn't vandalised, they arranged to meet him after he finished work, where he then brought them to his digs. This was where they were to stay until such time as they received word from the man in London, who was to arrange work and digs for them there.

In the meantime their sleeping arrangements were basic to say the least as they had to sleep on the floor on any space they could find. That alone would prove difficult enough under the circumstances as they were not the only ones needing somewhere to get their heads down. Approximately seven people were sleeping in one room. They were there for almost a week when some unwelcome news arrived. The man in London had got caught and was deported by British immigration officers; seemingly his dodgy documentation did not stand up to careful scrutiny, so now the pressure was on.

At this stage they had no choice but to forget about London and try their luck in Dublin. Over the next three months while they stayed there, as you can imagine, the tempers would flare now and again. But as always in situations like this, there were bound to be funny moments that you would never forget after having been told. I saw myself, for example, sitting on a train thinking of some of these extraordinary stories that they had told me and smiling at the same time, whilst the person sitting across from me would be thinking to themselves "God that poor man, he must have got a bad knock on the head at some stage to end up in a state like that".

One night in the digs, one fellow who happened to be working night shifts in a cinema came home drunk as a skunk and had to step over Ivan to get to his spot on the floor, which he managed. Ivan, who sported a big beard and looked like a member of the Taliban, who when he laughed would bust your eardrums if you didn't hold your hands over them, was over six foot two, strong as a horse and built like a Russian tank. Ivan woke up in the early hours to find that he was wet all over his chest and down his side. He soon realised what happened and in a rage hit your man next to him who was asleep, snoring and talking to himself, a savage dig with his elbow nearly dismantling his ribcage in the process. This man let out a big groan, same as if you had just squeezed an overfed puppy, turned over then and began peeing on the man on the other side as well, who when he realised what was happening also gave him a hiding. That's what life was like in these types of situations, you had to take a chance now and again and hope for the best.

It was very hard trying to get work because of the language barrier. Victor was the first to break the mould and get a bit of part-time work, washing dishes in a restaurant for which he was paid £25. Victor always, without fail, had a roll-up hanging from his lips when you went into a room where he was working. It was like going into a tobacco factory in Havana. Anyway, odd jobs like this, while in no way making anyone rich, kept them going for the time being until whatever few pounds they had was slowly starting to disappear as the outflow was more than what was coming in. It was at crisis point when all they had between them was £27. They had return tickets from Dublin to Vilnius in Lithuania. Others told them that if they took them to the travel agents they would get a refund, but when they went to a travel agent they were told to go to the airport, so they got the airbus at O'Connell Street which cost them £4 for a single fare. They bought four singles not realising that you could get returns for £6, which left them with very little left over. They were counting on the refund and hoped they would get around £150 or £200 each. They got a right shock when they were told they could only get a refund at the airport where they purchased the tickets back in Vilnius. They had £11.80 between them now, so things weren't looking too bright. Just not enough to pay for their tickets back to the city centre.

They decided that the best thing to do would be to walk around in different directions, through the cafes and shops within the airport and see if they could find some money that may have been dropped accidentally at ticket or maybe cigarette machines. They spent hours at this when Ivan, who was as thrifty as you could get with money, finally owned up that he still had £50 in his pockets. They were annoyed that he had done this but glad at the same time. They got back to their cramped lodgings and spent every day out walking the streets looking for work. Finally Victor and Ivan got a job with a man from Galway who ran a small building firm. He looked after them, even giving them some money up front. He gave them plenty of work and paid them well; this lasted for about four months. He at this stage decided to move back home and even offered them plenty of work in Galway as well but they decided to stay where they were as they now felt more comfortable in their surroundings and thought the city was the best option for them.

They had learned a lot of the basics fairly quickly about the building trade in that short time and started doing small jobs like moving partitions, garden walls, or changing a window here and there, while all the time learning how to do things as they should, or were supposed to be done. Shortly after this they were able to move out and get better lodgings in Donnybrook, where the two of them shared a big room. Things were looking up, but at the same time they had to be on their toes. They had a few close calls with immigration; this was one of the reasons for them moving to a place where they felt that bit safer.

A couple of days after moving into their new lodgings they saw a builder's van parked outside a house just down the road from them. It had writing on the side. The only word they could understand was 'construction', so they knocked on the door of the house and asked for the boss, who was off on one of his weekly or monthly round-the-world trips. He had that much air miles up he could or should have had his own 747. As he is a qualified pilot anyway, no problem. They were told to write down the telephone number off the side of the van and to ring and speak to the boss, which they did, and the result of that was they were starting work the following week on a building site in a very nice area on the Southside, Blackrock.

They hurried back to the house, got the local travel map out, and studied it carefully until they had figured out how and what bus or mode of transport they had to use to get there. Preparing for the following Monday they did a trial run so they would not get lost on their first day on their new job. Work started around 8am but they must have been there at least an hour before we landed on the site. This was where I first came into contact with these men. Victor told me months afterwards they were amazed when the boss, nicknamed 'the Slapper' (how he acquired this can be left to the imagination) greeted them with a handshake. Each one kept calling him 'Boss'. He turned around and said, "Don't ever call me boss again," offered them tea or coffee, went off and made it the way that we would be accustomed to making it. They seemed to be expecting some sort of godfather gangster-type wearing a three piece suit who wouldn't waste any time talking to them, but instead it was the opposite. He looked like he was dragged up and down the chimney a few times with a cigarette stuck sideways in his mouth and one eye half-closed because of the smoke drifting upwards. Never judge the book by the cover is something else they learned.

A few months afterwards they showed me how they were used to making coffee. This was the first time in my life to see some-one drink coffee made just like treacle. They'd just grab the jar of coffee and shake nearly half into a cup and then nearly the same amount of sugar, add a little boiling water, and there you have it, pure poisonous treacle. You could turn the cup upside down and it wouldn't come out.

The Russians Become Legal

Iurii, one of the Russians who got caught at customs, spent a few months in prison before he was sent back home, but he tried his luck again and this time he succeeded in reaching his goal without any mishaps or nervous moments. We will have to take his word for it. Unfortunately he did not settle here and moved on to the Czech Republic, in the former Yugoslavia, so that he could be closer to his family.

Under advice and guidance from the boss, who had very little time for illegalities, it was insisted that Ivan and Victor had to return home the following week after starting work with the company, to apply for work permits legally. Not alone that, the boss flew over to Moldova to make sure that the proper procedure was followed through. That was an experience in itself. The plane was a draughty rust bucket and there were potholes on the runway resembling some of the roads in Donegal. Victor brought him to his pub but it wasn't like your pub here. No niceties. The toilet was in the garden as the boss soon found out when he had to do a quick visit. It was a small hut and when he opened the door he nearly got knocked over by swarm of bluebottles. It was a big hole in the ground and it nearly full to the lip with the content of the customers' bowels. There was a knack to this caper. You had to reverse in, hunker down and hold on to the door frame for dear life in case you landed in more shit than you were trying your best to get rid off. It was minus a light or toilet paper; that's unless you carried your own personal supply with you, a sort of a Wild West scenario.

Everything had a price. You could buy anything from a handgun to a tank, or go and arrange a visit to a dentist and get a complete Hollywood-style overhaul and be left with a set of beautiful gleaming white teeth that would cost no more than filling a tank of petrol.

The reason for venturing out there in the first place was the fact that these men had turned out to be experienced stonemasons, and stonemasons in Dublin at that time were like gold dust, not to be found high or low. Victor's brother Dima (who had the same habit of the roll-up hanging from his mouth) followed his footsteps to Dublin shortly afterwards. He was a lorry driver who travelled mainly throughout Siberia. He had some tales of hardship to tell. He told me of many times he met lorry drivers who had lost fingers and toes with frostbite. The Russian lorries at that time were draughty and without heaters and the work was extremely dangerous. There were highway robbers everywhere. Drivers were often killed because they did not hand over the keys of the lorry, which was their livelihood.

There was an instance when Dima took a wrong turning and had gone a long distance before he realised his mistake. You could travel for most of the day or night without seeing anyone but on this occasion luck was on his side when he came on a roadside shop. You could eat, drink, buy or sell about anything that you could think of. He asked two men outside for directions. They told him to keep on the road he was on and that it would bring him to where he wanted to go. He set off happy enough.

He had travelled a good few miles when he noticed that the road was beginning to get rougher. He had also noticed the presence of a car following him. It soon dawned on him that it was the same men who had given him directions. He was beginning to panic when he came to an area that was used by lumberjacks to let down their felled trees so he never took his foot off the throttle. He just swung the lorry and it bounced around. He still does not know why it did not overturn and he just drove at the car and ploughed it in off the road and kept going. His wing mirror went in bits. He thought it hit off a branch or something. It was a good few hours before he stopped for a wee. When he had finished he checked around to see if everything was still safe. He had no back lights. They had been shot off and the back door was full of bullet holes. It was the last time he stopped to ask anyone for directions.

All's well they are now able to travel back and forth as many times as they like to visit family and friends, if they feel the need for it. This makes it a more pleasurable experience for all concerned, living and working legally and all above board, no need for watching over your shoulder. Victor's wife, son and daughter are here now. The daughter is top of her class at school and learning to play the fiddle. The son got a start with another construction firm, while Jena does occasional work as a housekeeper for people who need their house looked after when they go off on holidays. Back home she worked as a fully trained anaesthetist. Dima's wife and daughter are now also settled here. Each one fully intending to return home when they saved enough money; that was their stated aim.

Moving House with Victor

Victor and his family had moved into a house just up the road from Tony the boss's house. He asked me if I would give him a hand with a delivery to his house the following morning. Next morning I was at his house around 7.30, but we were standing around for half an hour before we got a phone call that the delivery van was on its way with a three piece suite. The traffic was very heavy, but we saw the van coming over the top of the hill towards us. Victor started to wave at them to show where we were and he had kept a parking spot directly outside the house. A man approached me asking me where he was going to park. I assumed he was a helper accompanying the van driver so I indicated to where Victor was standing. But he kept repeating that he lived on the other side of the hill and that he was in a hurry because he had to take his daughter to school.

"That's fine," I said, "We're right outside the door so it will only take a few minutes". But this had a negative effect on him as he raised his voice and kept repeating that he didn't have any time left. By this stage I was in the process of helping get a seat out of the van and I was losing my patience so I told him to f**k off. He went into a rant that he was going up to his house and he would be back in a few minutes to sort me out.

The van driver and Victor were looking at each other not having a clue what was going on. I wasn't sure myself to tell the God's honest truth. I had a measuring tape and money in my pocket so I took it out and handed the lot to Victor. Then turned to your man and said to him that there was a nice grassy garden in behind the wall of the park on the other side of the road. We'd settle our differences in there. But that wasn't suiting his plans either and he headed off in the direction of where he lived, and him cursing and swearing at me the whole time. The comical thing was that it turned out to be a whole crazy misunderstanding. He was actually waiting for a delivery from the same shop around the same time, saw the van and was trying to direct it to his house and could not understand why none of us were paying any heed to him. So it really got to him thinking we were treating him as a lunatic, and there I was expecting him to give us a hand. I waited around for a fair while for him to come back but he never showed up, which was all the better I suppose.

The Slapper

'The Slapper' was no ordinary boss, a self-made millionaire, due in part to having more than his fair share of brain cells and to the birth of the Celtic Tiger, who headed off to London when he was barely out of his nappies; sixteen to be exact. The funny thing is he used to mix big buckets of plaster for me and another plasterer Pat Kelly from Monaghan. Pat was very careful with his money. It was like extracting teeth when it came to paying; he just did not like parting with it. But he was one of the most generous men and the complete opposite to being as tight as a duck's ass when out on the town. Pat would not hear of you putting your hand next or near your pocket

That was when we were doing our stint on the building sites across the water. That was a fair few years ago now. The boss was in no way mean in how he treated his employees. We all shared in the spoils, some more than others I would suspect, because when you're taking a piece of the cake its difficult to resist the temptation of going for the bigger piece. That's how these things work once there is a pecking order in place.

The Downside to Wealth

I feel that I must also give a rundown of my thoughts on an issue that has done a lot of untold damage to people who keep pushing the barriers and are never happy with what they have. That can be said about a fair chunk of society. There is always a downside as well as an upside to wealth, however it is acquired, whether it's winning the lotto or just having that golden touch, which sad to say evades most of us. If this money is not handled with the care it deserves, it can prove to be a hindrance rather than a luxury. How to distinguish between a friend and an acquaintance can be difficult in these sorts of circumstances. A friend will say no when it needs to be said, whereas an acquaintance will generally agree with everything you say if there is a chance of it benefiting them there and then, or along the way. There are those who have been reckless when the pockets were full, who may well be down but not out by any means and given half an opportunity will bounce back again

There is a hidden underbelly that corrupts in many ways as it stretches right across all parts of the island. No one is immune to it at this stage, where the small but important things get left behind and are replaced by a more valueless society. This is spurred on by the relentless goals of the immoral drug barons down to the nasty street corner pusher who targets vulnerable young school goers who were spoiled and given money and all the latest gadgets in place of parental control and direction. This leaves schoolchildren and the venues they frequent a target for those who wish to corrupt to satisfy their own goals.

There have been some nasty stains left by the greed-engrossed rush of the Celtic Tiger that will take a long time to remove. It's responsible for spawning a generation of fast food junkies, or the guard turning a blind eye to certain activities, or a politician who accepted brown envelopes stuffed with cash or the Rolex-wearing developer who provided the envelopes stuffed with bricks. A 'brick' is Celtic Tiger slang word used mainly by jumped-up developer-speculators on the golf course or partying. A brick meant a thousand in cash, which was considered loose change.

We have been left with plenty of court cases and tribunals as proof of what was really going on behind the scenes. Just like winning the lotto, money can without doubt change a normal down-to-earth person into acting in much the same way as the spoiled Beverly Hills elite. And worse, lead to temptations out there that are unlimited, and in the most excessive of these cases, glorifying and partaking in all forms of drug taking. Like low hanging fruit it is easily accessed.

It is well documented fact that some extremely intelligent people, especially those in the public eye deemed as celebrities by a gossip and scandal-mad media are as likely, if not more, to succumb to addictions as anyone else. There is no monopoly on what walk of life drug users come from. They chose of their own free will to indulge in this detestable pastime, if you want to describe it as such, and to say that it annoyed me or gave me the shivers to see this going on would be an understatement. To watch a person snuff large quantities of white powder of whatever description up their noses; if you threw a white sock down in front of some they wouldn't notice the difference as they'd try and snuff that up their noses as well. These type of circles camouflage an awful lot of falseness. Greeting each other like the best friends in the world, while in reality many would not know how to tell the difference between friends or acquaintances, the latter being the appropriate term in most cases, as it's a well known fact that you go through life with no more real friends than can be counted on the one hand.

The Russians Again

Back to the Russian part of the story again and what was in reality the baby stage of the Celtic Tiger. They would be highly offended if they were described in any way as scroungers. Of course there were those who did take advantage of our generosity and abused the system to get what they could out of it. That's human nature. We had and possibly have at this present time politicians that are as corrupt as be damned so that makes it more difficult to point fingers or apportion blame on anyone else in that category.

If you were to direct any sort of a derogatory term towards Ivan, make sure of one thing – that there is a plate glass or a ten foot wall between you and him. If not you're history. You don't want to end up in many small plastic bags left in skips throughout the greater Dublin area (his description of how he would deal with troublemakers, and I believed every word).

There was one other thing that took them a while to get the hang of and that was the Irish sense of humour. I have to say they were a right sour bunch when they came here first. But now you're greeted with "What's the craic boy?" When I got to know them pretty well and vice versa I began to gradually piece together their story. I found it very interesting. There was also the fact that we had a lot more in common than we first realised. Their work ethic was second to none. Take this for example: a reasonable-sized swimming pool, six and a half meters by three and a half and nearly three meters deep had to be excavated at this very large, posh house, which was surrounded by beautiful gardens.

This property, which turned out to be the epicentre of this ever-expanding construction firm, was owned by a very pleasant lady and her husband who was an out-and-out gentleman. They did own a few other properties in different parts of the country.

I think she enjoyed the thrills and spills of being surrounded by the multicultural workforce that was on site and ultimately overseeing the work that was going on. She believed that she was being directed or mentored in her work by the ghost of an old man, who had previously lived in the house. In my opinion his mentoring skills left a lot to be desired at times. I certainly wouldn't leave it down to a spirit to guide me on such serious matters. What if he/she was a spiteful soul, or was a bit of a comedian with a rare sense of humour? It could be a case of a long and twisty road to nowhere. Oh where would we be without a bit of humour?

Occasionally there would be loud banter between the men working on the site and obviously there would be some complaints from the next-door neighbours. One particular lady, who seemed to get annoyed more often than any of the others, was a bit heavy in her condemnation over the fence one day when the owner and Ivan were standing in the middle of the driveway and happened to be discussing work practices in different countries. He leaned over towards her and said, "I think it is wrong time of month" (in broken English) "You know when woman have climax?" He certainly got his words mixed up but it had the desired effect. This little gem has been repeated in conversation a good few times since.

Back now to the swimming pool. Tony the boss was having a look, trying to figure out what size of an excavator or digger would be suitable to gain access to do the job. Ivan was standing beside us listening. The man possessed a talent for shopping that would make any woman green with envy. It doesn't matter how fine anyone could cut their weekly groceries bill, Ivan could cut at least a third off it. One of the boys on the job made out that he was that tight he could live in your ear. Eventually he butted in and said in a very loud half-English/ half-Russian sort of way, that left your ears sore, "Why you need machine when we have machine here?" and stuck out both his hands which looked like well-worn shovels. There was, you could say, a quiet moment of reflection to make sure it wasn't some sort of Russian joke. "Okay lads it's your choice," says Tony, as he made a hasty exit with a wry smile on his face. Straight away they set about ordering whatever tools and skips were needed, and set about the task ahead.

The house owner decided to get a few tapes of Russian music to play for the men to make them feel at home. I suppose it's the thought that counts. Much later they told us that the music gave them sore heads so maybe that was why it was completed in a very short period of time indeed. How many of us if we were to be honest, would have been so quick to put up their hands and volunteer for such hard labour when there was an easy alternative? It must have been the coffee they were drinking that gave them the energy. There would be more caffeine and energy value in one cup than a lorry load of Red Bull.

I have never come across a man like Ivan. Never enough hours in the day, or enough days in the week. He was here barely a year when he started to branch out. It was normal for him to finish at five and then go straight onto some small job, building garden walls, bits of concrete work, etc. This was every evening and every day, including Saturday and Sundays. You just could not but acknowledge the work ethic involved.

Ivan told me a story about another man who was a captain in the police force at home, left his job and made his way over to work on the building sites. I met him at one of the Christmas parties after Tony gave him a start. He was a pure solid block of a man, even sturdier than Ivan, and that's saying a lot. His name was Gregor and it turned out he was a fantastic singer. He had lungs like Dolly Parton and would have given Pavarotti a run for his money. Each time they went home for a short break, they returned with a good selection of wine, I'm talking a dozen bottles or more. I asked how they got that many through customs. "Ha, ha," one of them said, "Very simple. I have two bottles for myself and write the names of all my Irish friends on each bottle so I explain to the customs person they are not mine, as you can see for yourself, they are presents; works every time.

Ivan had got him a small job in Foxrock to repair part of a stone-built garden wall that had been knocked down when a car crashed into it. The bits of English that Gregor had weren't worth talking about, so the owner, who knew nothing about building or construction, showed him the wall and what he wanted done, then left him to get on with it. When he returned from work in the evening, he found Gregor with a big smile on his face thinking he had done a great job after knocking down the whole wall. Your man was speechless and phoned Ivan, who immediately left his own work and made his way there with beads of sweat on his forehead trying to think of what went wrong. When he got there and saw a perfectly good wall turned into rubble, the owner was inside, possibly in shock. The two of them agreed then that maybe they could turn a bad story into a good one and went on to tell the owner when he came out that this was the best thing to do because when the car hit the wall, it shook the whole thing and that it could be dangerous for children. Not knowing whether it was right or wrong the owner agreed that it was better to be safe than sorry. That night Ivan got a phone call from Gregor who was in the pub and him as drunk as Brezhnev when he couldn't get out of the plane at Shannon while on a state visit. "Why are you drinking?" Ivan asked him. "I'm drunk because I'm happy now that I have lots of work building a new wall."

The same Gregor went on to meet a lady doctor while visiting the hospital for treatment, and like the end to some sort of Mills and Boon novel, they are now happily married.

Another of Ivan's friends came here to work a few years after Victor and Ivan. He was always in pursuit of the good life. He would work hard for a while then live it up until the pockets were nearly empty. He was well known as a ladies' man, always buying flowers, would wine and dine until he spent the last cent.

He would get very bad tempered and anyone who knew him would stay out of his way when he had to go out to work again. One night in particular when things did not seem to be falling into place for him he decided to pay a visit to a lady of the night somewhere along the Quays. They went back to her place where they formalised their unsigned contract. Normally, from what I've heard, it's money up front in these sorts of transactions, but when it came to paying he had other ideas, so he made off, leaving a very angry lady behind.

As it happened he didn't get very far before he was stopped by two heavies employed by the lady to prevent such things happening. "Pay up," he was told, but he pretended not to understand why they were looking for money from him. "She did not give me anything or cook me any food so why would I pay," he says in broken English. "In my country you never pay for sex" and proceeded to turn his pockets inside out showing that he had no money. The heavies got so fed up with threatening him that they told him to eff-off and never come back. He has now moved on to Canada on a false passport.

Ivan told me another story of strange happenings back at home when he was a doctor in the hospital that he was responsible for. A friend of his worked as a gamekeeper in a state forest that was full of wild boars and deer. He was responsible for its upkeep and the protection of the wild animals roaming around inside it. He came upon some poachers one day while on his rounds. He told them that if they left immediately that he would not make a fuss, but one of the poachers wasn't going to be told what to do and started getting all heated up. This man in particular wasn't to be messed with as he had connections with people who were involved in mafia-type criminality and life wasn't very precious to them, especially that of a gamekeeper.

Ivan was at home when he got a frantic call from his friend the gamekeeper asking him to come to the hospital as quick as possible. When he got to the there the gamekeeper explained to him what happened. When the poacher began to threaten him back in the forest, the gamekeeper had a big dog, something like a Rottweiler, with him that if it sensed any danger to its owner would react immediately. It did just that and gave your man a bit of a mauling in a place that would really hurt, in the nether regions to be more exact. The gamekeeper was so afraid of the consequences that he wanted to make sure that your man got the best treatment possible. Ivan got him up onto an operating table, cut the torn trousers off him and set about cleaning and stitching where necessary. He had two female nurses to work with him so he put out his hand and asked for whatever tool he needed.

On getting no reply or tool he looked at the nurses. The two of them were standing with their mouths hanging open staring at the patient's manhood. As Ivan explained himself it was no wonder the nurses had reacted the way they had, because even as a doctor he had never seen a thingamajig as big before. He had a simple way of explaining the size when he said, "I think the dog went to bite his leg below the knee and got its teeth into this instead".

The poacher's wife rushed into the hospital some time later when she found out what happened. All she was worried about was "Is it still connected and is it working?" She never asked about his face, arms or legs. Ivan said, "I was left in no doubt about what was at the top of her list of priorities."

More About the Boss

A bit more now about the boss, as there is a lot to tell. He bought his first house in London when he was barely seventeen. He was one of those people that whatever he touched he would be able to turn into money because he could see something in it that most people would miss. Whether it was buying or selling cars, motorbikes buses, toys, or second-hand tools, going into his apartment was like going into a storage area for a car boot sale.

It was not unusual to hear chainsaws and garden strimmers starting up at four or five in the morning after returning home from the night club. This was his party piece. If there were women present or not the chainsaw would get started and revved up to the last to get the dancing started. It's funny there was never a complaint from any of the neighbours on the street. I don't know why? Maybe when they could see all the different rough-looking Irishmen coming and going at all times of the day or night they thought it was better to say nothing than to draw trouble on themselves. See no evil hear no evil; as good as any insurance policy.

Working in Dublin

Tony decided to head for Dublin at the behest of a few boys he had met in London through his wheeling and dealing with cars and so forth. They had been doing some renovation work and needed a plasterer. He borrowed a plastering hawk of mine and headed off. They were a couple of interesting characters as well, both highly-skilled tradesmen who worked on and off on gardening projects for TV shows. This was how he got introduced to the charming lady who insisted on quality rather than quantity and needed someone capable enough to oversee the construction of a large extension to her house.

So that started a sort of domino effect. Tony brought up mates of his from Cork, carpenters and block layers, Mickey, Big Dom, Snowball, Carney, Tart and Johnny, then me the plasterer. I then brought along my brothers Joe and Martin and quite a few Donegal boys after that – Benjy and Seamus. Others came and went over the next number of years. Pat Kelly came over from London and did a stint as well. After another while two more lads from Cork arrived on the scene, two carpenters – David and Jake. Later on David turned out to be better with a pen in his hand and so took over the running of the office. Jake on the other hand, having come from a farm, was always interested in any conversation that centered around story telling, milking, spreading manure, or silage, in that order. He was the best man you could ask to run a job. The reason being he had bundles of straightforward common sense and was able to convey that to those around him. He was very people-friendly, a thing that garners respect wherever you are. Sometimes the right person can discover that the wrong person is in the position where they should be.

The house next door was bought as part of the extended plan. We stayed there and worked on converting it all into one huge period residence. The amount of work involved was hard to gauge as plans were not set in stone, which meant they changed quite frequently, but you did as you were told. I did on several occasions over the years offer my advice, which seemed to fall on deaf ears. So rather than insult a person's intelligence I found that it was best to nod your head in agreement and leave it at that.

I found out that a member of a traditional Irish band that's famous all over the world was living just around the corner from us. He always came in and gave us a few tunes at the Christmas parties. We carried out lots of repairs and alterations on his house as well, leading on to a few other large houses after that. But if the walls of our main house could talk it would create that much interest that Hollywood directors would be beating a track to the door to sign up the film rights. It would fit in somewhere between One flew over the Cuckoo's nest and Nine and a Half Weeks to try and get the frolicking and the laughing in the one set. Another comparison would be with The Commitments, which might be even better again, but who knows. Hindsight is full of ifs and buts that only seem to complicate life more than is really needed.

Benjy

Benjy, who was from near me at home, was part of the crew that worked with us in Dublin. He was one of these boys who was very talented with his hands and could do just about anything, whether it was welding, carpentry or farming. He was always part of any windups at work or back at the house, or taking the mickey shall we say. He contracted a serious illness, which resulted in his death. It had a devastating affect on all who knew him. Ivan, Victor and Dima attended his wake and stayed for his funeral. Something that was much appreciated by his wife, family and friends.

The Trip of a Lifetime

I missed out on the trip of a lifetime one weekend by coming home on the Friday night. If I had stayed I would have been part of this story I'm going to tell you now. I got a phone call on the Saturday from Tony telling me that they had flown down to Cork on a private jet with an American multimillionaire, for a meeting that had been arranged through a third party. He had wanted to look at a house that he was interested in buying and Tony had been recommended to the American by one of his friends. So before leaving Dublin they had a few drinks so that they could all get to know one another, because there's no point in traveling anywhere with a stranger. Better to become an acquaintance first and friendships will follow.

A taxi was called for that took them to a private airfield where the jet was waiting. It landed at Cork airport in a very short time indeed, no queues, very little custom checks. A taxi took them from the airport to view the house, which was a fair distance away. Two of the boys who had decided to stay in Dublin for the weekend were with them as well. After a quick dander around the house without going inside, it was decided there and then that it would be the ideal house for him and that was that. He was not looking forward to the return trip in the taxi so he made a phone call and had a helicopter come to pick them up. On the way to the airport he decided to go the extra mile, or should I say, a bit further afield as he had not been to London before so that's where he wanted to go for a quick visit.

Of course the rest of the boys were nodding their heads and agreeing wholeheartedly with him, still not believing their luck. So off on the jet to Gatwick, where they were picked up by a stretch limousine and brought into one of the most expensive hotels in London. From there it was all red carpet treatment and all the hoity-toity stuff. After they had a meal in the restaurant the next port of call was the hotel bar where the drinks were flowing freely. One of the boys was wearing a t-shirt that had some unusual writing on it, which in turn started a bit of a debate that went on for a while, finally ending up with your man saying that he knew where to get the best t-shirts in the world and that he was going to take them there tomorrow.

There was a fair shot of drink taken at this stage but in the morning true to his word after a very light breakfast the stretch limo was outside the door waiting for them. Once they got whatever bits and pieces gathered up off they went to the airport again. This time however there's a bigger jet sitting on the tarmac waiting for them to board. None of the three boys could believe that this was really happening, but wait for this, where do you think they were going to look at the t-shirts? A shop in America, not far from where he lived. To shorten the story a bit, when they got to this supposedly fantastic shop, there were none of the t-shirts that he wanted to show them left in the shop! As far as he was concerned that was no reason to feel let down, so to cheer them up a bit he brought them to Trump Tower and the roulette tables of the casino where he bought a pile of chips and proceeded to share them out among the boys to use as they liked. This was fairy tale stuff from start to finish. After getting their fill of losing a lot more than they were winning and more than enough to drink he brought them to his house. This now was another story of how the other half lives. The house was something else altogether. The dining room had a small island in it surrounded by water with a few small boats that you could get into and row your way around the island, with even a small bridge making the connection. You could watch big TV screens from whatever position you wanted, and the description of the bedrooms and their en suite bathrooms matched in every way the extravagance and opulence of the rest of the house.

When they had to leave the lavishness of their surroundings and fly home to face the reality of a fairly normal existence it really brought it home to the boys how lucky they were to have experienced such a life, even if it was only for a short spell. When they came back they were able to produce more that enough evidence to prove beyond all doubt that they were not dreaming or hallucinating. I saw all the photos and I know of the man in question and how he acquired his vast wealth so there is no question of it not being believed. If I had stayed behind in Dublin all I had needed was my passport and a toothbrush, but for me it was not to be.

The Madhouse

We found out that there were a number of other very nice parks in the area, which was great as you wouldn't get bored so easily going out running in the exact same one during the long evenings. I remember the first day I landed at the house was a Sunday. I got a taxi from O' Connell Street, where I was dropped off after I came down from Donegal on McGinley's coach. As I approached the door, which was wide open, there was music blaring but no sign of anyone. I made my way inside, downstairs into the kitchen where I came upon some nice tasty homemade cake that tasted lovely. I made myself a cup of tea so that I could eat more of what I found before venturing upstairs to where the sitting room was.

The TV was blaring away and a body was lying there, obviously sleeping off a bellyful of alcohol. I did not make any attempt to disturb him, as if I could, so I made my way outside again as it was a glorious sunny day. Then I thought I heard a different kind of sound, singing. I look out around the gate and see this gang coming towards me and them singing for all they were worth and each one hanging on to the other. After the introductions were made by way of saying "If he's a friend of yours he's a friend of mine," it was inside for more singing and the man who was fast asleep minutes before was now up dancing on the settee.

What a madhouse. I have never lived in a house like it. It was non-stop craic throughout the whole summer. It was just happy, happy days. Theresa, the owner of the house, would lay on a big barbeque at least three times a week out on a big flat terraced roof with a Caribbean sun shining down on us. A few of the lads had returned from Australia and were used to this kind of weather and were kitted out with the shorts and wearing the shades, and were quite comfortable with the bottle of beer in one hand and a barbequed chicken leg in the other. Many's the day the owner said, "My goodness boys it's far too nice to be working on a day like this," and insisted that we go to the beach for a swim, or go diving at a place called the Forty Foot out at Dunlaoghaire. It was very hard to say no when it's the person who's responsible for paying your wages at the end of the week is telling you to do it. It's hard to describe the whole scenario. It was like going to heaven without having to depart this world in a box.

I would give Joe and Martin a ring if I was under a bit of pressure with the plastering. So they would head for the bright lights of Dublin's fair city where all the girls are not so friendly or in some cases not so pretty, especially when you'd see the amount of makeup that looked like it was spread on with a butter knife. It suited them to do a few weeks on and off as well. The sparring gloves were never too far away and used to appear a few times during the week, especially in the evenings, so all present got the chance to defend their corner. It was more of a laugh than anything else. There was a sports centre that had a swimming pool and gym ten minutes walk away, which was very handy. If I was feeling lazy, or under pressure for time, I would take the work van. One evening it needed diesel so I pulled in to the petrol station and filled it up, went into pay and ended up chatting to the man serving behind the counter. While this was going on, a young fellow walked in with a hefty looking wallet in his hand that was completely stuffed with fifty euro notes, threw it on the counter and says, "I found this laying at the petrol pumps" and walked out without leaving his name or anything.

Your man behind the counter shook his head in disbelief and said, "It's wrong to think that all young people should be tarred with the same brush," meaning that that was proof that there were honest young people around. He got a phone number in it and rang it up. It was one call that the owner was glad to get because at that stage he still had not missed it. He had taken money out of it while putting petrol in at the same time and left it sitting on the boot. As he pulled off it fell on the ground.

The Wrong Changing Room

I had a bit of a routine going at one stage, where I would go to the gym then go into the sauna. One evening I went to the gym, did my stuff as the man says, then into the changing room for a quick shower before the sauna. So there I am standing in all my glory, all wet and not a stitch on me. Normal enough you might think. Next thing the door opens and this lady walks in from the direction of the swimming pool. Now it's about fifteen meters through the shower area to the adjacent locker room. She walked the full distance with her mouth wide open and staring straight at my Godzilla. I'm thinking "You're in the men's changing room dear, for what looks like a bit of window shopping". But I think "So what, I'm not shy;

whatever floats your boat". She goes out the door leaving me there smiling away to myself. Next thing the door opens and she sticks her head in again this time with a smile on her face and says, "You do know this is the ladies' changing room and if I were you I'd get out of there as fast as I could because there is a horde of women coming in from the pool".

I would have passed out a Porsche 911 with the speed that I grabbed and gathered my towel and belongings, nearly doing somersaults on the wet tiles in the process. When I got out into the hallway she was there pointing at the sign on the door saying that the changing rooms had been swapped because of work being carried out in the ladies and her in convulsions with all the laughing. I must have looked a sight with a towel half around me, and trying to hold onto a bag and the rest of my clothes. God was I embarrassed. When I made it into the proper changing room I placed my belongings on a bench, put on my swimming trunks, wrapped the towel around myself properly and sat down and thought about what could have happened if she had not put her head in again to warn me. Now if things had been on the other foot I would not have warned her. That at least brought a smile to my face as I headed for the sauna.

You had to walk alongside the swimming pool to where the sauna and steam room were. There were classes of some sort going on in the pool, but I did not take any notice, because I was still feeling the heat of my previous encounter. I went into the steam room first. There were two women already inside yapping away, so of course I joined in as well, and started to tell them what was just after happening to me. I had them in stitches laughing. Little did I know what was still in front of me. The craic was good with them as they were country girls and we had plenty to talk about. There was a full length glass door on the steam room so I glanced out when I heard a lot of loud laughing and joking. It was women coming in from the pool. The unthinkable happens then. They started to peel off their swimwear right in front of the door.

A warning bell started to go off inside my head, I asked the girls was this a ladies only night or what? One of them says' "Yes. Why did you not know?" and the two of them went into an uncontrollable fit of laughing. I went into a cold sweat as one of the women is now standing naked chatting away to one of her friends, not knowing that there was a man within touching distance and him praying "Please don't open the door, because I don't know who's going to get the biggest fright," and I did not want to be caught in that sort of a cringe worthy situation. It was only for a minute or so but it seemed like hours before they all got dressed and left. God what a relief it was. Only then the girls told me they were only joking about the women only night. Since that I never go through a door without looking to see if there is a sign stuck up anywhere, just in case.

House in Cavan

The lady whose house we did all the work on in Dublin had bought a house in Cavan to take advantage of tax breaks which were available to anyone who bought or built houses in certain counties that would be considered sparsely populated and without much work going on. A good idea to create employment but it was one of the things that turned parts of the countryside into concrete jungles.

It certainly looked a nice building when I saw it first and it was in a fairly decent setting, but once I had a good look around there were some obvious problems that had been overlooked, like the floor levels inside being lower than ground levels outside, which was causing dampness. The curing of one problem resulted in the discovery of another one. There had been a carpentry workshop run from sheds that covered a large area at the back of the house, so the idea was to redecorate the place and change a small lean-to roof. But lo and behold, that idea soon went out the window. It went from a quick makeover to building an extension at the back that was four or five times as big as the original house. All the sheds had to be knocked down and founds laid before any building could start. The demolition was all done by hand. It was at this stage of the proceedings that Tony sent me there. Out of the way I think, to give him a bit of peace and quiet, because with good intention I had acquired too much of a guardian angel role in giving directions on what I thought a person should or should not do.

I found it very hard to simply be a yes man, which is always the easy route to take in any situation. I liked to voice my opinions and go against the grain if need be, which was not always the most popular thing to do. We had a good big mobile home on the site that we stayed in, with Sky TV installed free of charge by one of three boys from Estonia who worked on the job as carpenters. Hedrick was his name; he was very good at that type of thing. As the job started to progress, so did the changes and even the changes were changed. It turned into the sort of job where it was very hard to get motivated about it, because no sooner than you had some part of it near completed, it would have to be knocked, chopped or changed. In a situation like this it's best if you can find another avenue to get rid of your frustrations so I went looking for a gym and found one in a town nearby. That's where I would spend a lot of the evenings. There were a few Latvians, Lithuanians and Polish around the area. A lot were employed in the hotel business, or in the quarries and cement works that were springing up everywhere. Obviously there were quite a few going to the gym as well and I got on great with them. A few boys there took the bodybuilding seriously. Steroids and more steroids were what they thought was necessary or needed in their attempt to put muscles on top of muscles. Whatever floats your boat I suppose.

One of the men who I hooked up with was an Englishman who happened to be going through a bit of marital difficulty and took to the gym to take his mind of his problems. With a fair bit of encouragement and advice from a few quarters over a period of about a year he went from being very overweight to being very fit and muscular, and with that came a lot of attention from the ladies. Boy did he get himself into some hilarious situations. He was going out with a few women at one stage because he just couldn't say no. That was okay until one of them found out. He phoned me and him in a panic. He was in his house with a Polish girl and another one landed outside and was trying to get in. I could hear the racket going on in the background. I could do nothing but laugh so he put the phone down. She broke one of the door windows and scratched his car before leaving.

A few days later when he came into the gym he had a frightened look about him. "God what's wrong with you, you would think you were after seeing a ghost," I said. "I wish it was a ghost, it wouldn't have done half as much damage." Then he went on to tell me what had happened. He had come home from work to find the inside of the house wrecked, the curtains cut in half, most of his clothes chopped, hi-fi system, TV, all wrecked. I said, "Well you know now what can happen when you try to set up a harem outside of Saudi Arabia, and that's your lesson. There is nothing more dangerous than a woman scorned".
I would love to put some more of the incidents in here but it would not be possible because of the people involved so I'll say nothing till I hear more.

The Things You'd See on the Road

It was always a bit of a rush to get home on the Friday from the job in Cavan, as there were quite a few schools on the way and if you left it that bit late it could put two extra hours on the journey. But there was always something along the way to be amused by. We were driving behind a lorry when all you could see was plastic bottles and all sorts of rubbish being thrown out the window. It annoys me to see litter louts discarding their rubbish like that so I started blowing the horn and flashing the lights; this was on the road from Donegal Town towards Ballybofey. I made numerous attempts to get him to pull over, even passed him a few times, but no way was he going to stop. He eventually had to stop when he got stuck in traffic in Ballybofey so out I jumps and opens his door. Well he nearly jumped out the other side he was that frightened. When I explained why I was trying to get him to stop, you could see the colour creeping back into his face. He told me then why he wouldn't stop. Apparently he had been the victim of a hijacking a few months previous and thought this was going to be his second. I nearly forgot about him throwing out his litter I was laughing that much, but he'll think twice about dumping his junk out the window again.

It wasn't too long after that incident that we were driving on the same road from Ballyshannon towards Donegal Town on a Friday evening on the way home, Seamus was in the passenger seat with the radio going. He had the phone at the ready to ring into Radio Na Gaeltachta answering some quiz, as he was great if it came to finishing any old Irish saying's that would be part of the quizzes. All in the hope of winning a set of golf clubs, his other pastime when he wasn't in the garden.

The road was quite busy as you would expect on a Friday evening. Everyone in a mad rush to beat the traffic on the way home. We started to take notice of this car in front. It would slow from 100 kph down to 80 then speed up again. Then it suddenly veered towards the white line and back. It was a silver people carrier, just about avoiding a potentially fatal accident when an oncoming car had pulled out to overtake the car travelling in front of it. The first thing we thought was that driver is on the phone or is blind drunk. We wanted to pass but we had to wait for the right opportunity to do just that. How wrong can you be? We took the next chance we got to pass and see what was causing the dangerous driving. Curiosity was getting the better of us at this stage. What we saw wouldn't do the cause of women drivers any good at all. It was comical and hard to believe, a woman driving at that speed with a makeup tray balancing on her knees and a mirror leaning on the steering wheel. I started blowing the horn, so that made her jump because she was oblivious to the danger she was causing. I think she shoved the lipstick up her nose, and God, if you saw the dirty look she gave us, you would think that it was us that was being a nuisance on the road.

In the interest of balancing things up a bit, I wonder who was the person that was responsible for the survey that said women were safer drivers than men? I was thinking of posting it on YouTube. It would look well alongside the boy racers that you see on the same site with some of the antics that they get up to. I could nearly put a bet on something strange or weird happening most days before leaving the job. This time it was no different, although it was nearer to Ballyshannon than any of my previous experiences. There was some major road works going on. It was a lukewarm sort of day with a glaring sun to contend with. I was coming near to where the road works were beginning. I was having trouble seeing the road in front of me as the sun was low in the sky so I had to keep my eyes nearly closed to enable me to see. But rather than keep an eye on the road where I was supposed to keep them, I fell asleep. The next thing I saw when I opened my eyes was cones flying in all directions and one of those big mobile neon signs with lights telling you to slow down. It was a bit late for me to be seeing the likes of that as I went full whack into it. I did a fair bit of damage to the front of the van, but was able to drive home no problem. Rather than accepting the blame for falling asleep, I put it down to the lady with the makeup the previous week putting a spell on me.

A Trip to New York

Tony was getting together a crew for a trip to New York for St Patrick's Day so a refusal would not be something he would want to hear. The craic would be good and that was all that mattered. His motto was, don't think about it, just go. That same policy was applied to all his transactions. Only for his persistence, I more than likely would never have done it. He had the whole thing organised in the blink of an eye. It was only for a long weekend, so me and Martin were part of the crew. The few weeks flew by before we found ourselves looking for our room in a hotel close to Manhattan that Tony had already booked. Then when we found our bearings the partying started.

Barry by this time had been living in Boston, where he had a good business in construction going. So when I let him know that I was for New York, he decided to come down from Boston for the craic as well. I was looking forward to seeing him as we had not met for a good number of years. He was in a bit of a predicament himself as he did not have the Green Card, and so was one of the thousands of illegals that were trapped in many ways. He could not take a chance in coming home in case he would not get back over again, as that would leave him rightly banjaxed. I remember being on the go all night between bars and nightclubs in and around Times Square, so around 9.30 am I thought to myself "I have to get some sleep" so I managed to sneak off and head for the hotel. I can't figure out how I remembered where the hotel actually was, so I must say I surprised myself and if I could I would have given myself a big clap on the back for doing so. Once I got my head down on the bed I was soon fast asleep but lo and behold it wasn't going to be for long.

At first I thought I was dreaming about someone being killed because of all the squealing and banging, but as I awoke from my slumber something sent a message to my brain telling me that this was no dream. The noises had a very familiar ring to them and were vibrating through my head, which was touching the wall. With that I shot up in bed, still not one hundred per cent sure of what I was hearing. There seemed to be only a flimsy enough partition separating the rooms and by God there was indeed some action going on next door. It sounded like an animal rights campaigner after seeing his cat being run over by a truck. It was going on that long that I was seriously thinking of knocking on their door in the hope of being invited in. Then I heard their door opening and a lot of talking and giggling going on. I went to the door and looked out the wee spy hole that's on all hotel room doors now.

What I saw made me drool with my tongue hanging out like one of them big St Bernard dogs. There was these three girls, partially clothed, prancing and posing around the hallway and two boys who had Italian looks about them holding camcorders and giving directions. As far as I was concerned my suspicions were confirmed. They were making adult movies. The two boys left the scene of the fun shortly afterwards and the cackling continued in the room for another twenty minutes or so before the girls left. How on earth could I go to sleep then? Next thing some of the other boys returned to the room drunk out of their heads. There were a few beds in the room so they just lay down and were asleep before their heads hit the pillows. Then the snoring started. I couldn't stick it any longer and went off out again and ended up in a pub and got talking to a bunch of American women from Arkansas who were in New York for the weekend but not specifically for the St Patrick's Day parade. They turned out to be God-fearing Christians who never cursed in their lives and were shocked with my use of the swear words, which were minimal to say the least. But they were curious as to why I would go all the way to New York without my wife. I fed them some quare yarns; so much so, I was nearly believing them myself in the end up. They were doing their best to save me from myself. It ended up with me corrupting them more than they thought they were saving me. It came to a point where I was laughing more than I was talking because I was that tired so I bade them a fond farewell and returned to the hotel.

The next day was the big one, or the El Gordo of parades, but by God, it was that cold it would freeze the barnacles off a sperm whale. I had often seen bits of the New York St. Patrick's Day parade on TV but it paled in comparison to being there in the flesh and seeing it snake its way up Fifth Avenue. Huge just isn't the word for it. It's even bigger than that. But you have an idea in your head of what I'm trying to say.

An ordinary taxi was not a good enough mode of transport for us to be traveling back to the airport in, so a fleet of stretch limousines were organised by Tony. It was my first time to travel in one, and after the journey I said it would be my last. We were running a bit late for the flights so it was all panic. A bit like doing a stage of the Donegal rally in a boat. It was a lady driver and she was going to make sure that we were not going to miss our flights, even though we were feeling seasick and you could not just lean over the side and be sick. She even had to get a generous tip, which is the custom after all that torture.

Another American Trip

The next opportunity to visit America came when Barry insisted on us coming over to visit him in Boston. It was during the summer time so we knew it was going to be very hot. Every house had these air conditioners sitting on their bedroom windows, otherwise you couldn't sleep a wink with the heat. It was all barbeques in the evenings when you came back from touring around doing a bit of sightseeing. We had gone to the beach one day. Me and Barry wore swimming trunks and Anne Marie had on her itsy bitsy teeny weeny yellow polka dot bikini. You should have seen the looks we were getting. You would think we were naked. Some youngsters shouted for us to put on some clothes. Well that's what it sounded like to us. It was then I noticed that everyone seemed to be wearing clothes that would be more suited to going for a walk in the park than going to the beach. Shorts that went below the knees and t-shirts that looked more like a blanket. We began to feel a bit uncomfortable so we packed up and left the beach to the hyena look-alikes. I don't know whether they were extremely prudish about exposing a bit of flesh or did we happen to pick a day when some strict religious groups were having their day out.

In the area where we were staying with Barry was a great Irish community. Cafes with all the Irish food, bakeries doing all the Irish bread, etc. We decided after a week to drive down to New York to visit a sister of Anne Marie's in a big flashy jeep that Barry had. It was a Cadillac Escalade and I got the short straw when I was voted in as the driver, never having driven on the right-hand side before. I was nervous as hell. Once we got on the motorways it was okay until we got as far as Manhattan.

I got a bit lost then because I wanted to cross the Hudson River to Weehawken, New Jersey, but with two navigators, one in each ear, and tempers beginning to fray, I struggled on, managing to jump a few red lights in the process before reaching our destination completely unscathed, which was a plus in anyone's language. Anne Marie's sister Jean travelled from Colorado for the gathering, with Pearl, another sister, and her husband Terry who is a painting contractor. They then went on to overload us with food American-style. New York is definitely the city that never sleeps. You can get anything you want day or night. It was something else wandering around Times Square in the middle of the night. There was one occasion when my jaw dropped that far that I nearly knee-capped myself. This man and woman were walking along the footpath in front of us, holding hands and eating hotdogs at the same time. Very romantic, but that wasn't what made my jaw drop. It was the size of them. The footpath was the width of our main roads and there was hardly enough room to get past. Living in cities like New York it's easy for some to become fast food junkies if you let your guard down.

We had a great time before setting off again for Boston, reaching it without any mishaps worth mentioning. Barry dropped us at the airport the next evening as our return flight was at night to Shannon with a connecting flight to Dublin. Tony had arranged for us to fly home first class; this meant that you did not have to join queues for checking in luggage or boarding. You went into a members' lounge where all drinks and snacks were provided free. Then once you boarded the plane, rather than your knees being stuck up against the seat in front, it opened up like a bed. The stewardess saw to your every need, apart from jumping in beside you, although if I made any suggestions along those lines with Anne Marie sitting beside me I could have ended up doing a free fall jump from twenty-four thousand feet without a parachute, so that idea made a fairly quick exit from my head.

Back to the Grindstone

It was back to the grindstone again once I got back to work. The boss was steadily moving up the ladder. He had purchased quite a bit of property in Estonia so the excuse to visit came when he got invitations for a do in the Irish Embassy in Estonia for St Patrick's Day. Me, Martin and the two wives among a large group of his friends ended up over in the capital city Tallinn. Very beautiful buildings along with all the cobbled streets, similar to the old town in Prague or indeed any of those old well-established Eastern European cities.

We were a bit nervous about going to the do, because we knew it would be very hoity-toity, so we were dressed in our best Sunday for the occasion. When we did make our grand entrance the Irish ambassador met us and shook hands with each and every one, a right gentleman with no airs or graces about him at all. There was one of the guests who put a bit of a sour taste in my mouth when he introduced himself to me while at the same time taking in the tricolour pin and badge on my jacket. He was the commanding officer of British forces stationed in Estonia, and unbeknownst to this obnoxious chap, I had already got the low-down on him from another source. After giving him an educational lecture on Irish history and the involvement of the British Army in atrocities committed in my country, with the intent of making him feel as small as I could in the process, he soon got the message that I wasn't going to be listening to him blowing his trumpet. Instead, he tried to be my best friend, even handing me over his name, number, address, the whole shebang, as the man says. In the peaceful times that were in it, these particulars were of no use to me so I stuck it in a phone box alongside telephone numbers for working girls and suchlike. I'm sure he would have had quite a few calls from interested parties.

There was a good gang of Cork boys, so when the free drinks started to take effect, the Céili dancing started with a few rebel songs thrown in for good measure. It turned into a real hooley altogether. I don't think a lot of the invited guests knew what to make of the whole thing, but they let their hair down a bit and got into the swing of things and enjoyed it anyway. Even the now 'demoted' general thought he was one of us. We spent two St Patrick's Days there and the craic made it well worthwhile.

The boss had been saying for quite a while that if he made enough money his next purchase was going to be a helicopter. There is a bit of truth in the saying "Small money small plans, big money big plans". The news at first was taken with a pinch of salt but he proved the doubters wrong by investing in one, started off then with a round of lessons immediately and over a short period of time got his first flying licence. It was just like going for a car driving licence; you get your provisional first, spend a while accompanied by a fully qualified driver, and so on. When I got the chance of a spin or two on it I wasn't going to refuse, because I might not get the chance to do so again too handy. It was a very enjoyable experience flying the whole way from Dublin home to Donegal one weekend. It was a beautiful summer's day where everything could be seen clearly with not a cloud in sight. The amount of lakes in the mountains surrounding Glenveagh to Gweebarra and the whole scenery was just unbelievable.

He invested in a lot of property, one of which he made available for anyone to stay in while they were working for him. It was an open house for those that he knew if they needed somewhere to stay while visiting Dublin. He had it done up to the last, and no expense was spared in the process. It included a proper basement bar and dance area. It was certainly different in a lot of ways. It had an old pre-war motorbike fixed up to the wall above the bar and on the ceiling a racing go kart in working order was firmly screwed up. Looking at the house from the outside it did not have anything that would make it stand out from any of the others on the street. It was only when you went inside that it became apparent that this was no run of the mill abode. The lighting created some special effects that would make you feel right at home. The sound system was as good if not better than you would find in most nightclubs. The first time we got the opportunity to try it out properly was for one of the Christmas parties. It started on the Thursday night and continued non-stop until it sort of died a death on the Sunday night. It was a party to celebrate the recession!

I landed up one Sunday and Cork and Kerry were playing in the hurling finals and the celebrations were in full swing. About 3.30 am I thought to myself I'd better go to bed because I won't be fit for work in the morning so in I go to the room and there in front of me in my bed is this fellow from Cork and a girl from Kerry with the two opposition jerseys and whatever other clothing laying in a heap on the floor. Your man looks up at me and says, "I won't be long now," and he keeps repeating this over and over. I'm standing there with my mouth open wondering what's the best way to cool the fire here when in between the oh, oh's, and the ah's your wan asks me if I could go out and get her a glass of rosé wine? How's that for bare-arsed cheek? I reversed out, closed the door and slept on a sofa in the sitting room.

Losing my Job

Losing my job in Dublin, getting sacked, paid off, made redundant, whatever way you feel like describing it, wasn't a nice feeling. I knew I wasn't alone in receiving the dreadful news.

Hundreds of people in similar situations to me were getting the heave ho every single day all around the country. Considering myself a bit long in the tooth to be thinking of following all the other redundants abroad the next step to make was the lonely trek to your local unemployment office to sign on, and join the dreaded, but necessary, dole queue. I often wondered what would become of all the yummy mummies who used to cause such havoc outside one of the schools close to where we worked. It was a sight to behold; the four by four's all jostling for parking spaces closest to the school gates to drop off the children. Depended on what day it was, they were dressed to the nines like Hollywood A-list stars. One day would be tennis day, then it was the gym day. What a hectic schedule. And the housekeeper back in the house doing all the work. Oh I nearly forgot the coffee mornings!

The day I was intending to make my trip to the local unemployment office, Anne Marie says, "Sure I may as well go too and make the one trip instead of two as I have to pick up some school gear in the town". "Fine," says I and off we go. We were a bit early so we decided to go for a cup of tea or coffee. Grand job, it's nice and quiet, only a few people in so we sit down and a girl takes our order. Meanwhile a mobile phone starts ringing, a bit of scrimmaging to get the phone from the pocket before this girl answers. After a bit of chit chat in a loud voice she then starts to describe how she had found this poor cat wandering the street all alone and decided to bring it home with her, but not to keep, although she was prepared to consider fostering it but first she'd have to have it neutered. There was another lady sitting at the table across whose ears had pricked up once she heard the girl mentioning neutering the cat. She gets up and started offering advice on the pitfalls of doing such a thing to a poor cat. We went in for a quiet cup of coffee and this is what happens right beside our table. The girl with the phone then tells the one offering advice to mind her own business in a very aggressive manner. "There's going to be a war shortly if one or the other doesn't back pedal," I thought. I was going to add some fuel to the fire by saying that I would shoot the cat for them but one look from Anne Marie told me that would be the worst move I ever made in my life.

Tempting as it was I decided to just keep smiling and enjoy the heated debate over a poor cat that was out for a stroll minding its own business in its own territory. It had quite possibly been fed by its owner and had decided to go for a short dander and was carried off by a total stranger and was now at the centre of an argument that could lead to blows by two highly-strung fur lovers. When sense began to prevail, we decided now was a safe time to leave. I went in to sign on. I was smiling like someone that might be slightly unhinged. The lady was giving me a rather strange look and she said people coming in to sign on are not normally the happiest looking. "What's making you smile?" "A cat," I says, without elaborating on the fact that I was thinking that the two heated up ladies should be neutered instead of the cat. Wouldn't that thought make anyone smile?

The Romanian Orphanage

A neighbour of mine who lived just down the road was in the process of building a house, so if me or Joe had a bit of spare time we would give him a helping hand. He worked for an oil delivery company and was the man you rang when you needed your house warmed up. One of the days he was selling some tickets to raise funds for a Romanian orphanage. Of course we bought some. Then he says, "Would you be interested in going over there to do a bit of voluntary work with the Northwest Orphanage Fund?" So myself and Joe said no problem.

I mentioned it to a few people about what we were intending to do, so another man, Seamus O' Collum, says count me in too. To cut a long story short, there were no direct flights so we had a stopover in Amsterdam where we had a few hours to spare. So as you do when visiting Amsterdam, you go window shopping. I have to say I hate shopping and would resort to underhand methods to get out of it, but do you know what I took to this window shopping lark like a hare out of a trap. Just imagine out shopping in Letterkenny and there are these very nicely undressed ladies inviting you in to try out the goods that you see looking back at you in the window. Of course it's not your normal shopping centre goods that are on display, and I can't ever see it taking off in Letterkenny. We refused all the enticing offers of two for the price of one that you see in most shops and headed back to get our connecting flight with a spring in our step.

We landed at an airport that was very bare of everything, even people. There was a taxi waiting there for us. I could not keep myself from staring at his head. He would have been a dark-haired man but must have been getting a few grey hairs because he started doing a do-it-yourself job with the dye. I have to say it was a disaster. The whole top of his head was a reddish color that was nowhere near his own natural color, but that did not stop him preening himself in the mirror throughout the whole journey. We spent two and a half hours squeezed into this funny-shaped car travelling at high speed, in sweltering heat, that had no shocks and it swaying like a boat going out to Tory Island on a stormy day.

He brought us to the same house that others who had come over to work stayed in previous to us coming. The greeting we got you would think we were oil barons. It was easy to see that she was glad to get the bit of business. It was a guest house but very basic compared to what we would be used to here at home. Once we got settled in we got something to eat, which was another story. The driver took us to have a look at the new orphanage, which was only a short distance from were we were staying, and what we were supposed to start work on. Well my God, never in all my life did I see a new building so crooked. It was that bad that we could not stop laughing for about two hours until the realisation hit us that these were the crooked walls that we were supposed to plaster and leave nice and straight.

It's no good trying to describe it, you would just have to see it to believe it. The North West Orphanage owned the car that we were being driven about in, so we had to put petrol in it and pay the driver out of our own pockets as well. We soon learned that you would be fleeced fairly quickly if you did not keep your eyes wide open. The driver was insisting that he would take us to and from work and anywhere we wanted to go. As this was making work for him and costing us money we declined the offer, but he brought us to the old building that would eventually be replaced by the one we were after looking at.

We had brought some toys, and various bit and pieces for the children. When we got there it looked like a prison of some sort. Huge wooden gates that were only opened when someone was going in or out. I had a feeling that the big gates had more to do with keeping predators out than keeping children or anyone else in. We met all the children, who were very exited and were obviously told about the foreigners coming bringing gifts. We felt like the three wise men, except there were four of us.

We were then introduced to the ladies who were looking after them. We went for a sort of inspection of the building, which was in anyone's eyes a few hundred years old with little or no repair work carried out in that time. Loads of toys and stuff like that were up in a large loft area. I thought it a bit strange because none of the children had anything along them lines apart from what we had just given them. Obviously there must have been some legitimate reason for them to be neatly tucked away in the loft. It was very hot weather, but looking around I was thinking you would have more shelter sleeping half way up the side of Muckish once the winter time came. So that certainly gave us an impetus to do as much as possible for the three weeks that we were to be there.

We did not get to see much that first day. It was around evening time and they wanted us to have lunch or whatever it was with them. It was cabbage soup and more cabbage soup. This was the diet that those children survived on. There was no fear of anyone being fat or overweight, that was for sure. Everything was as basic as you could possibly imagine. When we came home we were talking to a crew from Derry who were there two years previous to us going over. They described to us what it was like. The children were like skeletons and no one really to look after them. There were no shops of any kind. They had to go to the market and buy cabbages because that's all that was there. So that's what the children were surviving on. I have to say it was foul tasting stuff.

We got up early in the morning eager to get stuck into it. Before we came over we told them what was needed without seeing the place. The organisers didn't have a balls notion of what was involved in building work, no disrespect to them. As we made our way out to the job, there were young and old women wearing old torn clothes out with what looked like witches' brooms sweeping the streets. It seems the first at the council yard in the mornings always got the pick of the jobs, and none of them were very appealing. Walking on another bit there was this big dump, and it was covered with people scraping away looking for any bits of metal and even bits of plastic, bottles, just about everything in it was being collected for some reason or another. It was all horses and carts. All the carts were four-wheeled, not like our horse carts. Very few cars were to be seen. It was like looking at scenes of the famine.

The name of the town was Fagaras, right in the centre of Romania. We started to mix sand and cement and tried to do a bit of plastering, but the size and scale of what was in front of us became so depressing that we threw in the towel. Every wall from floor to ceiling was off plumb between four and ten inches. We decided that we would use plasterboard to dot and dab, as it was the only chance to get it near plumb. Once that decision was made it wasn't a simple matter of going to the hardware shop for materials, because there were no shops. The nearest hardware shop was about a hundred miles away. All we needed was bonding to use as adhesive as there was loads of plasterboard that had been brought over previously, donated by some hardware companies I presume.

After a lot of phoning we got the number of the hardware shop. They had bags of bonding in stock, but they did not know what it was or what it was for. In the meantime, our taxi driver managed to find an old van, so we set off for the hardware shop. When we did manage to reach it, it was a very modern shop stuck in the middle of nowhere. It was bonding alright, about a year old, and by God were they pleased to be getting rid of it. The whole time it was there no one knew what it was for, and if you saw the funny looks they gave us when we ordered more you would have died laughing.

I can't remember correctly but I think we got about fifteen bags, so that's what our work consisted of for the next three weeks. Sticking on sheets of plasterboard. The driver was sent on a few more journeys for bags of bonding. We had another job as well and that was keeping the spectators at bay. There was one thing that annoyed us about the whole thing and it just did not add up at all. These so-called architects would swan in now and again in their big Mercedes dressed to the last. It was obvious that they were not doing their work for nothing. They even thought that the plasterboard job we were doing was the finished work and they could not get over the speed we were working at. A lot of them could not understand why we were doing it for nothing.

Some evenings if we could not face any more bread and cabbage soup we would venture as far as this restaurant in the middle of the town where there was a fairly modern pub with a pool table. I was wondering why John Doogan always headed straight for the pool table but I soon found out. It was because he was good at it. The chest was always out on the way back to the house after thrashing us game after game. The restaurant was just a name over the door, because as restaurants go, it wasn't even a cafe never mind being classed as anything other. There was a menu, but only a few of the things on it were available. They were always glad to see us coming because we left them a good tip. Sunday was a day off. It was like Ireland years ago when people did nothing in the line of work, so we thought we'd play it safe and that way you upset no one.

Ceausescu, the Romanian communist president who ruled with an iron fist, was a very cruel leader who lived a life of luxury with his family while his people were dying with hunger. He was subsequently killed in an uprising. He had a big castle in the town that we visited but there was nothing in it but the bare walls as everything had been taken away by the people. What a site and what a building. We also visited Dracula's castle in Transylvania, which was a few hours' drive away. It was a tourist attraction and a very nice castle but not as big in reality as is shown on postcards and not half as scary as having to walk through any graveyard in the midnight hours.

The three weeks flew in and we found ourselves on the way to the airport for the return journey. As we threw our near empty bags onto the baggage slot at the check-in desk, the lady working at the desk tried to pull a fast one on us. She said that our luggage was overweight so we'd have to pay something equal to a €100, but we started to put up an argument. After a few minutes she waved us on without any explanation. This was one way of bumping up their wages, but her luck was out this time. That's why I was saying earlier that you had to be on the lookout the whole time. Most but not all of the people did not see the immorality in doing us to the two eyes. Even though we were there helping them. It was something that you could not dwell on for too long or the resentment would build up and you wouldn't do anything on a voluntary basis.

It was a few months before we were in a position to go back to try and finish what we started. When the plane landed at the airport, by this stage the frost was fairly heavy on the ground and all I could think of was "What the hell am I doing here?" But after getting another great welcome from those involved with the orphanage side of things and the children laying on more cabbage soup you knew what you had to look forward to for the next three weeks.

The four of us were confined to the one bedroom, so you had to be on the ball to get in quick to get the pick of the beds. Of course John had the big size ten stuck in the doorway first and fired his bag onto the bed of his choice. Between John's socks, James' s talking in his sleep, Joe snoring, and me... well I didn't have a problem with any of these things, so that's my story and I'm sticking to it.

In the mornings especially you'd meet people coming into the town with bundles of sticks that they collected in the forest to sell as firewood. The lucky ones would have a horse and cart. We always gave the most needy looking some money. If you had money and didn't you'd need to have a heart of stone, and even in that cold they would still be scraping through the big dump looking for bits and pieces that they might be able to sell. It was around the second week that we were there that we started to venture off the beaten track when we had a bit of time to spare. By this stage we thought we had seen all the poverty that we were going to be seeing, but we were to be proved wrong on that one. The town itself was fairly big, and the further out you moved, the bigger the divide between rich and poor started to became more apparent, to the extent that there were people more or less living out in the open.

We were making our way home after going away off the beaten track. That's when you saw the rough living conditions that a section of the people were living in. Corrugated tin shacks with barely anything covering the openings. At first we thought that it was animals that were being kept in the these huts until we saw smoke coming out of some of them. On looking a bit closer you could see people huddling around a small fire in the middle of the floor. There were areas you would not venture into after dark either because it was a bit too dodgy looking and none of us fancied meeting any undesirables who would think very little of making a few holes in you.

The evidence was all around that it was once a very wealthy place, the intricate stonework, the nice facades, roofs, but everything was in a terrible state of disrepair. Glass broken in windows of houses that people were living in. No one seemed to take responsibility for fixing anything. During the years of communism everything was owned by the state and was repaired by the state. So that mentality was there where you expected or waited for it to be done for you. The other thing that was noticeable was how young people dressed. Whatever money they could get their hands on went on nice clothes; it did not matter that the rain was coming in through the roof or that there was no glass in the windows, dressing up seemed to be the most important thing. I suppose one way of looking at it was that if you could at least feel good about yourself and how you looked, then maybe it made it that bit easier look further afield past the grey dreariness of the rundown landscape. In some unforeseen way it helped in choosing to make changes for the better.

It was like the Cinderella story in a strange sort of way. We went to a market one day. It was a strange, surreal sight to behold. It was as if you were transported back into the pages of a Tom Sawyer story. I've never seen so many heads of cabbages stacked along the road or so many pigs in the one place before. There were pigs in buckets, in barrels, in boxes. I saw one man walking down the road carrying three small pigs by the legs in each hand and them squealing away like mad. There were a few chickens as well but they were not half as plentiful as the pigs. I don't know what the animal rights people would have made of the whole thing, but I don't think they would have been too happy. That's all that was at the market, pigs and cabbages. It would not bother me too much if I was never to see a head of cabbage again.

We had at this stage got stuck into our plastering and were flying through it. We did not have too many options available to us for keeping warm, just keep the head down and work as hard as you could. We had the spectators to keep us company whether we liked it or not. The time flew in and it was time to go. We got a few bear hugs and whatnot off the children at the old orphanage and off to the airport we went. The job was completed by gangs of others like ourselves the following year, getting the whole shebang moved in, and all lived happily ever after according to the updated reports we received for some time.

This experience prompted us to think about keeping a child from Belarus for three weeks in the summer, where the after-effects of the Chernobyl disaster were felt most. We did and brought the same girl back for a number of years. She was seven when she first came over to us, and eleven on her last visit. Just like all those other families who kept children, it was for their benefit alone, ours came secondary.

Skiing

Never a dull moment. This is another funny story. My thinking is that if you're going to tell a story just leapfrog the boring bits if you can because you don't want people to fall asleep while you're going on about how great your mother-in-law is for example.

My next-door neighbour, who is originally from the Netherlands, suggested to me that we should consider going on a skiing holiday. I have to say I thought he was a bit mad for suggesting it in the first place, because I never even imagined any of my family with a pair of skis over our backs climbing up some slope in a snow-covered land. But gentle persuasion, telling us how easy it was, did the trick. I think we bought enough long johns and winter wear to last an Eskimo their lifetime. So both families set off from Belfast to the Czech Republic, landing in Prague.

The last time I got a flight to that city I had an awful rare up with a man sitting in the seat in front of me. I was sitting next to the window looking out as we took off. Once we were airborne he immediately puts the back of his seat back as far as he could. Maybe it was the plane we were in, but it seemed to come back a lot more than others; the head rest was right in my face, with his mop of hair nearly tickling my nose. If he had dandruff I would have ended up sneezing my head off. When the stewardess came around with the refreshments I prodded him on the shoulder and asked him to lift the back of his seat up a bit but he ignored me and pointed for me to move into the middle seat, which was empty. Well I flipped and banged his seat that hard he nearly catapulted up to the front. It was a good job I had my seat belt on because it stopped me going over the top of his seat to get at him. I gave him some mouthful. It worked wonders because he never relaxed the rest of the flight as he stayed leaning forward with the back of his seat up as straight as it would go. Rein (neighbour) had business interests in Prague so he knew the place like the back of his hand. We travelled by taxi on snow-covered roads at breakneck speeds as if you were travelling on a motorway in the middle of summer. My heart was in my mouth on a number of occasions. This was before I was told that all vehicles were fitted with snow chains. I was sitting in the front seat and I could see the driver smiling to himself when he'd see me going through the braking motions. It took a bit of getting used to. It turned out we were staying in a hotel up on the mountainside. If I remember correctly it was early enough in the day, so after getting booked in, fed and watered, it was out the door. There was no other option as you would have needed leashes on the children to have any chance of keeping them in. This was after getting fitted out with the proper boots and skis. I must have looked like Michelin man with all the layers of long johns, short johns and every other type of john I had on to keep the cold out.

Rein took the lead and led us out like the pied piper onto this gentle enough-looking slope. The children were off like rockets, while the nervous mummies were taking a back seat, being safe rather than sorry. Rein was floating around on the skis as if he was born with them attached to him. I thought "This can't be too hard," so I get all geared up trying to look all professional. That was when my legs went in all directions and I ended up in a mangled heap half in under some sort of seat. Try as I might there was no way on earth I was going to be able to get back on my feet. With the sweat running down my face, being cooked alive in under all my layers, cursing and swearing like mad, Rein managed to get me on my feet. The first thing I did was to go back into the hotel and get rid of half my clothes. Enough to fill a blooming suitcase.

I felt like a new man going out again, but that did not stop the falling over. The children were laughing at me, the wives were laughing at me, but at this stage I was beyond laughing, so after nearly a week of falling and getting up I began to get the hang of it. On this slope there was a small lift that kept going unless someone like me got tangled up in it. You had to stand in a queue unsteadily as you still had your skis on. When the empty seat came along you had to move into position quickly and straddle it, fitting it under your behind. After two seconds you got a jolt forward and if you weren't standing in your skis right for the takeoff, you ended up with a leg here and a leg there, and if you could not get out of the way fast enough the next person ended up on top of you, which happened to me a good few times. My face went all shades of red, but after a dozen or so times of ending upside down the embarrassment goes out the window.

The children had taken to it like ducks to water, and the mammies were doing very well but not intent on breaking any records. There were a number colours that determined what slope you should use: blue for beginners, red for intermediate, and black for experienced skiers. In the evenings we would go for a walk down into the village. You couldn't even throw a snowball because it was like powder. It would not stick together like here at home. This was dry snow.

We would have something to eat in one of the many restaurants after a wander around. Rein took us onto the blue slope at the beginning of the second week. This was scary, as it had a similar system with the lifts, but once the people in front took off, me, Anne Marie, Tara and Fionn had to get in line because it took four, and you had to get the timing right. It swept around the turn wheel. Once you felt it touching the backs of your legs you sat down as quickly as you could. Then a bar came down over you to stop anyone from falling out, and up into the air. Sometimes there was ten feet beneath you, next there could be sixty feet beneath. Getting off at the top was a repeat of getting on except in reverse. Once the bar went up and your skis touched the snow, all had to push forward at the same time for you to reach a safe distance from the next seat with Rein, Sarah, Theo and Jena coming along.

It took around ten minutes to go up and if you managed to stay upright, a two minute thrill took you down. After a few days getting the hang of that from morning till night, we were all beginning to really enjoy it. But Rein was up and down the black slope like the real professional and, worse still, you'd be watching young children coming down, and I mean down, then you would look at yourself and you having trouble standing in the one spot.

On our last day there Rein said we would have to go for a night ski. When it got dark the lifts worked up until twelve or until there was no one left to ski. It was beautiful when you were on top of the mountain looking down on the village with all the lights in the distance. He was making it sound very romantic. I was having doubts about it but then he says, "You could do it no bother; you're good enough now," so that gave me a bit of confidence. If only I had known what was in front of me. That night me and Rein set off up in the lifts. It was very quiet as there were very few people, but he was right, all you could hear going up was the whirr of the cable car. There was an eeriness accompanying the quietness, but it was absolutely beautiful. The scenery was breathtaking and if it was female company you could say it was indeed romantic.

But one thing I failed miserably in not noticing was that this was not the normal lift that we had been going up in; it seemed much steeper but I said nothing. As we slid off at the top I got a few yards away from the next seat in which there were two people. I stopped just to make sure everything was in place before I set off. I looked around for Rein but he was gone, and so were the other two. I was left there standing on my own. I thought I better get going so I begin to make my way to the top of the slope. But the closer I got to the edge the more it began to look like a cliff. "There is no way that I can go down there," I thought and I started calling Rein everything under the sun, under my breath of course. I took off my skis and decided that I would climb down through the trees alongside the ski slope but once I took a step or two off into the soft snow I nearly went down to my neck so I clawed my way out again, and wondered what should I do.

I had no other option. I had to get my skis on again, take a deep breath, close my eyes, jump off and hope for the best, and that's what I did. You could compare it to going down a very steep hill driving a lorry with a big load and you realised you had no brakes. There I was speeding down doing about eighty miles per hour when each leg decided to go different directions. That's exactly what happened. I don't know how I didn't split up the middle before somersaulting in all directions as my head bounced off the ice, packed hard as a rock by the thousands of skis going down all day.

When I did stop bouncing I was looking up at a lovely starry sky. I was able to move okay so nothing was broken but I had to slide and tumble down a good bit because one of my skis had gone ahead without me. When I managed to get hold of it and get it clipped into my boot properly I set off again. I fell about five more times, and none of them were gentle I can tell you, before reaching the bottom. Next thing Rein lands in nicely beside me having come down the second time. "Well f**k you anyway," I said, "Why didn't you tell me it was so steep?" He started laughing and said, "If I had told you the truth you wouldn't have come and you can't give up now". All I could do was laugh, so after some refreshments I was feeling brave again and up I went. It wasn't so bad the second time because I was expecting it, but boy what an experience. I would recommend it to anyone.

James Woods

The boss had been doing some practice sessions at the skiing in America when he was over, so he was itching to get away somewhere to try it out again. In between times I had mentioned it to Rein. He said that was no problem, he would arrange for us to go skiing for a weekend in the Czech Republic. All we had to do was to meet him in Prague. I told Tony what the score was so it was decided to go for a weekend. With the wife giving me absolution to go on my travels, the two of us landed over in Prague and were met by Rein, who then took us up into the same resort area where we had been before with the families, but the difference this time was we were staying in a house belonging to some friends of Rein's who were there for the same purpose.

Like Rein they were both very experienced on the slopes. Anyway, to cut a long story short we had an action-filled two days and then it was back to Prague where Rein had booked us into this hotel because he knew the manager who would give us a good deal. That was sound. We landed in the foyer of the hotel with our short stay bags. By that I mean a spare shirt, hairbrush, toothbrush, one extra pair of socks and the G-strings, so we were traveling light. We got up to reception, showed the passports and I couldn't get over how overly friendly and helpful the two receptionists were. One of them insisted on carrying my bag to my room after we had booked in. To tell you the truth I felt embarrassed. Me a big strong macho man walking along and this very attractive girl carrying my paperweight bag for me. I was cringing. She led me into my room, which was a single, very modern and stylish. As she began explaining where everything was and what it was for she was eyeballing me from top to bottom, then went on to tell me where I could go if I wanted to eat out and where the best music venues were, giving me the sort of smiles that would have melted a glacier.

Suddenly a thought came to me. She's after a tip, so I offered her a generous tip, seeing as my bag was so heavy, but alas she was having none of it and departed with another chocolate-melting smile. I was left standing in the middle of the room scratching my head. I certainly wasn't used to that sort of attention in any hotel before that or since. I was to find out why later on. After a cleanup I met Tony, Rein and some friends of his in the lounge for coffee and again the smiles and attention from staff were close on going over the top. Even the manager joined us for coffee. But things were beginning to get on my goat at this stage. I got up to pay for our coffees, which were refilled a number of times, but the manager jumped up as well and said they were on the house and then slipped his business card into the pocket of my shirt and said if I needed anything at all to ring him straight away.

"What the hell is going on in this place?" I thought to myself and glanced in Tony's direction only to see him with a big grin spread across his face as well so I made a beeline straight for him and said, "What the fuck's going on here?" Then he whispered out of the side of his mouth what all the fussing was about. Rein had told the manager that James Woods (Hollywood film star) was coming for a few nights and he wanted everything kept hush hush, and this was why I was staying in a single room. Oh my God. When he told me that I felt sorry for the poor manager, and the other staff for being taken in like that. When I handed in my passport they saw the name on it, and just assumed that I was who Rein said I was. The fact that it was an Irish passport didn't seem to register at all or that I didn't resemble him in looks either.

The receptionists had their own idea of how my looks could have changed. They had come up with the idea that it was down to all the plastic surgery that the stars of the big screen are so fond off. I heard all about these theories later on. Shortly afterwards as I made my way back from doing a pit stop in the toilets I met the manager, and him so courteous I began to feel so sorry for the oul eejit that I had to tell him what was going on. I could see from his reaction that he was sort of devastated and in a state of disbelief on hearing how he was the victim of a con job like this, but at the same time was doing his best to put on a brave face. As I made my way back to my seat, I thought of a way to turn it around.

When I sat down I acted all excited, said to Rein that I had met the manager and he told me he was upgrading me to a big executive room on the top floor because he said the room I was in was far too small. I could hardly keep myself from laughing as I saw the color draining out of his face, and to rub it in a bit more I said, "I wonder who's going to pay for that?" Tony was listening and smiling away as Rein went very quiet. He was thinking his bit of a laugh was starting to go horribly wrong. I let him sweat it out for a while before telling him that he was now the victim of a windup. With the relieved look that appeared on his face I'd say he didn't mind one bit. The only person I never laid eyes on from then on was the manager and you couldn't blame him for that, I'm sure that when the word got around there would have been a lot of piss taking.

Tom Jones

I was trying to do a bit of fencing close to the house and getting on good enough until I nearly tore the hand off myself on barbed wire. I just walked away from the lot and went into the house to look for a bit of sympathy. But it was in short supply. I got some tea made for me anyway to lift my spirits. "Here's something that just might be the right medicine to help cure you," says the wife with a smile on her face, "Would you like to go to a Tom Jones concert?" I knew that she was a big fan of his so I said I wouldn't mind. "That's good," says she "because I have two tickets that someone gave us for a present." He was appearing in the newly-done-up O2 venue in Dublin. It used to be called The Point.

Anyway when the time came we found ourselves in the queue. The place was huge. There was ten thousand people in it that night and seventy-five per cent were women. I thought Tom was getting past his sell-by date, but how wrong can you be. The show he put on was an experience not to be missed, even for men. I never saw so many women of all ages losing their inhibitions so quickly when an entertainer like Tom came on stage. He had the audience of mostly females worked into a frenzy with his hips, swaying and baring his well-tanned chest while strutting around like a peacock. If it was a good few years back when you had to answer to the priest or the bishop, and they got wind of the carry on that these wild women were capable of getting up to! There was no age limit.

A man was making his way to his seat, and as he passes one old woman who was near enough to eighty if she was a day, he says, "Keep them on now because it's cold outside!" She replies, "Sure I have none on." Everyone around busted out laughing it was so funny. There would have been an awful lot of excommunications going on, the amount of ladies' underwear being discarded, some not big enough to make a patch for your eye, and some big enough to cover a marquee or a hot air balloon. One lady beside me, who was a bit under the weather, even took off one of her expensive looking red stilettos and threw it up onto the stage. That did not stop her dancing away with one shoe. Lucky for Tom there was a good strong barrier between all those ladies and the stage, because if they got within reach he would have ended up looking as if he was just after going through a paper shredder.

The Funny Things that Happen when you Live in the Countryside

It's funny the things that happen when you live in the countryside. John, another brother, was up around the hills one day when he came on a baby deer. Something must have happened for its mother to leave it on its own, maybe it got shot or something, but he brought it home with him. So he then had the job of how to start feeding it. He bought a baby's feeding bottle and used that for a while. He then had to use a coke bottle because it was getting a bit greedy. He nearly had to take out a mortgage to buy milk for it. It used to wander in and out of the house of its own free will, just like a dog, and more often than not that's what the dog did, follow it around.

It grew fairly quickly. I remember one instance where we had visitors who were just after having tea and were sitting chatting. Next thing this big deer walks in around the kitchen and lifts a few slices of bread off the table and walks out. We knew what was going to happen, but you should have seen the look on their faces. They did not know whether to laugh or scream, but we knew what to do and burst out laughing. When they recovered they did the same.

Me, Fionn and Tara were out through the fields for a walk one day when the dog came back with something in its mouth. Fionn managed to catch it. What was it but a baby rabbit. After looking around for burrows we couldn't find any so we brought it home with us and put it in a cardboard box beside the fire. The following day it began to drink milk from a syringe and as the days went by it grew bigger and bigger. I was thinking to myself "That's a funny looking rabbit". It had very big paws and long ears.

Our neighbour Paddy came in with eggs one day and Tara showed it to him. He started laughing and says, "That's not a rabbit that's a hare." I felt a bit stupid myself for not realising it sooner. We'd let it out for a run around the kitchen. There was a rug on the floor and it would make for that straight away and start this crazy break dancing of flipping upside down, laying on its back with the feet in the air going flat out. It was a lot better than watching the Late Late Show. I eventually fenced off quite a big area in the garden because I don't like the idea of keeping wild animals locked up in small cages. It grew that big that our cat would not dare go near it. It was a big black cat and a great hunter. By this stage we were thinking it was time to let it go free again. We had told Tara and Fionn to expect this so that they would be prepared for the big day.

We took turns in carrying it wrapped in a blanket up the hill and let it go. We never saw it again, but the neighbour who told us in the first place that it was a hare rather than a rabbit had an encounter with it a week or so after its release. He was out feeding the hens when this big hare came hopping right up to his feet. He got a bit of a surprise alright, but he copped on straight away that it was our lodger. It sniffed around for a few minutes before hopping off again nice as you like. That was the last time he saw it as well.

Airing your Dirty Laundry

Talking about Tara, here's a funny thing she did one bright sunny day. Anne Marie told Tara to hang the washing on the clothes line so the dutiful Tara did as she was told, hung the lot nicely on the line. A few hours later when Anne Marie went to take the clothes in she made a discovery that made her screech like a banshee. In the middle of the hullaba-loo, who walks around the corner only the parish priest and finds Anne Marie reading the riot act to Tara. "My goodness what's going on here," he says to the now-blushing mammy. "Well I'll tell you why," she says, "I told Tara to hang up the washing. What did she do but pick up the dirty washing in a basket beside the washing machine and hang it up? What should be on the line is still in the washing machine". You couldn't blame the priest for going into a fit of giggles. Since then it's a bit of a joke, don't hang up the dirty clothes.

Errigal Arts Festival

I happened to pick up a free pamphlet while out doing a bit of shopping one day. It was advertising what was on for the Errigal Arts Festival in Letterkenny. There were so many interesting things on that you'd want to be in a few places at one time. But one thing caught my eye. It was a writers' workshop in a hotel in Rathmullen, a must-see part of Donegal. Brian Keenan, who spent a few years as a hostage in Beirut, was in charge of the workshop, so I was interested in seeing what the man was like up close. I rang up a friend, Martin Jim, and got him to come along as well.

It was for a Saturday at 1.30pm, which was grand. It suited the two of us down to the ground. But lo and behold things do not nun smoothly where Martin Jim is concerned. He rings me up on the Saturday morning saying "I can't go". "Why not?" says I. "Well I had a front brace in and it came out but I know a dentist who may be able to do a temporary repair job on it and if he can do it I'll see you there."

I wasn't looking forward to going to one of these things on my own as I did not know what to expect, but as I was about to go in the door I heard the shout. It was Martin with a big smile showing the teeth. We got seated around the middle, a sort of a hiding place in case you were out of your depth. The proceedings got under way as Brian brought out two big pictures, one of a church and a large bridge the other a bus full of people. Both these pictures were based on places in Mexico. We were asked to describe what we could see in the pictures and how they were relevant to each other. It was unbelievable the stories that some people were able to conjure up just by looking at them. I felt quiet comfortable after a while and I was able offer up my views on what was in front of me. One way of summing it up was that the old church looked like a scene that you would see on a fine day looking down over Dun Luiche. The other one could have passed for a group of all ages going out the Dun Luiche road intending to climb Errigal, which in all honesty brought me to the part that I wanted to tell.

I started off by saying that if he asked everyone in the room to write a story about what they could see, everyone's story would be different, so now I upped the ante by saying that if you looked up at the sky on a cloudy day, you would see all sorts of images. I went on then to tell of meeting a man who could see strange things in water. This is how that happened. One nice sunny day I decided to climb Errigal. On reaching the top there was this middle-aged man who looked like he was used to climbing mountains as he was well geared for it. He was standing there in another world, gazing down over the lake. A very picturesque scene indeed. As I moved close to him he says, "Can you see anything down in the water?" As I strained my eyes I could make out the boat leaving Ionad Cois Locha, but alas that was not the answer he was seeking. "Can you see any shape?" he says. Then I says, "I can see the outline of a dinosaur," but again I was dismissed as some sort of a dimwit. I was getting a bit fed up at this stage so I says, "What do you see?" All that I can say is that his answer left me gobsmacked.

Pointing down he says proudly "Queen Victoria". Now I have to say without being able to give the man an intelligible answer, while in a state of shock, that the only consolation

I got from it was that I wasn't too far out when I said dinosaur and better still she was in the deep end and unlikely to surface in the near future.

The following year I went back again for the craic. This time it was being run by Dermot Bolger, Karl Gebler and Paul Perry. Again it had its funny twists, but was that little bit rushed for me. What a pity. We had a break where we went for a bite to eat, which was included in the price. I sat down at a table with three others, and had a good chat about the various speakers and so on. We were offered coffee after we finished our meal, which we accepted, and the waiter returned after a few minutes to present us with a bill for the coffee, which it turned out was not included in the price for our meal. A little bit underhand I thought myself. It was discussed and regurgitated a few times until I got fed up listening to the whinging about the cost. I discreetly took the bill and paid for the four coffees before returning to my seat.

As we got up to go back to the workshop, I could hear change rattling so I told them that it was paid for. Well you know, it would have been nice to hear a thanks, but no they disappeared so fast that I just wondered to myself, "Why the hell bother trying to be nice to people?" There is one old saying that would relate nicely in this case. "It's not what we give, but what we share that makes us great, and what you're good at never seems hard".

Our Next Outing

Our next outing was a bit on the rare side of things as well. Martin phoned me up and asked me would I be interested in going to some do in Letterkenny. He said that he got an invite but wasn't sure what it was. That it was in some bookshop and that was all he knew. It was a Friday night with nothing else to do so the two of us headed out the road. We had a bit of trouble finding a parking spot as the town was extremely busy. As luck would have it a car pulled out on the main street allowing us to park not too far from our destination, the bookshop. Something happened then that I will refer to further on. As we approach the door a gentleman opens the door and me being in front asks me "Are you reading?" Me thinking he was just being smart, says, "Yes of course, I'll read anything you want or tell a story," and continued on my way in.

It turned out it was a poetry night. I think Martin knew all along, but knew if he told me what it was, that I wouldn't have gone. It was fairly packed with a friendly bunch of people of all ages. We were offered tea or coffee and some nice cakes. We got seated and someone started doing a poetry reading. After that the gentleman who had greeted us at the door, turns to me and says, "Right it's your turn now." "What!! you want me to read a book?"

Everyone is looking at me now clapping and cheering, so up I get, completely blank. All I could do for the time being was scratch my head hoping that something would come to me. It did, I told a story and went down a treat even though it had a raunchy twist to it. Then it was Martin's turn. His story was pure filth and would never pass any of the barometers set down by the broadcasting standards commission. But it went down a treat. We told a few more stories based on fact and had the crowd in stitches. I think we turned the poetry night upside down. When we said our goodbyes at the end of the night and made our way to where the car was parked, we talked about what we had been confronted by earlier on when we had just parked.

Lying on the footpath was this very good looking girl drunk out of her head exposing a lot of flesh that would not normally be on display to onlookers. The Guards arrived minutes later and had her taken away by ambulance. So I wrote a poem about it, seeing as it was because of poetry that we were there in the first place, and this is it:

Poetry on a Friday night

One quiet Friday evening I settled down with
a cup of tea and a slice of half-burned toast.
My phone began to ring, from Martin Jim it came.
Did you forget about the date we had, In Letterkenny town?
God, says I, sure I did indeed, but panic we shall not,
What about herself? says Martin Jim, a worry line appeared.
But not for long, as I did declare, for tell her I shall not!
As we drove along, says I, what does our date entail,
For tell me not, was Martin's plan, until we were there.
As we alighted from our car, our eyes looked on in glee,
Before us lay a beauty drunk, with all her wares to see.
No need for a second look, as we were well aware,
For Universal Books was up the street,
where we were supposed to be.
Once inside, we got heated up, with hot coffee,
buns and tea,
Poems, poems, we did not recite, for the one painful reason,
As we considered ourselves, not that type.
But funny stories, and experience galore,
Left the ladies with wet pants, as laughter filled the air.
When I got home and told the wife,
She glared at me with her fists clenched tight,
With choice words, she told me that I'm no poet,
And by God, did she let me know it.

I wouldn't hold my breath expecting to win any prizes for my first attempt at piecing words together in this way, but it was the best I could do so I'm more than happy with it.

I read a book written by, or on behalf of, Mickey MacGowan, who originally came from a townland just down the road from me. His book, *The Hard Road to Klondike* tells the story of the hardship and suffering that he and others alike went through in the quest for a better life mining for gold in the mountains of Montana and Alaska in the late 1800s.

My story, while interesting, is not comparable in the sense of the hardship that he encountered before or during his travels, but it planted a seed that I hoped to be able put something into print one day. Everyone has a story to tell, and everyone is capable of putting the ups and downs of their life down on paper, if they put their mind to it. Take me for example. I could write my name, address, and not a whole lot more when I left school, but I did read and talk a lot, which combined to help me on the way to something that started out as a hobby, turned into a bit of a dream and which in turn may help someone else do the same.

This story should hopefully fill in some of the gaps for anyone who may have been suspicious of some or all of the foreigners that came looking for work when it was plentiful in Ireland, most of whom have moved on to greener pastures since. Of course you will come across the odd bad apple or two in the bucket, but so what, that's life. The old saying that Ireland was a land of saints and scholars is beginning to fade into the mists of time, don't you think?

It should create a better understanding of the harsh surroundings that we all seek to leave behind in the past, especially those before us, a large percentage of whom crossed over to England and were confronted with unwelcome signs that read "No Irish, no Blacks, or no Dogs". Hence we should keep this fact in mind when dealing with strangers to our shores who seek work and shelter, "to treat them as we would like to be treated ourselves."

Now as I begin to wind down, bringing this writing business to where I think I can end it, I never realised that I had so much fun until I had to start thinking about all the things, some good and some not so good, that have happened to me in the course of reaching the age that I'm at now. Which is for me to know and you to find out.

The Rooster

There is another wee story that may be worth telling. Earlier on I had mentioned about killing hens and so on when I was younger. Well it turned out that Joe had two lovely roosters that someone had given him. As he had intended to get a few hens but never got around to it, the two roosters had the run of the place, shitting all over tools, tractors, just about everything for a year.

Me, Fionn and Tara decided to stage a kidnapping, because we needed a rooster for our broody hens. We equipped ourselves with a torch and a couple of bags to put them into. This was a big adventure for them. As we made our way towards Joe's shed, the plan was all laid out by the two of them. Fionn was going to hold the torch and blind them because he knew where they liked to perch. I was going to catch them. Tara's job was to hold the bag open for me.

The whole operation went like clockwork. We headed off home with our hostages and took them into our shed where I told them to pick whichever one they fancied because we only needed one and the other unlucky one is going in the pot. I went inside and got a good sharp knife. By the time I came back to the shed they had made their choice. I showed them how to kill a chicken humanely.

Fionn kept running in and out between the shed and the house giving his mammy the low down and what was to happen next. I showed them how to pluck and clean and then turn it over a flame to burn off any hairs. I then hung it up for three days in the shed and every day I got the same question – "When can we eat it?" and I would give the same answer – "When it's ready." Eventually it made its way to the oven. Well it wasn't me that put it in the oven. It was herself and she left me to keep an eye on it and peel the spuds as she went to pick the children up from school. While I'm peeling I got a phone call that lasted longer than I realised, which meant I was still peeling spuds when they landed in from school.

Anne Marie says, "Did you check the oven?" It dawned on me all of a sudden that that crackling sound should not be there. She opened it before I even had time to react. Smoke and flames followed by the time I got a look at what was left in the oven. It had shrunk into the size of a cup and burned to cinders. It wasn't a happy ending for the rooster and neither was it a happy ending for the poor hungry souls who were looking forward to eating it.

A week later I went into the hen house in the morning to give them their feeding. I reached over to lift one of the chickens that seemed to be having a problem getting down off his perch. The next thing I ended up on my back-end in hen shit. The bloody rooster had attacked me and stuck one of his spurs right into my wrist. I felt he was giving me the evil eye for a while so whether this was revenge for me putting his mate in the pot, or for me daring to put my hands on one of his chicks, there's one thing for certain. He's just used up one of his three lifelines.

A week later his lifelines were cashed all at once. Fionn comes running in saying "The rooster just dropped. I think he's dead". We rushed out to see what the problem was, and yes he was dead as a doornail. Whether the poor hens were too lively for him or what, I don't know, but it looked like a heart attack. This posed another problem. Where to get another one. I knew a man who lived a few miles away who had loads of hens so we decided to pay him a visit. When we got there, there were all shapes and sizes running around through the yard. After knocking on the door and having a look about the place, there was no sign of the man himself. I decided to try and catch one, but it wasn't going to be that easy, but lo and behold the crowing started in a shed beside me. I opened the door and there sitting on a piece of timber were two of the finest, biggest roosters you ever did see. In I go and in no time at all I had bagged myself one of the boyos. With our second bout of kidnapping over without being spotted, we headed for home.

I was fairly smiling to myself thinking about your man scratching his head trying to figure out where it went or how the hell it got out, and the door bolted. I told a friend of his about what happened, and he had some laugh about it, but said nothing to see how he could wind him up about it. Your man was raging when he found out that one of his big daddies was missing; it's a wonder that he didn't go to the guards about it. But one thing is for sure, if he ever reads this he'll certainly know who took it and where it went.

Fionn Builds a House

My son Fionn, who was nine at the time, came in one day shouting for me to come out and have a look at the house that he was after building all by himself, and of course I have to admit that I did not expect much. I thought that it would be nothing more than a piece of plastic thrown over some of the branches of the trees, but oh boy was I wrong. He had got hold of two bandstands that I had lying around which I had used when building a shed. He layered the bottom with short scaffold boards. Then he did the same for the roof, but covered it over with the plastic I had seen him dragging around after him earlier. He had fencing posts sloped up all around the outside. To be honest if it was on a bigger scale, considering the thought involved, it would have put a lot of these so-called architects that I've come across in me travels to shame. I was sort of taken aback with all the work he had put into it in such a short space of time. The bandstands were heavy for a wee buck like him, as were the soaking wet scaffold boards, not to mention the fencing posts which he had dragged more than a hundred yards and lifted over a high fence that I was only after putting up as well.

He must have grown at least a foot in height when I praised him up and down about the great job he had done, knowing full well that I would have to dismantle it at some stage. He was like a drowned rat; the rain had been drizzling lightly, but was now starting to come down in bucketfuls so I said, "It's time for you to come into the house to see if we can find something nice for you after all that hard work".

So it was a race then to get in. He was first of course, and he began whistling away like the cat that got the cream.

In case I forget, Fionn got his reward – hot chocolate.

Recession, Recession, Recession

In the meantime everything is doom and gloom. Recession, re-cession, recession is the talk of the day where people from all walks of life have suffered. Some a lot more than others. As long as you have your health no matter how bad things look, there will always be the chance of a bit of light at the end of the tunnel. It's a bit like the story of the two mice that were perched on the rim of the bucket of milk trying to get a sup of milk, but they leaned over a bit too far and fell in. All they could do was keep swimming. After going round and round for ages, one thinks "What's the point sure I'm never going to get out," and gives up and drowns. The second mouse says to himself "I'm getting out of here if it's the last thing I do," so he swims even harder until the milk turns into butter. He climbed up and got out.

It's like my struggle with this book. There were a few times when I lost between fifteen to twenty thousand words fiddling about on the computer and felt like throwing the lot out the window, but I didn't and the moral of me and the mice story is never give up. I hope in this process I haven't been the provider of too much stale or bad writing.

So on that note I'll let things be without getting myself into any unforeseen difficulties that may come back to bite me, or trip me up. The highs in this recollection of my life's ups and downs, so far, outweigh the lows by a mile.

♦♦♦♦♦♦♦♦♦♦